Long Road to Harpers Ferry

People's History

History tends to be viewed from the perspective of the rich
and powerful, where the actions of small numbers are seen to
dictate the course of world affairs. But this perspective conceals
the role of ordinary women and men, as individuals or as parts
of collective organisations, in shaping the course of history.
The People's History series puts ordinary people and mass
movements centre stage and looks at the great moments of the
past from the bottom up.

The People's History series was founded and edited by
William A. Pelz (1951–2017).

Also available:

A People's History of the German Revolution
1918–19
William A. Pelz
Foreword by Mario Kessler

A People's History of the Portuguese Revolution
Raquel Varela

Long Road to Harpers Ferry

The Rise of the First American Left

Mark A. Lause

First published 2018 by Pluto Press
345 Archway Road, London N6 5AA

www.plutobooks.com

British Library Cataloguing in Publication Data
A catalogue record for this book is available from the British Library

ISBN   978 0 7453 3760 9   Hardback
ISBN   978 0 7453 3759 3   Paperback
ISBN   978 1 7868 0324 5   PDF eBook
ISBN   978 1 7868 0326 9   Kindle eBook
ISBN   978 1 7868 0325 2   EPUB eBook

This book is printed on paper suitable for recycling and made from fully managed and
sustained forest sources. Logging, pulping and manufacturing processes are expected
to conform to the environmental standards of the country of origin.

Typeset by Stanford DTP Services, Northampton, England

Simultaneously printed in the United Kingdom and United States of America

Contents

EPILOGUE

Introduction

The once prominent African American physician James McCune Smith took up the nom de plume of Communipaw from one of the earliest Dutch settlements in Jersey City. Some of the first Europeans in the area of New Amsterdam camped alongside the Hackensack Indians on a peninsula extending into the Hudson River. There, near what became South Cove, Smith envisioned Africans living and laboring alongside native peoples and whites. By the early nineteenth century, the market demands of capital overwhelmed those of the people, and Jersey City had long since obliterated the old settlement.[1] The complex origins of an anticapitalist American Left were inseparably related to a vision beyond that of the "white republic" to the possibilities of a civilization that could value liberty, equality and the willingness of different races to cohabit a place such as Communipaw.

This is a concise history of those origins. Such a work has been needed since I began looking for one half a century ago. The economic collapse of 2008 and the political management of massive bailouts and corporate subsidies created numerous radical critiques of capitalism, particularly among the young. So the time seemed ripe to bring this project to term.

* * *

Historically, conditions predisposed these works to become rather stinted institutional histories of radical organizations. Some of the earlier efforts were predisposed to become the annals of a Teutonic fraternity clinging to its explicit mathematical appreciation of "surplus value," with little attention to the world moving around it. Not without reason have such preoccupations failed to generate a more powerful and widespread challenge to American capitalism.

This work has a more amorphously "movement" focus. When real rather than aspirational, movements are innately fluid and "move" in differentiated layers based on pace and viscosity. While a movement may have different—even contradictory—effects, several factors distinguish the core of a movement from the periphery, the most important to me in this work being its dynamic.

Such an approach, of necessity, reflects the fundamental complexities of American civilization and its hierarchies. That civilization, as it now exists, grew from clearly racialized foundations. Shortly after three million residents of Anglo-America attained independence, about 600,000 native peoples lived within the claimed borders, and this fell to less than 340,000 by 1860. Its foundations are no less independent of an "African Holocaust" that seized an estimated 18 to 20 million Africans from their homes from the sixteenth through the nineteenth centuries, of which half a million labored in Revolutionary America, growing by 1860 to nearly four million, the vast majority of which lived as slaves. These harsh realities framed an American understanding of liberty, equality and inclusiveness.

Scholars have reasonably extended Caribbean models to underscore the legal determination of "whiteness." However comparable, conditions on the North American mainland differed significantly from that in the plantations of the Caribbean, where the relatively small population of self-defined "whites" had to cooperate in the subjugation of a massive black majority. The Black Codes from colonial times to the color bars of the nineteenth century represented legal strictures formulated by the rulers and imposed on the entire society.

Then, too, everywhere in the New World experienced "maroons." Some native peoples occupied the least exploitable niches, and large numbers of runaway slaves of both sexes joined them in the swamps, mountains, and other isolated areas. They built homes, raised crops and livestock, organized their defenses, and, provided a place to which others might flee. American slaveholding societies, by their existence, created these "maroons."[2] Participants included white renegades, intellectually and culturally defined.

These inspired a series of challengers. These included Christian Gottlieb Priber, as well as black leaders such as Cudjoe, Lewis, and "General of the Swamp," who headed their maroon towns in Georgia and North Carolina. For James M. Smith, for example, Communipaw represented a maroon internalized.

One of the most prominent of the antebellum labor radicals borrowed the "comprehensive phrase of a black writer" to describe the exclusions of the society that developed. It had been a white king and his authorities who "stole the black man from his land," took land "from the red men," and apportioned "the stolen bodies and the stolen land among a few of his own color, to whom he made the remainder of the whites as dependent for the means of existence as were the blacks themselves."[3] The inequalities Euroamerican society imposed upon outsiders reflected the inequalities imposed within. Men remained more likely to immigrate to America and, more so, to head to the frontier, but women constituted nearly half of the two million white residents of the colonies. Almost all women in America remained essentially civic nonentities and, in some cases, little more than domestic slaves. While patriarchal relationships within the family pre-dated capitalism, power turned increasingly on property ownership, custom and law further marginalized half the human race.

More than this, capitalism required the vast majority of the entire people to labor. Conditions on the frontier or in areas characterized by subsistence family farming—especially mountainous districts not conducive to large scale farming—required few hired workers, but the large well-settled commercial farming regions that produced grains in the North or tobacco in the South required a work force beyond the family. The roots of a recognizably modern working class took form in the twenty pre-Revolutionary towns with a population over three thousand and, especially, in the five over ten thousand—Philadelphia, New York, Boston, Newport and Charleston. Such communities needed carpenters, bricklayers and masons for construction or shoemakers, tailors, hatters and others for things to wear. Beyond such artisan crafts, the docks, warehouses, and ships required maritime labor and large numbers of the unskilled as well. Workers and their households accounted for a bit over half the population of the smaller cities and as many as three-quarters of the big cities.

Such mercantile centers became the points of friction between the British Empire and the colonial merchant elite which relied heavily upon the numbers and coherence of working people in the streets. Too, immigrants disproportionately clustered in the large port cities, which mingled numerous Scots and Welsh newcomers and a growing portion tending to be Irish, even as Germans constituted about a third of Pennsylvania. Not surprisingly, many had no great love for the empire, though they found themselves subject to its maritime or military service, the taxes, and the cost of taxes imposed on merchants and employers passing on their cost. Households, of course, carried this load, including many women struggling to support themselves and their children on their own. So, too, "the market women" prominent in preindustrial bread riots and similar "disorders" reappeared with the "leather aprons" of workingmen in the streets.

Tackling the origins of an American movement against capitalism must recognize the stratifications and ripples in social structures, as they exist in the real world. Indeed, Indians, unpaid black slaves, and the maroons or even women constrained to the spheres of the household superficially existed beyond the developing monetized world around them. To the extent that any of these groups cherished values more important to them than market forces, they could be said to be non-capitalist, if not anti-capitalist. Nevertheless, none of their priorities avoided their ultimate subjugation to the Euroamerican power structure and its economy.

Focusing simply on a structure of "class" read into the very real conflicts between the bosses and workers misses the fundamental unity of a complex process. Although the burdens of empire—and class hier-archies—obviously fell on all those subject to its power, the realization that the weight fell differently on native peoples, Africans, women, immigrants, and workers generally is essential to the project.

So, too, understanding that origins of an American movement against capitalism has to grow from an understanding that transcends the evolution of a vocabulary. Those of and for the "unwashed masses" regularly spoke the language of liberty and equality, using the same words the imperial authorities and colonial elites used. Increasingly, it became clear that those with the wealth and power advocated a liberty to gain more wealth and power, regardless of what it does to other people. They sought a freedom not just to own property, but to buy or sell, acquire or disinvest in that property to best expropriate more of it. Equality acquired a legal meaning that assured access to buying privileges to those with the wealth to do so. On the other hand, this narrow perspective had little meaning for those without the wherewithal to participate, those who embraced a more expansive version of liberty and equality.

Too, the possible impact of such differences turned on one's definition of community and the obligations of solidarity around that community. Elites generally found themselves rather contented to see themselves as part of a natural hierarchy, with notions of a community and solidarity turning upon the legitimacy of their authority. Obviously, the emergence of socialist communities, anarchist ideas, cooperatives, trade unions, and political parties challenged this. Over the generations from the Revolution to the Second American Revolution, growing numbers of Americans developed a new realization of what "solidarity" meant ... or what it had to mean.

Most importantly, the story of how growing numbers of Americans turned against human slavery was ultimately inseparable from how they thought about the prospects of abolishing capitalism as known and practiced in the United States. Read from the inside out, the debate over slavery turned on the argument that economic profitability had priority over people, that the property rights of the owners superseded the most basic human right for those who did not own property.

Obviously, not every person who said something positive about land reform or women's rights came to articulate radical abolitionist ideas. Nor did all abolitionists generalize their assault on exploitation into matters of gender or class. Nevertheless, the dynamic of events created a common agenda between the core of land reform and early socialism with the more militant, political, egalitarian abolitionism.

This study of that convergence and its impact offers us a recognizable "first American Left." The first part traces the debate around the standard Revolutionary themes of "liberty, equality, fraternity," the last of which essentially meant solidarity. The second part traces efforts to build permanent organizations and movements around distinctive versions of those themes, with a focus on the overlapping concerns of radical land reform and abolitionism. The third part discusses the distillation of what looked increasingly like vanguards and cadres.

It might be that keeping to this course within the limits of a readable book may leave much to be desired. No doubt. Rightly understood, though, a study like this is always an invitation to a discussion.

*   *   *

The execution of this project reflects the fact that my predisposition is to write people into the broad sweep of historical currents. Readers will hopefully find some entertaining eccentrics here—from the "Walking Stewart" through Russell Comstock to Eliphalet Kimball. *Long Road to Harpers Ferry* also casts some deserved light on a number of unappreciated figures, such as Gilbert Vale, James McCune Smith, and Ernestine L. Rose. It also offers a different appreciation of some well known in other contexts, such as John Brown and Susan B. Anthony. In the process, we have hopefully done some posthumous justice to figures often misrepresented in their own day and misunderstood by later scholars, such as George Henry Evans and Hugh Forbes.

This book largely represents an attempt to synthesize earlier work, including my own. Where those secondary works provided them, I took the liberty of not bogging down the manuscript with primary sources. I made exceptions for most direct quotes, and where I was introducing material that was not necessarily previously cited, particularly in the closing chapters of the book.

As in earlier projects, I wish to acknowledge the help of my friend and colleague, Janine Hartman, who has long provided me a second pair of eyes on the manuscript. We have both gotten better at this over the years.

In closing, the book is appearing at this particular time due to the goading of my old friend and comrade, the late William A. Pelz. We had been discussing these sorts of questions for decades, and he finally persuaded me to submit the project to Pluto Press. The last exchange I had with him was my informing him as to its progress, after which he texted his ever-encouraging words. In a matter of days, I was told that he had collapsed with a fatal heart attack and we had lost him. It could hardly be more appropriate than to dedicate this work to Bill.

PART ONE

Working Citizens:
From Ideas to Organization

With some the word liberty may mean for each man to do as he pleases with himself, and the product of his labor, while with others the same word may mean for some men to do as they please with other men, and the product of other men's labor.

—Abraham Lincoln, Sanitary Fair, Baltimore, April 18, 1864

Let it not be said in future generations that money was made by the founders of the American States an essential qualification in the rulers of a free people. ... For they are now planting a seed which will arise with boughs, either extended to shelter the liberty of succeeding ages, or only to skreen the designs of crafty usurpers.

—*The People the Best Governors*, 1776

1

Liberty: Eighteenth-Century Transatlantic Legacies and Challenges

Since the seventeenth century, the debate among English-speaking peoples over the nature of "liberty" periodically spilled out of the salons of the Enlightenment into the streets and onto the battlefields. When business concerns used what they called their liberty to create scarcities that raised prices, and five hundred Bostonians exercised what they called liberty to turn out with drum and fife to escort four merchants out of the city. Shortly, Abigail Adams reported that when "an eminent, wealthy, stingy merchant" who had refused to sell coffee under six shillings per pound, a hundred or so women descended on his warehouse with their carts and truck, insisting on it. When he snubbed them, one of the women grabbed him by his neck and tossed him into the cart, from which he gave up the keys. The women tipped him into the street, unlocked the warehouse and seized the coffee they wanted. Throughout, "a large concourse of men stood amazed, silent spectators of the whole transaction."[1] Revolutions for liberty required mobilizing broad social currents with diverse and often conflicting interests and ideas of "liberty."

In contrast, the owners and rulers of the society translated this diversity of perspectives into the institutionalized standards of a white republic, said to subsume and codify the aspirations of that Revolution. The issues of the War for American Independence and the establishment of a new government of the United States pose a broad range of complex issues, so many of which have become hard to distinguish from the subsequent course of the nation. To understand the process from the inside out—from the bottom up—a serious appreciation of the revolutionary content of the movement and the aspirations of the people should be the starting point. Still, the elites in each of the thirteen colonies would define its specific and often contradictory impact.[2] The limits on the potential of the Revolution become particularly evident in considering its reaffirmation of the mass exclusions endemic to the colonial condition.

Revolutionary Stirrings

The Stamp Act in 1765 got the independent craftsmen—and those artisans and laborers rampaging through the cities of British America—chanting "Liberty, property, no stamps!" Though many officials complained of "the mob," one British official opined that "the inferior people would have been quiet" had their social "betters" not agitated them. He thought that the sailors "are the only People who may be properly Stiled Mob, are entirely at the Command of the Merchants who employ them." The gentlemen dominated the "Sons of Liberty" which hoped would mobilize the craftsmen and laborers of the port cities where they might block the collection of the taxes. Still, it became quickly obvious that the "mechanics" meant something rather distinct from the merchant princes when they spoke of their "liberty, property." "What will it avail to secure a nominal independence," asked one rebel, "if we suffer our property which is the essence of it, to be wrested from us?"[3]

Once mobilized to resist the Stamp Act, the crowds set a course of their own. The Boston's Sons relied on Ebeneezer Mackintosh, a twenty-eight-year-old cordwainer. The descendant of Scottish rebels and the son of a man so poor he had been "warned out" of several Massachusetts towns, Mackintosh had deep roots in the community as a veteran and a member of the militia leader, the fire company, and the South End gang, which had clubbed its way to victory in the annual "Pope's Day" brawl the previous November. In August 1765, he led a large crowd from "the Liberty Tree" on the Commons and to the Town House, as planned, but then began a three-day rampage by continuing to the docks where it reduced the half-built warehouse of a local Loyalist to kindling. At Newport, John Webber, a young sailor led a similarly independent rampage, after which the local Sons arrested him only to find the threatening "mob" on their own doorsteps.[4] The Sons of Liberty learned early that the people they sought to use learned how to act in their own interests.

From his refuge in Boston Harbor, the royal governor warned that once one permitted popular challenges legitimacy, "Necessity will soon oblige and justify an Insurrection of the Poor against the Rich, those that want the necessaries of Life against those that have them." "Both employers and the employed," wrote another, "much to their mutual shame and inconvenience, no longer live together with anything like attachment and cordiality on either side; and the laboring classes, instead of regarding the rich as their guardians, patrons, and benefactors, now look upon them as so many overgrown colossuses, whom it is no demerit to wrong."[5] Similar fears moved many resistance leaders to revise their approach to the problem.

It would be the working people of the city that faced down the imperial authorities. On March 5, 1770, British soldiers opened fire on a civilian crowd in Boston. Said to be the first American killed in the Revolution, Crispus Attucks remains a terribly obscure figure, though certainly a man of color. Almost certainly a seaman of mixed African and native background, likely held as a slave until his escape around 1750, after which he went to sea. Attucks stood at the fore of a crowd armed with clubs advancing on redcoats at the Old State House. When the troops opened fire, Attucks and four others died and six were wounded. Many years later, William Cooper Nell and other black abolitionists started the celebration of a "Crisups Attucks Day."[6] In the immediate aftermath, both sides pulled back from open conflict.

Yet, "anarchy" of "the mob" unfolded most clearly in the larger Mid-Atlantic cities—Philadelphia and New York—which concentrated them in the most numbers. At the latter, "The mob begin to think and reason," wrote Gouverneur Morris at New York.[7] Yet, the British occupied the city early in the war, providing an immediate common enemy that stymied the debate among the revolutionaries about the nature of the liberty for which they contended.

Certainly, some of the resistance embraced the possibilities of a thinking "mob."[8] After his training as a physician, Dr. Thomas Young had settled in rural New York, where he faced prosecution in 1756 for declaring Jesus Christ "a knave and a fool." By then, his travels had already taken him across the state line into Connecticut where he befriended the youthful Ethan Allen. Together they completed a massive tome entitled *Reason the only Oracle of Man*, later more popularly known simply as *Ethan Allen's Bible*.

Having suspended assumptions about the divine origins of human institutions, men such as Young or Allen anticipated a rational reconstruction of society and saw a role in this for the "New Hampshire Grants." Royal officials in New Hampshire had liberally distributed lands west of the Connecticut river although also claimed by New York, which doled out land there in larger swaths to speculators. Young made *Some Reflections on the Disputes Between New-York, New-Hampshire*, defending the settlers against both New Hampshire and "the great land-jobbers in New York." For settlers on the Grants—which Young would later name Vermont—the fight over home rule actually began as a fight over who should rule at home as well. Young became the most noisily peripatetic of the radical resistance, participating in the movement across New England before ending up in Philadelphia.

Philadelphia, the largest city in the colonies—with some 60,000–70,000 residents—avoided an early British occupation until September 1777 and the redcoats left in June 1778, which left the people there with the greater possibilities for action than their peers at Boston, New York City, Newport, and, eventually, Charleston. Moreover, the colonial elite there functioned through a peculiar Proprietary government that had long enjoyed greater autonomy than other colonies and felt less an impulse to take radical action.[9] In the absence of occupation forces, these legions of people who cared little for the *status quo* and less for the past began to act on their own aspirations for the future.

The small circle of genuine radicals coalesced, not just to oppose British policies but around a common faith in human reason and the capacity of that "mob" of so-called ordinary citizens to govern themselves through an enlightened self-interest. Not the least memorable was the remarkable Anglo-American radical Thomas Paine, a native of Thetford already approaching forty years of age.[10] Biographers have long covered his life, starting as an avid student in the Quaker tradition, continuing to read avidly even after he left the school at thirteen to enter his father's trade as a staymaker. After shipping out to sea several times, he returned to pursue his intellectual interests, attending regular evening lectures before marrying and opening his own shop, returning to Thetford as a collector of the excise tax.

Understaffed and overworked, excise officers rarely settled easily into the civil service, being almost forced to take bribes. Paine taught school, preached and even thought about entering the clergy, before taking a second appointment to the excise in 1768 at Lewes, and his peers had sent him to the Parliament in 1771–2 to lobby for a pay increase. At

London, his *The Case of the Officers of the Excise* secured meetings with Whig leaders such as Edmund Burke, and the writer Oliver Goldsmith introduced him to the colonial agent, Benjamin Franklin. By then, he had become familiar with the iconoclastic ideas of Deism and the fraternalism of the Masonic order. In 1774, when the Crown answered the petition by firing Paine, Franklin persuaded him to take ship to Philadelphia. Taking a position as the editor of the *Pennsylvania Magazine*, he pondered and denounced slavery, the subject status of women, dueling, and cruelty to animals, while studiously avoiding the troubled relationship of the colonies to Britain. Those who knew Paine, however, became increasingly aware of his views on the subject.

In addition to Young and Paine, the radical circles there included Doctor Benjamin Rush and the teachers James Cannon and Joseph Stiles, as well as the druggist Christopher Marshall, the storekeeper Timothy Matlack, the shoemaker Samuel Simpson, and David Rittenhouse who had yet to make his reputation as a scientist.[11] Through the winter of 1775–6, as armed bodies began clashing with the British Army, Paine scribbled *Common Sense*, his remarkable plea for breaking the colonies from Britain in January 1776. It wove an impassioned rhetoric into an unanswerable succession of reasoned arguments for launching a new nation. At its core, however, was Paine's insistence that the construction of a rational and humane society freed from the stifling traditions of the past would justify American independence, displacing colonial hierarchies with a genuinely representative political order.

As the Continental Congress warmed to the idea of independence and prepared for war, the delegates of Pennsylvania's Proprietary government thwarted both. Eager to find some way around this, Young's old friends like Samuel Ward of Rhode Island and the Adams cousins— Samuel and John—from Boston assured Young, Paine and others of their private advice and assistance. The local radicals petitioned the Assembly, took their case for independence into the February elections for the Committee of Inspection and Observation, and called for a state convention to elect its own delegates to Congress. Such pressures forced an apportionment of more seats to the underrepresented back country and the city for the May elections to the state Assembly. In consultation with the militia's Committee of Privates and the artisans' Patriotic Society, the radicals sought to make independence the key issue in the voting.

The effort failed. Perhaps ill-advised by their allies, the radicals picked their Assembly candidates from the same "silk-stocking" crowd as the conservatives, even as adherents warned of betrayal by those who had become "rich from *nothing at all … engrossed* every Thing," and sought to "*keep* every Thing." Defenders of the old order had great difficulties in justifying previous electoral practices like early closing at the polls to minimize the impact of artisans and the direct exclusion of many Germans. Paine, Young and their cothinkers later attributed their defeat to traditional deference, Quaker pacifism, Catholic fears of New England influences, the continued exclusion of many Germans from the polls, and the absence in the army of many voters favorable to independence.[12] For whatever reasons, though, the May election sustained the conservative perspective, albeit by tissue-thin majorities.

Removing the persistent obstacle to the plans of the Continental resistance required new strategies.[13] Within days of the election, as the sounds of battle drifted upriver into the city, the military necessity seemed to justify the move of the Continental Congress against the very legitimacy of the Assembly. In mid-May, John Adams secured the passage of a resolution authorizing the replacement of governments not "sufficient to the exigencies of their affairs." One of its delegates protested that this placed Pennsylvania "instantly in a state of nature," and Maryland actually walked out of the Congress, but New England, Virginia and South Carolina carried the measure.

Meanwhile, military conditions demanded that Pennsylvania have a functioning government. The Associators—the popular militia—defied the Assembly and appealed directly to the Congress for assistance. By early June, the Committee of Privates instructed officers to poll each battalion on the Congressional resolutions and issued a circular titled *To the Several Battalions of Military Associators*, warning against "an Aristocracy, or Government of the Great," and advised that "great and over-grown rich Men will be improperly trusted" to structure the new government. The builders of the new government should have "no Interest besides the common Interest of Mankind," and take measures to insure "an Annual Return of all Power into your Hands." "Honesty, common Sense, and a plain Understanding, when unbiased by sinister Motives," it argued, "are fully equal to the task."[14]

Radicals everywhere sought to place the people at the center of the debate over this new government. "The people best know their own wants and necessities," declared one Yankee pamphleteer, "and therefore are best able to rule themselves. Tent-makers, cobblers, and common tradesmen composed the legislature at Athens."[15] Such impulses could certainly provide the American Revolution genuinely revolutionary content.

On June 18, as Congress in Philadelphia debated independence down the street, a state convention at nearby Carpenters' Hall drafted a new constitution. Few had played any prominent role in colonial politics, and one of them, Franklin had stayed home to nurse his gout. A week of deliberations established a single-chamber legislature, abandoning the old English goal of institutionalized "checks and balances" upon the representatives of the people. They also extended the vote to all Associators of twenty-one or older who had lived a year in the state, paid taxes, and defended government "on the authority of the people only ..." Except for the insistence of rural delegates that civic rights required faith in the Christian trinity and the divine source of the Bible, they produced the most democratic government of the Revolutionary years. John Adams recoiled at its "spirit of levelling" that gave voice to "every man who has not a farthing," and forced "all ranks to one common level."

Nevertheless, the new government replaced Pennsylvania's delegates in the Continental Congress, which quietly resolved on July 2 that the colonies were "and, of right ought to be, free and independent States." On July 4, it approved Thomas Jefferson's draft of a declaration, and, two days later, crowds gathered in the State House yard to hear a proclamation to which their representatives had been moving for months. Crowds cheered its public reading, as military Associators ripped the King's arms from the entrance to the State House.

Although content with this result, Adams feared that the inexperienced nobodies who had seized power in Pennsylvania might down more than the symbols of monarchy. Blaming much of this on Paine's *Common Sense*, he penned his own *Thoughts on Government*. It favored a suffrage virtually as restrictive as in colonial days and a system of mediating or warping representation into various governmental bodies that would check and balance each other as well as the transitory whim and "excesses" of the people. Adams later recalled that, upon its appearance, Paine showed up "to remonstrate and even scold me for it, which he did in very ungenteel terms." Still, Paine, Young and others found themselves drawn into military efforts and played no role in the new government at that point.

As if to confirm Adams's worst fears, the New Hampshire Grants took up the Pennsylvania model. With Ethan Allen imprisoned in Canada, his brothers Ira and Heman agitated not only for independence from Britain but from New York and New Hampshire. In May 1776, Heman took the cause of the Green Mountain towns to the Continental Congress, where New York delegates forced the Congress to table the matter, but Allen left Philadelphia with radical advice to go back and simply form a new government of their own. When New York adopted a new constitution that retained colonial quit rents and a narrow suffrage, settlers on the Grants, "almost to a man," declared their own independence and sent Heman Allen back to the Continental Congress demanding a seat. Young issued a circular supporting the effort, citing the Congressional authorization to overthrow local authorities not up to the tasks of revolution, and using "Vermont" for the first time, but he shortly died of a disease contracted at his hospital.[16] Vermont—along with sparsely populated Georgia—joined Pennsylvania in establishing governments aimed at representing the will of the people.

Would revolution reconstruct the hierarchic Anglo-American "civil society" or launch some genuinely new social experiment? Would an independent America build a truly New World or merely provide a new site for the same timeworn practices and policies of the Old?[17]

Defining the Revolution

The concept of a general human "liberty" raised serious questions as to whether the overwhelming majority of the propertyless could exercise freedom if the rich and well-born exercised an exclusive authority to define what it meant. Had not developments on the Grants demonstrated that the wholesale seizure of property followed civic equality for the poor and "middling" citizens? Already the colonial legislature of Massachusetts complained of "alarming symptoms of the abatement of the sense in the minds of some people of the sacredness of private property, which is plainly assignable to the want of civil government and your Honours must be fully sensible that a community of goods and estates will soon be followed with the utter waste and destruction of the goods themselves." On the other hand, radicals identified their natural opposition among those whose "immediate views and interests it will thwart."[18]

The foundation of English thought about such things left ample ground for challenging the dominant views of property. The Quaker John Woolman had reminded readers that, ultimately, "the Creator of the earth is the owner of it." Benjamin Franklin described property as "a Creature of Society, ... subject to the Calls of that Society, whenever its Necessities shall require it, even to its last Farthing," suggesting elsewhere that individuals had the right to enough property for subsistence and reproduction, wealth beyond which could ultimately be seen as "the Property of the Publick."[19]

Paine, Young, the Allens, Joseph Warren and others came to see that the diffusion of political rights would be essential to securing substantive civic economic and social power and a practical check against its abuse. Delegates to Pennsylvania's constitutional convention sought to embed such an understanding in their new bill of rights: "An enormous proportion of property vested in a few individuals is dangerous to the rights and destructive of the common happiness of mankind and, therefore, every free state hath a right to discourage such property."[20] The defeat of the proposed amendment hardly eradicated the ideas behind it.

Popular responses to the war-related shortages often reflected these views. The burden of the war fell heavily on the base of society, especially in the cities, while those in a position to accumulate "enormous proportion of property" did just that. Continually depreciating currency and the shortage of such items as flour, sugar, and coffee enabled investors to make quick fortunes by purchasing and withholding such items from the market. "Awake my countrymen!" warned one critic, urging action against "the avarice and abandoned arts of an inconsiderable number of your fellow citizens."[21]

Americans once more clashed with each other over these questions less than a year after declaring dependence. As we have seen, Bostonians raised a "great cry against the merchants, against monopolizers, etc." and the costumed figure of "Joyce Junior" who had been ubiquitous in the street actions against the British reappeared on horseback to lead demonstrators against the "profiteers." The action by market women in that city, reported by Abigail Adams was hardly unique. Similar outbursts took place elsewhere, such as East Hartford, where the popular vengeance came down "on the heads of monopolizers, as it did on the odious stamp masters."[22]

To some extent, these concerns appeared beyond the northern colonies. "Are not many, under the delusive character of Guardians of their country, collecting influence and honour only for oppression?" asked one Yankee radical. In Virginia, "AGRICOLA" described British oppression as a temporary affliction that "only mutilates a limb" while the financial skullduggery of America's own "spurious citizens … aim directly at the heart." The writer proposed "that the whole trade of the continent be taken out of the hands of individuals (during the present contest) and carried on for the benefit of the public, by persons authorized by the legislature under stated but liberal salaries." He proposed a "considerable money tax on all property in America" to pay the army, navy and government. That might eliminate "the cause of the evil" rather than its results. Revolutionary authorities on the local, state, and continental levels did try to retrain the entrepreneurial spirit with a series of regional conferences that decried profiteering, monopoly, hoarding, and engrossing, but left practical action to generally powerless local bodies.[23]

The more naturally volatile conditions at Philadelphia inspired attempts to discourage hoarding. Radicals there won authorization for a Committee of Inquiry into the flour shortage allegedly created by forestallers. In 1778, Paine served as the Congressional Secretary to the Committee of Foreign Affairs, leading to his charges against Silas Deane, believed to have lined his own pockets with help from his business partners in and out of government. Robert Morris and other of Deane's friends then began pushing to get Paine out of the office, getting his resignation in January 1779. "There are not throughout the United States a set of men who have rendered more injury to the general cause, or committed more acts of injustice against the whole community, than those who are known by the name of *monopolizers*," concluded Paine.[24]

Sailors continued to play a notably radical role. On January 12, 1779, within days of Paine's resignation, about a hundred and fifty seamen "assembled in a riotous manner and proceeded to unrig outward bound vessels, in order to distress the merchants into the raising of their wages." That evening the state's Supreme Executive Council heard of further "unwarrantable acts of a dangerous tendency, unrigging Vessels, and taking away by force the Workmen employed on board them." The

Council ordered local authorities "to exert themselves in suppressing the said Riot, and bringing the offenders to Justice," so General Benedict Arnold provided the military muscle when they "made strict search and took fifteen" strikers "at their lodgings, and as many more the next day, and secured them in the county jail. This entirely quashed the mischief."[25] Not quite.

As spring warmed pressures increased. An angry crowd of Philadelphians confronted a merchant who had transported his flour from a hungry but regulated Pennsylvania into Maryland which had little effective regulation; local authorities jailed him for his own protection. The artillery of the city militia criticized military standards that allowed the rich to buy substitutes and denounced the growing power of speculators. Finally, a May 25 meeting of the Constitutional Society became "a Mob … assembled to regulate prices." Paine headed the committee to wait upon Morris, who declared it "inconsistent with the principles of Liberty to prevent a man from the disposal of his property on such terms and for such considerations as he may think fit." At Paine's direction, the committee seized an entire cargo of flour from his stores.[26]

Within days of his confrontation with Morris, Paine denounced the Continental Congress for its inaction, and offered the half-serious suggestion of a "Censor-General" to oversee its financial dealings. Through the summer, the people carried the issue beyond the parliamentary debates. "We have arms in our hands and know the use of them; nor will we lay them down till this is accomplished," threatened a local artillery unit which warned that *our drums shall beat to arms* should profiteering remained unchecked. In the August elections, voters returned proregulatory candidates by a margin of ten to one.[27]

On October 4, the anger of "the lower orders" erupted against Tories, opponents of the constitution, and profiteers in the city. After marching three businessmen through the streets to the Rogue's March, they converged on the home of James Wilson, Deane's ally and the long-standing foe of "the mobility." A heated exchange of words turned to gunfire, only ending when Pennsylvania's president arrived at the head of the "silk-stocking" Light Horse. The day after this "Fort Wilson Riot," officials dissuaded a German militia unit in the county from advancing on the city, but Wilson and the unpopular General Arnold went into hiding. Officials released the militia leaders who emerged from prison on bail, but urged petitioning as the rightful means for the redress of such grievances.

From this point, the authorities backed away from issues likely to encourage "the mob," but promulgated a series of measures aimed at quieting its discontent. This included placing Paine in position as clerk of the Pennsylvania assembly, in which position he worked on a bill to eliminate slavery in the state, which passed the following March. For him, though, as for most, the problem of funding the army and making foreign alliances to assist that process seemed to take priority.[28]

Through these months, the struggle for the economic well-being of ordinary citizens shifted to the Continental and militia forces that had participated in the earlier struggles both for a radical constitution and an assault on profiteering. Notwithstanding agreements at the time of their enlistment, soldiers of the Pennsylvania Line found themselves regularly without provisions or payment. 1780 forced a resolution of a conflict implicit in the 1777 recruitment of the army, when men enlisted "for three years or during the war." Soldiers from New York, Massachusetts and Connecticut sought redress of such grievances to the point of "mutiny," the last broken only by the arrival of Pennsylvania troops.[29]

On January 1, 1781, radicalized members of the Pennsylvania Line called what one historian called "a well-managed strike." They had been in winter quarters on the Jocky Hollow Road near Morristown, New Jersey, where leaders from the ranks persuaded the men to wait for the New Year, after which everybody who had enlisted in 1777 would have been in the army for three years. That night, cheering and gunshots galvanized the camp, followed by an unauthorized assembly on the parade ground. Soldiers told General Anthony Wayne and other officers that they had no quarrel with any of them nor any desire to shirk their duty, but they sought to bring their legitimate grievances to the civil authorities. A board of sergeants supervised the Line's orderly march through the New Jersey countryside, while General George Washington and others fretted over the security of "persons and properties of the citizens" at Philadelphia where "there are numbers who would join them in such a business." On January 9, Pennsylvania met and reached agreement with the sergeants, who turned over two British agents sent to bribe leaders of the mutiny. (Wayne seems not to have understood why the sergeants refused his reward for the spies of a hundred guineas, the equivalent of over two years' wages for a journeyman.) Soon after, long-overdue clothing and blankets arrived and a commission began mustering out the three-year enlistments, while reenrolling many with the offer of month's pay, a sixty-day furlough with travelling provisions and a bounty worth nine and a half pounds.[30]

By mid-January, the success of the Pennsylvania Line seems to have inspired the memorial of twenty-two Massachusetts sergeants protesting unpaid bounties, poor food, inadequate clothing and back pay kept "beyond all reason." Washington had already sent nearly a thousand New Englanders to crush the Pennsylvanians' rebellion, and his protégé, the Marquis de Lafayette wrote wistfully that the Continental soldier should not expect his reward in this world but in the next. When, on January 20, the New Jersey Line at Pompton tried to follow the Pennsylvania model, Washington and Lafayette told its officers to promise anything to keep them in camp. Five days later, Massachusetts troops encircled them and the officers convened a court martial on the spot, sentencing to death one of the leaders from each regiment. Yankee muskets covered a firing squad composed of twelve other "mutineers."[31] The authorities hoped they left the threat of Continental revolt lying in the bloodied snow.

However, the soldiers did not just await their heavenly reward. That spring at York, officers of the reconstituted Pennsylvania Line tried (or shot without trial) six men for pointing out that the government had failed to keep its January promises. Later, they posted placards in South Carolina asking "Can soldiers do their duty if clad in rags and fed on rice?" Arguing that their indiscipline could spread, officers killed another former "mutineer." At the close of the war, in June 1783—when the government dismissed Pennsylvania troops without providing the large amounts of back pay—several hundred of them marched on Philadelphia. In response, the Congress and its new Bank of the United States barricaded themselves in their "public" buildings. By then, even in radical Pennsylvania, the authorities ruled that a government regulation of prices constituted an "invasion of the rights of property"[32] Yet, the city mechanics, market women and Continental soldiers remained unconvinced that the right of property for the few required their own immiseration.

Reaffirming the Exclusions

With the aid of France, the Netherlands and Spain, the British colonists in America emerged victorious from their War for Independence. The governing bodies of the now-independent thirteen states—and that of Vermont—assumed power and began making arrangements to codify what view of liberty the American Revolution had won. More obviously, the separation of Church and State amounted to the legal emancipation and civic equalities of Roman Catholics, Jews, and unbelievers who had no standing under the established churches in the colonies.

Abigail Adams famously wrote her husband John to "remember the ladies and be more generous and favorable to them than your ancestors. Do not put such unlimited power into the hands of the husbands. Remember, all men would be tyrants if they could." "If particular care and attention is not paid to the ladies," she continued, "we are determined to foment a rebellion, and will not hold ourselves bound by any laws in which we have no voice or representation."[33] In easing access to divorce and other measures, incremental changes took place in the deplorable legal non-personhood of women.

One might have expected African Americans to have emerged with more. From Crispus Attucks forward, they had contributed greatly to the Revolution, participating in large numbers. By the close of the war, blacks constituted a large portion of the Continental Army, numbers out of all comparison to their portion of the population.[34] This translated very unevenly into any kind of inclusiveness into the wider society.

The Revolution did deliver a serious blow to slavery, though the institution paradoxically seemed to emerge stronger than ever. Vermont never had the institution, and the other states north of the Mason–Dixon Line followed the leads of Pennsylvania and Massachusetts until, in 1804, New Jersey abandoned the practice. The colonial status of slavery in the South had made the institution less viable there as well, but independence freed the tobacco planters from their colonial debt, actually making slavery more viable. Revolutionary slaveholders such as Jefferson discussed the institution as a "necessary evil," imposed on the colonists by Britain that left the American economy inexorably bound to black slavery. The rise of the textile mills, as the cutting edge of the so-called Industrial Revolution made slavery even more lucrative and rooted it even more deeply in the South.

The elimination of slavery in the North and its periodic weakening in parts of the South produced a growing population of free blacks. That diffused a new kind of exclusion based not on their enslavement but on the very fact that they were African Americans. As cotton began to grow in importance towards the close of the century, apologists for slavery abandoned Jeffersonian rationalizations about an unwanted but necessary evil and began discussing slavery as a positive good, for the slave as well as the slaveowners. Too, scholars began formulating a new explanation of black inferiority—what would become "scientific racism."

Finally, for all the talk of the universality of human rights and the right of self-determination and revolution, the rulers of the new nation shuddered with the mass revolt of the plantation slaves on Saint-Domingue in the West Indies. Their principal leader, François-Dominique Toussaint L'Ouverture terrified slaveholders with his skill in defending the perilous course of revolution in his small country between the great powers. Then, in 1800, Gabriel Prosser in Virginia validated their forebodings in an attempted slave rebellion, that was brutally suppressed by the whites, a process quickly repeated at Igbo Landing on St. Simons Island, Georgia in 1803, and Chatham Manor Virginia in 1805.

One did not have to look so far to see the impact of the Revolution on the native peoples. White colonists wanted the liberty to expand west and that brought them into conflict with the British Proclamation of 1763, intended to insure peace with the indigenous peoples of the interior. When war broke out, both sides accused each other of massacres and atrocities. On July 3, 1778, white Loyalists and Iroquois allies attacked the Continental defenders of Forty Fort in the Wyoming Valley, which ended in the butchery of prisoners. In March 1782, Pennsylvania militia massacred nearly a hundred Christianized Lenape Indians, mostly women and children in the Gnadenhütten massacre, sparing only two young boys. Two months later, Indian allies of the British attacked the family of John Corbly, a minister in Greene County, murdering his wife and three children, though the two daughters they scalped survived.

In the face of real pressures from the British along the coast, the Continental forces dispatched a force against the Indians in upstate New York. Massacres took place on August 31, 1778 that left nearly forty native people dead. On November 11, the British and Seneca forces attacked the village of Cherry Valley, killing sixteen armed Continentals and around forty settlers. On September 1, 1781, Iroquois allies of the empire massacred the family of Johannes Dietz in their home at Berne, New York. Conflict also broke out beyond the mountains to the west. In the "dark and bloody ground" that became Kentucky, desperate Indian allies of the British seized a caravan of settlers in June 1780, killing seventeen of them and selling their scalps to the British. In September 1781, fifty Miamis killed thirty-two settlers in the Long Run Massacre, later ambushing a similar number that had ventured out to bury the dead. To the south, settlers responded to the 1788 massacre of the Kirk family south of present-day Knoxville by using a flag of truce to lure Old Tassel and four other leaders of the peace faction of the Cherokee to where they could be butchered.

Spearheaded by Virginia—with its old ambitions in the Ohio valley—Continental forces moved ruthlessly against native peoples in what would become the western part of that colony, what would become West Virginia a century later. In April 1774, Daniel Greathouse led rebel troops against Chief Logan's people along the Ohio, killing members of his own family in the Yellow Creek Massacre. Native peoples took their chance for revenge when it presented itself on September 26, 1777, when they ambushed and killed a company of militia in the Grave Creek Massacre. The McMechen creek narrows only a few miles from the monumental Grave Creek Mound. The subsequent Virginia expedition of George Rogers Clark in 1777–9 secured the territory west of the mountains and north of the Ohio river.

Nevertheless, a few native leaders cast their fate with the colonists. Born to an African father and an Abenaki mother in what is now Quebec, Akiatonharónkwen—later known as Joseph Louis Cook—grew up in a New York village of the Mohawks who took him and his mother into the tribe.[31] He grew up to fight against the British and colonists during the French and Indian War, and most of the Iroquois leaders reasonably allied with the Crown against the colonists when the Revolution came, hoping to thwart the colonists' drive to move west. However, Akiatonharónkwen led a band of Oneida warriors to the Continental army, which gave "Colonel Louis" an officer's commission, a singular honor for either an Indian or an individual of African descent. After joining Arnold's unsuccessful bid to take Canada, he even joined the brutal Continental campaign of extermination against the Indians of the Mohawk Valley. Cook—who spoke English, French, and multiple native languages—sought to negotiate arrangements between his peoples and the new government, which, however, had little interest in any negotiations that they would have to honor.

In fact, the success of the American Revolution marked a century of escalating war against the native peoples. One of the first acts of the U.S., the Northwest Ordinance, organized its territorial acquisitions north of the Ohio River in preparation for statehood. It became quickly evident that these plans had no place for the indigenous peoples. The Wyandot, the Delaware, the Ottawa, the Chippewa, the Potawatomi, and the Sauk people participating in a December 1788 meeting with General Arthur St. Clair had hoped to secure an agreement that would reserve some of their lands, but the U.S. wanted all of them removed. In 1791, they send a small force supplemented with partially armed militia to burn out the villages and the natives responded with armed resistance in the Miami valley.

After Indians killed fourteen settlers on January 2, 1791 in Morgan County, Ohio, the government responded in force. On November 4, near Fort Recovery, General Arthur St. Clair, whose troops had mutinied on him in the Revolution, lost half of his army of 1500 to Little Turtle's Miami insurgents. Now with their own central government, the U.S. mobilized another army and sent General Anthony Wayne with 2000 men, who decisively defeated the native forces under Blue Jacket and Buckongahelas on August 20, 1794 at Fallen Timbers.[36]

For years, the U.S. justified this shamelessly lopsided war against the native peoples by citing some desperate Indian atrocities and ascribing them to the influence of the British in Canada. Through the generation after the war, clashes with native rebels escalated across the region, blighting with massacres the founding of cities such as Chicago and Detroit.

The most prominent native leader of the day, Tecumseh came to the leadership of the Shawnee in the Ohio Valley and counseled united action against the white encroachments. With his brother Tenskwatawa, the Prophet, they founded a new multi-tribal community near present-day Lafayette, Indiana. "The Prophet" then set off to establish ties with the Creeks and other nations of what was then the Southwest 1811.

"Brothers—the white people are like poisonous serpents: when chilled they are feeble and harmless, but invigorate them with warmth and they sting their benefactors to death." When William Henry Harrison's force approached Prophetstown, Tenskwatawa persuaded his people to attack, initiating the battle of Tippecanoe, resulting in terrible losses and the destruction of the town.

American ambitions to eradicate the Indian presence and assimilate Canada was virtually suicidal in the U.S. declaration of War in 1812. Just as the U.S. had hoped to take advantage of the British preoccupation with Napoleon, the Red Stick faction of the Creeks hoped that the U.S. conflict with England would permit the success of their own rising. Later, with his role reduced to that of a figurehead ally of the British, Tecumseh lost his life in October 1813 in the battle of the Thames. Through all of this, the old Continental ally, Akiatonharónkwen had learned enough to urge Indians to remain neutral in this conflict, though he himself could not resist joining the U.S. army's push into Canada; caught in the fighting around Lundy's Lane, he fell from his horse and died in camp.

Over the generation after the founding of an independent United States, the liberty ceded the Indians hardly amounted to acceptance of their right to live. Another generation would lead to the large scale removal of the native population from east of the Mississippi River, the first stage in a national ethnic cleansing of unprecedented scale, duration and brutality.

In the end, most Indians and many African Americans would have likely preferred rule by a distant empire over a land-hungry white republic just down the road. Perhaps they understood the nature of the Revolution more clearly than the plebeian whites who had expected or hoped that the logic of the revolution would unfold a more expansive liberty.

The elite of the new nation had long recognized what it needed to secure the allegiance of the landless white majority. In the midst of the war—even as the Continental Army revolted—General Wayne urged the government to "give your soldiery a landed property, make their interest and the interest of America reciprocal, and I will answer for their bleeding to death, drop by drop, to establish the independency of the country. On the contrary, should we neglect rewarding their more than Roman virtue, have we nothing to fear from their defection?"[37]

From the beginning, far-sighted and pragmatic men of power, as well as radical visionaries, understood the potential of reform. "Land is the most solid estate that can be taxed, and is the only permanent thing," declared one Revolutionary pamphleteer, who continued: "Let that therefore be divided into equal convenient parts in a State, as is the case with our townships and let the inhabitants possessing the said parts or townships be severally and distinctly represented. By this means the plan of the legislature will be fixed, and an earnest version of it handed down to posterity, for whom politicians were rather made, than for those who live in their time."[38] Then, too, Paine's *Agrarian Justice* offered very concrete proposals for translating the idea of equal access to land into social benefits for the young, the elderly, the unemployed and those physically unable to work.

On a much more modest level, the Swiss-born Abraham Alfonse Albert Gallatin also saw land as a means of promoting middle-class proprietorship. Though a persistent critic of slavery, he served the longest tenure in office of any U.S. Secretary of the Treasury, serving under both Presidents Jefferson and Madison. He fostered passage of the Land Act of 1804, which reduced the amount of land a settler needed to purchase as a means of fostering land ownership and settlement.[39]

Nevertheless, the vast territories won in the Revolution allegedly belonged to the people, destined mostly to remain landless. An American Agrarianism emerged where those citizens dissatisfied with this arrangement concentrated in sufficient number to sustain an ongoing, organized and radical opposition to the predominant course of national development. Paradoxically perhaps, that located the origins of Agrarianism in the early American cities.

*　*　*

A people marginalized by the liberty accorded them by imperial institutions thought that they had freed themselves from the cultural and social weight of tradition and superstition. Paine anticipated a democratization of rights and land as "the real riches of the habitable world, and the natural funds of America—the common right of all," and claimed it as "collective property." Although he never became a full acknowledged member of that select assemblage of wealthy white worthies that became the legitimate "Founding Fathers," his concerns about slavery, women's rights, and an "agrarian" critic of class society made him something of a founder for those not in those exclusive circles.[40]

To the dismay of many, the new United States itself institutionalized a liberty that often meant little more than the right to buy, sell, invest and disinvest their capital. This rationalized the course of the civilization and could then be seen as following the demands of a mythological "free market," defining an imperative rule of capital that essentially defined "capitalism." For those who lacked any substantive capital or who placed a greater priority on the needs and will of the people, it seemed to be a system that licensed those with wealth and power to plunder the rest of the society. In the end, the divine right of kings re-emerged as the rule of King Cotton, the unquestionable dictatorship of an allegedly "free" market, and the presumably immutable and natural weight of property over people.

However, the question had hardly been settled.

2

Equality: The Mandates of Community and the Necessity of Expropriation

Late in life, Thomas Paine passed on a copy of his *Age of Reason* to a servant girl. The artist John Wesley Jarvis took it from her and chided the old radical. While he himself embraced the rule of reason in religion, politics and social standards, he denied that it applied to all. Jarvis warned Paine that without the fear of divine retribution "which now govern her conduct, she may cheat me; she may rob me; she may be undone." When the old staymaker persisted, the painter took him to a window and pointed out one man with a particularly disreputable past in "a congregation of people of color" near their lodgings. Paine again scoffed at his concerns.[1] For him, as for later radicals, our best future acknowledges a common human capacity for reason, regardless of class, gender, or race.

Some who endured the first generation of U.S. history realized that equality mandated the abolition of class privileges, if not class itself. Early American critiques of capitalism naturally bore a relationship to kindred spirits in Britain and elsewhere. As Northern states began dropping the property requirement for voting—even as they clarified citizenship as being white men only—growing organizations of workingmen tried to take the issue of class into electoral politics. Some of the growing numbers of organized workers turned to political action as they faced the courts. In formulating a more thorough program, they began to pose the necessity of expropriation.

Resisting Inequality

The dynamic that created the republic continued to shape it. Even as British defeat removed those barriers to further western settlement,

29

the merchant and planter elites along the coast established a central-ized government of the United States. In the process, the promoters of national expansion found one voice in addressing what they determined to be obstacles. They needed no new deliberations as to how to treat the troublesome remnants of the native populations. So, too, the dominant faction of the embryonic ruling class—the planters—agreed what "domestic tranquility" would mean in dealing with their slaves. This institutionalized inequalities accorded the subject peoples—resident populations barred from a role in governing—could not be separated from the official view of those who formally held citizenship.

The initial authorship of the U.S. government shared a general concern about managing the proliferation of paper "continentals" and bonds from the Revolution, whatever the cost. As the representatives discussed constitutional solutions to their problems in Annapolis, news arrived that sections of the former army had once more gone into armed revolt. On September 12, 1786, a Paper Money Riot or the Exeter Rebellion reflected the demands of New Hampshire townsmen for printed currency.[2]

A former cobbler at Albany, New York, Abraham Yates had studied law and entered local politics, becoming a leader of political fight against the self-proclaimed "Federalists." While their proposed Con-stitution drew support from the misguided artisans of the city and the larger farmers of the country, he charged that it represented the interests of urban merchants and large upstate land speculators, including many former Tories. His own later history of the origins of the U.S. charged that Alexander Hamilton and his clique demonstrated their faith in "a Common Maxim among Tyrants 'that no free government was ever dissolved or overcome before the Manners of the People were corrupted,' by securing adherents among the Rulers in several states."[3] From his perspective, the U.S. itself represented a triumph of the upper classes over the poor farmers, mechanics and laborers.

Most memorably, from August 1786 into June 1787, former Captain Daniel Shays led a rising of several thousand rural men from western Massachusetts. They closed the courts and fought several battles with militia sent from the coast, aided by troops from neighboring states. Nearly two thousand of them, with sprigs of hemlock in their hats and arms in hand followed Captain Daniel Shays and other former officers in the Continental army in an attempt to seize the Federal arsenal at

Springfield on January 25, 1787. Government artillery opened fire on the crowd, killing several freeborn American citizens. The "Shays Rebellion" faded into the back country with troops at its heels.[4] Further rebellions contributed to building a deep legacy of agrarian unrest that lingered for years, if not generations. Pennsylvania saw similar revolts over taxation in the Whiskey Rebellion of 1791–4 and the John Fries Rebellion of 1799–1800. The former involved Maryland-born Herman Husband, who had already led a the colonial insurgency of the western North Carolina "Regulators."[5] While more commercially profitable agricultural areas tended to support the Constitution, the people engaged in subsistence farming areas remained suspicious.

The Federalist repression of dissent in the wake of the French Revolution further fueled agrarian discontent. Born in Bethlehem township, Litchfield county, David Brown—a rural carpenter, sailor, and Continental veteran—became a self-educated proponent of the French Revolution, and a self-appointed agitator against the "new aristocracy": based on wealth which was crushing "the labouring part of the community." We only know of him because he got arrested after the raising of a liberty pole at Dedham, and sent to prison under the Sedition Law. Describing work as "the soul parrant of all property," William Manning, a Billerica innkeeper complained that "the Few" with wealth had subjugated "the Many" who worked. A sympathetic observer of the back country rebellions, he proposed a "Labouring Society" to battle for popular justice, even suggesting its organization on an international basis.[6]

In the cities, some original thinkers saw beyond the profit system, particularly in the case of what critics called the "Columbian Illuminati" at New York City and similar circles at Philadelphia. Conservatives were hardly happy to see Paine return to the U.S. unapologetic after his efforts to spread the French Revolution to Britain, and to encourage rebellion in Ireland. Beyond his political offenses, his *Age of Reason* challenged religion and his open letter to George Washington criticized the iconization of the general.[7]

Perhaps most deeply, Paine's *Rights of Man, Part Second* and *Agrarian Justice* proposed a social blueprint for the new governments emerging from under the old monarchies. These proposed to mediate the growing inequalities of wealth with a series of measures that ranged from unemployment insurance, health care, education, government old age pensions, graduated income taxes, and a "patrimony" from the state given everyone upon reaching the age of twenty-one.

While he wrote these things overseas, some Americans rushed them into print here. Most notably, John Fellows, a native of Sheffield, Massachusetts, a Minuteman in the Revolution, before becoming an auctioneer and bookseller in New York. He published *Agrarian Justice* here and readily befriended Paine when he got back. A prominent Jeffersonian critic of the emergent urban injustices, Fellows wrote for years as "Aristedes," deriding "monopolies," while taking up the cause of radical reforms.[8]

Paine settled on a farm at New Rochelle, though he soon found himself more at home in Greenwich Village, just beyond the city. There, he befriended prominent artisan leaders such as Alexander Ming and the Bruce brothers, among the printers, and Charles Christian the furniture maker. Christian had been the president of Philadelphia's Federal Society of Journeymen Cabinetmakers and the founder of a 1796 cooperative furniture shop that mobilized societies in other crafts in its support.[9]

The fact that those skilled workers with sufficient leisure had been organizing and going on strike since the Revolution measures the extent to which the structure of power defied its egalitarian rhetoric. Veterans of the Continental Army, such as Samuel Lecount of that ever-troublesome Pennsylvania Line participated alongside their coworkers. In doing so, workers simply followed the example of their employers, who regularly met, collaborated, and combined in pursuit of their self-interest.[10] Still, in the first years of the new century, unionists found themselves on trial for criminal conspiracy.

These Paineite circles at New York and Philadelphia also published John Lithgow's 1802 account of life in a fictional Lithconia. There "the acquisition of property was every thing, and the cunningest knave was the best man," and an upper class maintained "hired deceivers ... to teach the people that all the evils which afflict the generations of men were appointed by God the Supreme Ruler." Eventually, reformers among the Lithconians inspired a rebirth of their civilization with the decision to share the land and the bounties of Nature.[11]

America's first major literary figure, Charles Brockden Brown of Philadelphia contributed to this as well. An avid student, he had witnessed the Revolution and took up the study of the law before leaving it in hopes of earning a living as a writer of fiction. Influenced by the British radicalism of Mary Wollstonecraft and William Godwin, Brown imbued the fictional protagonist of his two-volume novel, *Arthur Mervyn*, appearing in 1799 and 1801 as the epitome of the "natural man" who left the rural Eden of Chester county for the big city of Philadelphia in the hope of finding "other manual occupations besides that of the plough."[12]

Criticisms of capitalism, like its nuts and bolts of capitalism itself—technologies, legal structures, and managerial practices—benefitted much from developments elsewhere. 1817 saw the first publication in English of writings by the martyred French revolutionary leader Gracchus Babeuf, gathered by Maria Aletta Hulshoff, a Dutch exile in New York. According to some accounts, Emile Babeuf who shared his father's views brought them across the Atlantic.[13]

Radical German émigrés were present early on. Karl Theodor Kristian Follen, a leader of the student *Burschenschaften*, sought refuge in Massachusetts, becoming a Transcendentalist and abolitionist. Heinrich Ludwig Lampert Gall scouted the New World in 1819 for a planned socialist community, though the effort produced little beyond an emigration society formed at Harrisburg the following year. Peter Kaufmann, the young immigrant teacher associated with the Harmonists in Pennsylvania continued to plan for such a community.[14]

British influences naturally had the most important influence in the U.S. An American edition of David Ricardo's *On the Principles of Political Economy* appeared in 1819. It distinguished between utility and a "measure of exchangeable value" based upon "their scarcity, and from the quantity of labour required to obtain them." This distinction between a commodity's use and its price identified a fundamental implicit injustice in the economy. Further, his use of labor as the ultimate measure of value planted the seeds in classical political economy of a sweeping moral critique of the capitalist system.[15]

Even earlier, John Stewart, a British veteran of service in India pitted nature against capitalism and parochialism in general. Having worked for the East India Company, he determined to walk back from Madras. He regularly set off again, crossing much of the United States and Canada in two visits. In the course of all this, he befriended Paine, Thomas De Quincey, and Robert Owen, while George Henry Evans, the most important antebellum voice of labor radicalism in America published his own edition of Stewart's multi-cultural musings.[16]

Too, Thomas Spence, the radical English critic of land monopoly had a certain, though confused influence in the U.S. He argued that selling the land presumed a "right ancestors are not supposed to have over their posterity," and amounted to selling "all their children to be slaves, massacring them with their own hands." Repression in 1817 and after the Cato Street conspiracy of 1820 drove many Spenceans across the Atlantic, where they certainly had some influence. Most importantly, though, their presence eased the immigration of working-class radicals from Britain such as Benjamin Warden and William McDiarmid over the next quarter century and beyond.[17]

By 1820, Americans certainly knew of the work of Robert Owen, certainly the most well-known critic of capitalism in the English-speaking world. William Duane, the editor of the Jeffersonian *Aurora*, reprinted extracts from *A New View of Society* in 1817, and W. S. Warder, an American Quaker sent his short sketch of the Shakers to Owen who published it in 1818. Joseph Gales, Jr., the Washington editor, former trade unionist, and son of a British republican also "endeavored to become acquainted with his [Owen's] system, as developed in the British periodicals."[18]

Gales's *National Intelligencer* published an 1819 declaration by "The Friends of Natural Rights" endorsed by such first rank economic thinkers as Matthew Carey and Hezekiah Niles. Following Owen's perspective, they suggested a system whereby "all goods, wares, merchandise, and estates" would be "granted in fee simple, forever" instead of being privately controlled. A common board might then plan the economy so "that thenceforth neither the capital nor labor of this nation should remain for a moment idle." They repudiated the "vulgar notion that the property which a citizen possesses, actually belongs to him: for he is a mere tenant, laborer, or agent of the government, to whom all property in the nation legitimately belongs." Their proposal would enable the nation as a whole to "manage this property according to its own fancy, and shift capitalists and laborers from one employment to another ..."[19]

Yet, Americans had already formulated their own version of such critiques. On one level, their Revolution left a continent of the discontented. Indeed, it professed to acknowledge the right to life even as it engineered the mass extermination of native peoples. None of its rhetorical faith in "liberty" precluded domestic slavery in the home, chattel slavery in the field or "wages slavery" in the factory. It sanctioned "the pursuit of happiness," but neither defined nor assured the means necessary for its exercise.

Grounding Equality

For many adherents, the Judeo-Christian traditions in western societies mandated equality. When protesting Christians challenged the hegemonic authority of the Church of Rome, their Reformation unleashed a dynamic that seemed to sanctify challenges from any professed believer. A few Protestant currents gained support from one or another section of the ruling classes, but a wide variety emerged to face serious repression.

One of the later and most important of these in the Anglo-American world drew largely on the Quakers to establish the United Society of Believers in Christ's Second Appearing. These "Shaking Quakers" prepared for the imminent Second Coming by organizing celibate, pacifist, communities, uniquely shaped by a remarkably strong series of female prophets, such as Ann Lee, whose revelation brought a small group to the American colonies on the eve of the Revolution. In the aftermath of American independence, the original colony at Mount Lebanon created new settlements across the northeast, and the revivals of the early nineteenth century—what became "the Second Great Awakening"—spread the Shakers societies into the Ohio valley, leaving about twenty communities with as many as 5000 members and 6000 supporting "believers" by 1840.[20]

As with many religious communitarians, the Shaker contribution to the wider society went far beyond their numbers. The communities produced a distinctive style of art, music, and construction, involving a series of innovations and inventions. Its faith required a theological hierarchy in which women governed equally and alongside men, but celibacy represented self-imposed restrictions in terms of growth. They divided work traditionally, with males in the field and shops and females focused on domestic duties.

Moreover, they marked one of the first of a series of religiously motivated Christian communist societies. The same New England and upstate New York districts that sustained the Shakers also produced the Yankee "Perfectionists" of John Humphrey Noyes at the Oneida community or the Mormons who carried their way west to Nauvoo, Illinois. Protestant Christianity continued to inspire communities.

German models included the Ephrata Cloister in Pennsylvania, Separatists or Zoarites at Zoar, Ohio, "Harmonists" of George Rapp at Harmony, Indiana and Economy, Pennsylvania, with several spinoffs in Louisiana. Later in the century, organized Inspirationists eventually established the Amana colonies in Iowa, as did Swedish Janssonists at Bishop Hill, Illinois.

Beyond religious motives, the sense that the American Revolution may have somehow misfired took a particularly strong hold in the early Ohio valley, where educators such as James Maxwell Dorsey sought to found schools and new societies. Dorsey opened his own "Select School at Oxford Ohio in 1811, out of which he and William Ludlow built Miami University in 1816. Fascinated by the Shakers near Lebanon, Ohio and the German Pietists at Harmony, Indiana, they also launched the "Rational Brethren of Oxford," hoping to build a secular socialist community centered on education. The following year, Ludlow moved to Lebanon, where he revived the project in 1819 as the "Rational Brethren of the West." Four years later, they established the Coal Creek Community in Fountain county, Indiana.[21] Later historians of the town and the university would incorrectly dismiss their interest in socialism as a whim.

They early rivaled the ascendancy of a new town at Cincinnati, in the Symmes Purchase, land acquired by a well-connected eastern family hoping to dominate the future of the region. Soon, though, one of the scions of the ruling clan, Captain John Cleves Symmes inspired his own visions of a utopia. A military man, he had served at several posts on the lower Mississippi River before the War of 1812, during which he served in a company of Missouri Rangers commanded by Nathan Boone, son of the famous Daniel Boone. He carried his military title through life to distinguish himself from his uncle, Judge John Cleves Symmes. Soon after the war, the Captain struck upon his "Theory of Concentric Spheres, Polar Voids, and Open Poles," describing the earth as hollow, open at the poles and inhabitable in the interior. Indeed, he described five concentric spheres, before returning to the Cincinnati area in 1819 to resume promotion of these ideas.[22] In 1820, an unknown writer, using the name of "Captain Adam Seaborn" described his voyage through the hole in the north pole into *Symzonia*, an internal world of equality, justice, peace and prosperity.

More respectably, if less spectacularly, Daniel Raymond took up the pen at Cincinnati to write what one historian called the "first systematic treatise on economy published in the United States." A Baltimore lawyer, Raymond had taken a courageously anti-slavery stand in that slaveholding state with *The Missouri Question* in 1819, before moving to Ohio. His 1820 *Thoughts on Political Economy* aimed not only at understanding economic relations, but offered suggestions for their rational reconstruction.[23] It ran through a series of editions.

Further transmountain utopian musings came from Edward Postlethwayt Page, an eccentric Irish Protestant and a veteran of the British army in India. Staying on after the Fourth Anglo-Mysore War, he worked for the East India Company, and studied "Brahmanic and occult science" before a severe sunstroke there left him "a wreck of a bright intelligent man." Coming to America in 1807, he settled in New York, offering numerologies to his fellow Mason, President Thomas Jefferson. Unable to return to the antiquities of India, he settled among the mounds of Marietta, Ohio left by the earlier inhabitants of the area. Neighbors described him as a pleasant man, though obsessed with "squaring the circle and its accompanying vagaries." Declaring himself the "High Priest of Nature and Emperor of the Sun and Moon," Page went to Washington to petition congress "for a grant of a million acres of land in East Florida in behalf of my 'Scientific Commonwealth.'"[24] The government demurred.

In 1816, George Flower and Morris Birkbeck, a couple of well-financed English philanthropists came to America in hopes of establishing a colony in America for the more venturous but disadvantaged of their countrymen. Flower toured extensively before wintering in 1816–17 with Jefferson at Monticello and deciding to organize his colony in the West. In the Spring, he learned that a small party of English immigrants had landed at Richmond headed by Morris Birkbeck, who had been convinced to look towards Illinois. The combined group made their way to Princeton, Indiana, before heading on to Harmony, then Shawneetown in Illinois. They settled upon Boultinghouse Prairie in Edwards County, which became "English Priarie." By the spring of 1818, two parties of about 150 people left Britain for Illinois. By their arrival, the colony had already divided into Albion under Flower, and, two miles distant, Wanborough under Birkbeck. Birkbeck becoming especially instrumental in blocking the 1824 effort to introduce slavery into Illinois, though he drowned in the Fox river the following year, but many from both became absorbed in a larger colonization endeavor in southern Indiana.[25]

Organized Socialism and the Advent of Owenism

The first permanent American organization to promote communities as a general social response to capitalism appeared in New York City. There, by 1817, Dr. Cornelius Camden Blatchley worked as a physician among the poor of New York City. A Hicksite Quaker from New Jersey whose Yankee father had participated in the Revolution, took up the cause of "the most needy class of society, who, oppressed to the utmost, starve, or toil night and day, winter and summer, in foul and fair weather, year after year, till they drop exhausted, poor and wretched into the silent tomb unless previously slaughtered by their severities." He had earlier written President James Madison urging an end to the war with Britain. Shortly after, Thomas Branagan, a Quaker philanthropist, described a letter from Blatchley that "lamented, in the most pathetic manner, the distresses of the poor, and pointed out some causes that naturally produce these fatal effects, which I read with much interest, and in a moment recognized their utility as well as their originality, and forthwith requested him to write me an enlarged dissertation on the same subject, which I proposed to introduce in my next publication." At his request, Blatchley elaborated upon "Some Causes of Popular Poverty," which Thomas Branagan appended to one of his books, recommending its views to "the investigation of the first men in the United States, not excluding the President."[26]

Then the Panic of 1819 dropped the United States into its first economic depression. All the old assumptions that the elimination of monarchy would unfetter human industry and ensure prosperity collapsed.[27] The panic also imploded a range of the mythologies on which capitalism is based. Market forces devastated the society, leaving honest, hard-working and sober wage earners out of work without having actually done anything themselves to cause it.

Almost immediately, Blatchley found cothinkers ready for organization. The New York Society for Promoting Communities appeared at the time of the depression. Its participants were liberal in religion, and secularists in that they believed in the united efforts of all of good will, regardless of their faith. Members included: Rev. J. Solyman Brown a schoolteacher and a pioneer of modern chemistry in the U.S., Samuel Huestis a member of the New York Typographical Society since 1810, and James B. Shey, a freethinking lawyer. In 1822, these pioneering socialists issued *An Essay on Common Wealths*.[28]

The socialists won a sympathetic hearing among many of the local freethinkers, who believed that superstition threatened an emerging democratic social order. In 1824–25, old Paineites like Fellows, Ming, Thomas Herttell joined veterans of the British movement like Ben Offen and William Carver, as well as the socialist Shey in an effort to reorganize their long defunct Deistical Society. In doing so, they shared their meeting place with several of the city's journeymen's societies at Harmony Hall, annually commemorating Paine's birthday.[29]

By the fall of 1823, a similar group of radical freethinkers around the local Academy of Natural Sciences at Philadelphia formed a small but active association headed by William Maclure. The scion of a Scottish mercantile family, Maclure had accumulated his fortune thirty years earlier and used it to travel widely and make serious contributions to science, especially geology. After studying vulcanism and dabbling in Spanish education, Maclure toured Owen's community at New Lanarck, and became an ardent supporter of organization at Philadelphia. A visit to an experimental school at Yoerdon convinced Maclure that the children of the impoverished could learn as well as those of the ruling class, and he became a lifelong educational reformer.[30]

Those around Maclure found themselves swept up in his enthusiasms. These included Thomas Say, the Acadamy's librarian, and the most accomplished entomologist and conchologist in the country, Gerard Troost the mineralogist, the French-born Charles-Alexandre Lesueur, an artist and naturalist, and John Speakman, Say's former partner in the drug business. Their plans for a school tapped into the innovative reforms of the already aged Swiss educator Johann Heinrich Pestalozzi who had mapped out an innovative series of school reforms aimed at meeting the need to teach "the people." Maclure recruited Joseph Neef and Madame Marie Louise Duclos Fretageot, veteran Pestalozzians.[31]

In terms of reaching the people in general, they had Theophilus R. Gates's paper, *The Reformer*, launched in 1824 to "expose the clerical schemes and pompous undertakings of the present day and the pretence of religion, and to show that they are irreconcilable with the spirit and the principle of the gospel." With New York's Society for Promoting Communities, Philadelphia's Common Wealths Association at Philadelphia provided the mainstay of a movement that also organized at Pittsburgh, Cincinnati and, perhaps, elsewhere.[32]

In that year, Robert Owen and his son William came to the U.S. with the intention of finding a site to construct his "New Moral Order." Early in the next year, he agreed to purchase Harmony from the Rappites, renamed it "New Harmony," and invited any interested to join the experiment. By the time he returned from a recruitment trip in April 1825, nearly a thousand had arrived, including many seeking an escape from unemployment in the depressed conditions of Cincinnati and Louisville.[33]

Most famously, Owen recruited a "Boatload of Knowledge" for the community. On January 26, 1826, the keelboat docked with a remarkable group from Philadelphia, included the educators Madame Fretageot and Neef, as well as the scientists Say, Troost, and Lesueur. The schools there became simply legendary, being the first to open public schools to both boys and girls. In the end, Maclure brought almost all of the prominent participants in that circle around the Academy of Natural Sciences. The project enlisted the involvement of such prominent scientists as Sir Charles Lyell and Charles A. Lesueur, as well as those around Maclure's group. Eastern socialists such as William Stillwell of the New York society who, years later, still had a farm east of town. John Christopher Fory, a New York freethinker moved there later, and married Caroline Maria Warren, the daughter of Josiah Warren, a Cincinnati stovemaker who began developing his own distinctive perspective on the abolition of capitalism.[34]

While on his way there, one of the founder's other sons, future Congressman Robert Dale Owen received a green calling card followed by a man dressed in a specially made green suit, seeking an interview with Robert Owen. "My name is Page," he told Owen's son, "I am the page of Nature. She has enlisted me in her service." Unrolling a manuscript of green paper, he began to proclaim his mission of social regeneration, which involved an astrologically determined millennium, which he proposed to merge with Christianity into a new church of Nature, over which he would preside, donning green and living on "cold vegetables and water." The Owenites listened politely, though, after his departure, one of them wondered aloud, "Have we been poking into great subjects and thinking of a world's reform, until our brains are addled and we are fit inmates of a lunatic asylum?"[35]

At this point, though, the spotlight remained on Robert Owen and his venture. He promoted his own militantly materialist critique of early capitalism, but also spread an awareness of other English critics of the economic and social order. While spreading an awareness of other Old World thinkers—Charles Hall, William Thompson, Thomas Hodgskin and John Gray—Owen courted the good will of prominent men of power like Jefferson. Twice, Owen himself dashed off to Washington to address both houses of Congress, and to meet with presidents, statesmen and foreign diplomats.[36]

Beneath it all, New Harmony faced deep and pervasive problems. Its preliminary constitution required members either to render service to the community in return for credit at the store or to purchase those credits. Then Owen left others to sort it out when he returned to Scotland in June to sell his works there. In his absence, many more people crowded into the town, which lacked enough housing or the means to organize the newcomers to establish self-sufficiency. Tensions developed between those who worked for store credits and those who could purchase them.

The town attempted a restart on February 5, 1826 with "The New Harmony Community of Equality." The community delineated the general responsibilities of participants through their lives. Almost immediately, though, various splinters broke away from the larger community over the year, forcing its reorganization. New Harmony reordered the work to cover agriculture, manufacturing, domestic economy, general economy, commerce, with a last category on literature, science and education. The superintendent over each of these—together with an elected secretary—formed a governing council, but it limped on into March 1827. Piece by piece, the features of the community faded away until 1829.

Through this, Owen's eldest son, Robert Dale Owen taught school and published the *New Harmony Gazette* with Frances Wright, the young Scotswoman who had come to the U.S. a few years earlier as a traveling companion of the aged hero of the Revolution, Marie-Joseph Paul Yves Roch Gilbert du Motier, Marquis de Lafayette. By the time of the community's dissolution, though, the effort had exhausted them. In

February 1828, Wright wrote Robert L. Jennings that communitarian experience "has well nigh killed us all ... We have all had our share of sufferings and exertions."[37]

The failure has been largely attributed to the various categories of the unwashed masses turning up to freeload off the gullible philanthropists, but none of the organizers of the community ever entirely agreed on what they were doing and how they should go about doing it. Maclure's leadership led to multiple unique achievements in education. Neef headed a school of two hundred children, which became the first public school in the country to admit females to the same classes as males. Maclure also planned and started one of the first industrial schools in the country. He also moved his massive library and geological collection from Philadelphia, establishing—in 1838—the Working Men's Institute, which started a small museum as well as what became the oldest continuously operating library in the state. Maclure knew what he wanted and strained against Owen's attempt to manage his work through the community.[38]

Notwithstanding the uneven results of the New Harmony experiment, Owenites went forward with other communities. Among the more famous were those at Blue Springs in Indiana, Wanborough in Illinois and Massilon and Yellow Springs in Ohio, as well as Coxsackie and Haverstraw in New York. Then, too, former communities such as New Harmony tended to sustain radical politics for generations afterwards.[39]

Wright launched the Nashoba community outside of Memphis to harness the communitarian impulses to the service of antislavery. She planned to buy slaves out of slavery and have them work off the cost of their liberty and enough to buy others, after which they would be emancipated and allowed to go to Africa or Haiti. For all the obvious shortcomings of this overtly paternalistic approach, interracial life rather quickly broke down barriers among the participants, which, in itself, doomed such a project in a slave state. Conditions were so miserable that Wright herself caught malaria and had to leave in 1827 to recover, leaving the colony in the hands of trustees that included Lafayette, Flower, Maclure, Owen, Robert Dale Owen, and her sister Camilla Wright. By her return, the community had collapsed.

However, Owenite influences became pervasive through the society. Whites in Texas recaptured a boy taken and raised by Indians years before. In a remarkable effort at rehabilitation, they gave him a good education, after which he traveled to England, and became an admirer of

Owen. As with so many other such attempts, though, John Dunn Hunter left to rejoin the western Cherokee in 1825. They sent him to negotiate for a secure place in newly independent Mexico, but returned in May 1826 with the offers of private grants for individuals, but a refusal to give them tribal territory with self-government. Thereafter, Hunter and the native leaders sought allies among the Anglo settlers for the doomed Fredonian Rebellion. When abandoned by the Anglos, the Cherokee council repudiated the plan, and the authorities seized and executed Hunter in February 1827.[40] Visions of utopia were never simply cerebral.

The Emergence of Class

Owenism—particularly its bold criticisms of capitalism—raised important questions for the laboring people who stood to be the most to win from its implications, though its answers left much to be desired. The more confrontational Cincinnati schoolteacher at New Harmony, Paul Brown bluntly declared that the community had opted not to be a community. He insisted that a new social order required not paternalism but self-government. Brown complained that Owen never had sufficient faith in the enterprise to sign over his local assets to the community.[41]

Josiah Warren formulated a distinctive alternative. Born to old Yankee stock in Boston, Josiah Warren was an ideological kinsman, if not a relative of Joseph Warren of Revolutionary fame. Back in Cincinnati, he had made stoves and invented a lamp that burned from lard, before leaving it all for New Harmony. Perhaps the experience gave him a particular insight into the paradox of wanting those with the greatest interest in changing society—its most impoverished and oppressed— to assume the risks of leaving their jobs and migrating someplace like New Harmony to rebuild society. Warren embraced Owen's critique of capitalism but saw the solution as cooperatives that could be established where the workers currently lived and labored. His "Labor-for-Labor" or "Time Store" distributed goods in return for paper "Labor Notes" redeemable for specific amounts of time spent in specific work. Warren's successes ultimately exercised an influence that far outlasted Owen's results.[42]

Back at Philadelphia, a new "Friendly Association for Mutual Interests," formed at Valley Forge, the site of the legendary hardships of the Continental Army. Its articles appeared in the American edition of Gray's *Lecture on Human Happiness*. While the English publisher failed, the tract went through second and a third editions at Philadelphia in 1826. Describing labor as the source of all wealth, Gray described the emergent capitalists as "dependants" upon productive work. Dismissing explanations of the alleged ignorance and maliciousness of "the higher classes," Gray wrote about an "unjust system" to be largely dissolved by worker self-organization into cooperative labor. The appendix to the American edition substituted the founding document of the Valley Forge community for those of "the London Cooperative Society."[43]

However short-lived, the effort of the thirty families at Valley Forge involved those who had been active earlier with those who would be fighting for radical change over the next forty years. Page, for example, participated, later talking about "the Community I was three months associated with at Valley Forge, near Philadelphia." He thought the effort "overwhelmed by a rush of importunate applicants, and there was not fortitude enough to refuse them."[44] Small and short-lived, the Valley Forge effort had a tremendous impact, largely by virtue of its location near a major city.

Others involved included Peter Kaufmann, an immigrant schoolteacher from the city and Page who had resumed his work on the "Scientific Commonwealth" in Ohio. His conjuring predicted the fall of civilization, after which he stopped using them because "the results of his sciences are so terrible in their nature, that we desire to learn nothing more of them." His efforts not only included the Valley Forge effort but a community called Emblem Place, five miles from Marietta between Duck Creek and the Muskingum River where "several families are now in full cooperation, one for all:—all for one!" Many years later, he met with James Gordon Bennett of the *New York Herald*, and issued a few final astrological screeds on the advent of the millennium.[45]

More pressing realities moved workers in New York. In 1810, the city had surpassed Philadelphia as the nation's largest early in the century, and the impact of the Panic of 1819 clarified the mixed blessing such an achievement represented. The conservative estimate of the local Society for the Prevention of Pauperism acknowledged that the crash had dropped over a tenth of the city's 120,000 residents into a condition of immediate and dire want. Church groups, with local butchers established soup kitchens to save thousands of the homeless, unemployed and destitute.[46]

Shortly thereafter, New York's freethinkers became confident enough to launch *The Correspondent*. For this project, they enlisted George Houston, "a half-educated genius" who had been jailed for blasphemy back in England, and Robert L. Jennings, a former Unitarian minister with ties to both the *New Harmony Gazette* and to Frances Wright's Owenite community at Nashoba in Tennessee. So, too, their president, Henry A. Fay became associated with the Owenite Franklin community at Haverstraw, along with Houston, Jennings and Abner Kneeland, the Universalist minister who later became the subject of a major prosecution for blasphemy in Boston.[47]

By the end of 1827, the freethinkers coaxed to the city the twenty-two-year-old George Henry Evans. A native of Herefordshire, his father had been an officer in the Napoleonic Wars, and proprietor of a brick yard and his mother the daughter of a well-off but declining family of the lesser gentry. After her death, the family emigrated in 1820 to join relatives at Chenango Point (now Binghamton), New York in 1820. A year later, the family settled on a farm on the road to Oswego near Ithaca. Later, when the Democratic editor Bennett hinted that Evans had been "indoctrinated with agrarian principles in the English radical districts," Evans replied that he had "served my time to the printing business on a *bucktail* paper in this State before Bennett *came over*, and I afterwards got my agrarian notions from a *Native American*."[48]

Evans and his brother, Frederick William Evans, became apprentice printers in the shop of Augustus P. Searing, the printer-editor of the *Ithaca Journal*. Even tiny Ithaca had residents like Searing and Ebenezer Mack who had formerly been active in the typographical societies of the hired men at New York City or Albany. Upon finishing his apprenticeship, Evans established a partnership with L. B. Butler, another journeyman who had been a member of the union at New York City. By arrangement with Searing, they used his press to issue the *Museum and Independent Corrector* in April 1824, but both continued to perform wage labor at Searing's shop. At least into July, they twice weekly issued what one scholar described as a "chatty free thought paper," though it also covered the unionization of tailors in London.[49]

Their work came to the attention of the New York City freethinkers. They drew him to the city where he spent "about eleven months of a rather irregular bachelor's life in an attic up some half a dozen flight of stairs." He tirelessly encouraged the interest of freethinkers in social reform. When, for example, a thoroughgoing materialist and a Deist clashed in the columns of the paper over the immortality of the soul, Evans editorially framed the debate as constructively as possible, and later offered his own convincing argument that such speculative and insoluble issues faded before the social and political tasks facing free-thinkers in contemporary America. By early 1828, "George H. Evans Printing Co." began publishing *The Correspondent*. After its demise later that year, he began printing the *Free Enquirer* for Robert Dale Owen and Frances Wright.[50]

By then, the efforts of local radicals centered on a "Hall of Science." The first real "movement center," it sponsored meetings, lectures, and classes fostering critical rational thought, not merely about Biblical miracles but the secular articles of faith on which the capitalist system rested—the assertion that people compete on a level playing field, that the market produces the best solution. The project became successful and well-known enough to where, by 1829, E. P. Page discussed plans for "Halls of Science throughout Ohio, similar to Miss Frances Wright's at New York."

* * *

Radicals espoused a liberty that required an egalitarian respect for the general capacity of each human being for rational decision-making in a representative, republican civilization. Conversely, their advocacy of checking unaccountable power as necessary to liberty included the checking of the unaccountable power that came with the unchecked power to accumulate unlimited amounts of wealth. Then, too, the prevailing orthodoxy in the English world saw the leveling of political power as a prelude to a general leveling of social and economic privileges, because it left power in the hands of a propertyless and near-propertyless majority.

Real equality would require what they called "fraternity" in Revolu-tionary France, but might more accurately be rendered as "solidarity," the social and political empathy of people with others similarly excluded from wealth and power. And its achievement would require the coherent mobilized power of the working citizens.

3

Solidarity:
Coalescing a Mass Resistance

In February 1831, the shadow of the moon swept across the Virginia countryside in broad daylight. What the owners of that world saw as a solar eclipse appeared as a vision to one of the most downtrodden of the workers they exploited. For him, the light and darkness fell on all together and the shadow across the land seemed to be that of the collective hand of his class. When a second eclipse came in August, Nat Turner realized that the time had come to act. Across the United States, other workers had begun to have similar realization, but the legally defined "whites" had difficulty seeing Turner as one of their own. However, what was central to George Henry Evans about the attempted slave rebellion was that "they expected to emancipate themselves," so "their cause was just."[1] Few, even in the explicitly abolitionist press, placed the right of revolution and the demands of solidarity above any considerations of race.

The old slogan of the French Revolution had been "liberty, equality, fraternity," but the last, meaning solidarity, explains their connection between them ever more clearly. Solidarity as something other than a religious abstraction begins to grow from a practical social empathy applied most immediately among those nearest. Conditions in a local craft fosters cooperative action, and an identification with those in the same work elsewhere in the community, extending beyond to workers in a similar situation so a sense of class grows from practical cooperation with local crafts.

The Building Trades, the Law and the Workingmen's Party

At the time, the building trades probably provided the most obvious example of work that usually required the active collaboration of a range of different crafts. For a generation, they had organized and, at times, clashed with employers over wages, hours and working conditions. However, most of the really heavily invested new projects often required the cooperation of various trades, such as house carpenters, masons, stonemasons, and bricklayers, so the tendency over time fostered coordinated actions and made a sense of solidarity essential to success.

Then, too, the ideology of a workers' movement appeared early among them. A strike of New York carpenters in the spring of 1810 offered a written statement of labor's common demand of the capitalist order. Modeled on the Declaration of Independence, they described a "social compact" of the workplace in which workers conditionally participated in the expectation of fair treatment, decent conditions, and wages competent to the costs of living.[2]

Conflict flared periodically over the next fifteen years, culminating in a series of annual clashes at Philadelphia. Through two seasons and eventually involving six hundred men, the carpenters waged a major strike to win the ten-hour day. Arguing "that all men have a just right derived from their Creator, to have sufficient time in every day for the cultivation of the mind and for self-improvement," they declared that "ten hours industriously employed are sufficient for a day's labour." Employers reacted to the "inexpedient and altogether improper action" by resolving that "any Journeymen who will not give his time and labour, as usual" would not be employed. The strikers established a committee that not only organized the strike but issued an appeal to the "citizens of Philadelphia" with whom "rests the ultimate success or failure, of our cause." When employers advertised for three or four hundred workers to come to the city, the organized workers of the city offered a united response.[3]

Members of the shoemakers' union provided the crucible for much of this discussion. As later described, the "present effort of working people" had "originally developed in part in the fall of 1826, in a trade society in this city." Its leadership included veteran organizers like John J. Dubois, Sr., an active unionist since 1794 and convicted of criminal conspiracy in the 1806 trial of the old Federal Society of Journeymen Cordwainers. One the other hand, younger men like William English, "a mechanic born to toil from early childhood," would influence the local labor movement for years to come. William Heighton, a Southwark shoemaker who had emigrated from his native Northamptonshire as a youth, became the spokesman for their conclusions.[4]

Abner Kneeland, formerly the Universalist pastor on Lombard Street near Southwark, began opening his church to the workers. At one such gathering in April 1827, Heighton delivered his *Address to the Members of Trade Societies*. Several weeks later, Owen spoke at the Franklin Institute, recommending Heighton's *Address* to "every producer in America" and praising it as more valuable than "all the writings on political economy that I have met with." Owen's arrangement of an English edition attests to the sincerity of his remarks.[5]

As the militants proposed a citywide Mechanics' Union of Trade Associations, the carpenters' demand for a ten-hour day spread to house painters, glaziers, and bricklayers. The last group commended the *Journeyman Mechanic's Advocate* to "the patronage of journeymen mechanics generally." In turn, proponents of a Mechanics Union argued that concerted action by discontented craftsmen could secure the shorter workday and other reforms that would benefit them all. "When the different branches or occupations of the working class have formed societies, and properly organized" declared Heighton, "the first difficulty in our way will be overcome."[6]

Shortly thereafter, a mass meeting formed the Mechanics' Union. On November 21, 1827, Kneeland's Universalist church provided the forum for Heighton to give *An Address ... before the Mechanics and Working Classes Generally*, urging the participation of local trade societies in a common movement. The Mechanics' Union that formed shortly thereafter actively recruited the trade associations that had not immediately affiliated and urged "those trades who are as yet destitute of trade societies" to "organize and send their delegates as soon as possible." It established a library company with rooms for reading and for meetings and sponsored projects within the association, like a "Labour for Labour" club, based upon Warren's Time Store. The Union also established the *Mechanics' Free Press* with Heighton as chief editor to provide information on the movement, provide workers with a forum and reprint Gray's *Lecture*, Heighton's *Address*, and Warren's letters.

The recent trend of eliminating the property requirement for voting turned the Mechanics' Union to its new opportunities by May 1828. Its adherents decided to secure candidates "to represent the interest of the working classes" in the City Council and the state assembly "to take the management of their own interests, as a class, into their own immediate keeping." Based on "their experience of past errors and misfortunes, they concluded that "some of the most prominent evils which have found place to the detriment of the welfare of society, but especially of the working classes" grew from "an injudicious use, or a criminal abuse of the elective franchise." Also, "ambitious and designing men, by means of intrigue are enabled to secure to themselves those immunities and privileges guaranteed alike to all by the wholesome provisions in the great charter of our rights." Finally, "the ordinary mode of effecting nominations of candidates, and of conducting elections for officers in the several departments of the city, county and commonwealth, tend only to concentrate in the hands of a few what should be the property of all."[7]

Associations of the hatters, the carpenters, and, of course, the cordwainers (with Heighton as their secretary) led the way. In July "delegates from different trade societies" met "without respect to party politics or sectional names" in July "to confer with any committee of mechanics or working men that might meet them on the subject of the next general election." After meetings in the Northern Liberties and Southwark, as well as the city, the union formally adopted a by-law in August for political action.[8]

From the beginnings, the new party linked electoral action and cooperation, the two immediate responses to the limitations of Owenism. However, electoral politics were fraught with other dangers. How would candidates be selected? How could the movement avoid breeding professional politicians among its number? Should candidates be workingmen like themselves, or should they nominate their "friends"? If the latter, how could the party know their true opinions. Were candidates of the other parties to be included on the slate, as frequently happened to early nineteenth century electoral tickets of all sorts? What were the possibilities and pitfalls of fusion with the older parties? Aspiring to represent the workers as a whole, the party naturally hoped to avoid even the appearance of serving as a vehicle for fostering the careers of professional politicians.

Delegates elected by these district meetings convened in late August, but adjourned to await the nominations by the major parties. All expected the slate to lose, but expected a strong showing, the more optimistic anticipating as many as a thousand votes in the county. The

Workies themselves later noted that partisans tried with some success "to direct the strong current of excitement now acting on the working people, into their different party channels." Indeed, "both of the great political parties had attached to their carriages, and stuck up these words, 'The Working Man's ticket,' coupled with the names of Jackson or Adams. Both candidates for a Federal Congressional seat uncontested by the Workingmen made "an open acknowledgement of the justice of working people's attempt to lessen the established hours of daily labour," actually issuing election bills declaring "in conspicuous characters, the words 'From Six to Six'." Perhaps most importantly, the presidential election minimized the impact of any new party.

The county convention reconvened early in September. The "city delegates" and the "county delegates" issued their own "Addresses," appointed "committees of vigilance" and a special body to organize Southwark, Moyamensing, and Passyunk, and called a mass meeting of "the working men of Manayunk and its vicinity." The results shattered the complacency, if not the rule, of Philadelphia's Jacksonians. Assembly candidates exclusively on the Workingmen's slate got 239 to 539 votes with an additional three to six hundred going to those jointly nominated by one of the larger parties, with the highest totaling 1391 votes. None exclusively running as Workies or jointly on the Administration tickets carried the day, though all twenty-one jointly supported with the Democrats won election. "The result," announced Heighton, "has been equal to our most sanguine expectations; yet it may not be equally as satisfactory to our friends."[9]

The Workies hoped to broaden the movement to other areas. In January 1828, Heighton received a warm reception when he repeated his November address before Baltimore craftsmen. The movement at Philadelphia also spread to Wilmington and into New Jersey. Dozens of communities fielded political tickets of "workingmen" over the next few years. Even those that represented no more than the repackaging of an established political party by some astute local politicians demonstrated a widespread desire among workers for an independent political expression of their grievances. Moreover, some of these parties of "workingmen" shared a constituency and orientation similar to that of the Mechanics' Union.[10]

Earliest critiques of capitalism had been implicitly coupled to the establishment of communities on the less expensive lands far from the cities and the class most vitally interested in formulating and encouraging an alternative. Very quickly, Owenites and others began to translate their counterinstitutional strategy into the advocacy and formation of various cooperative ventures that would involve workers and demonstrate the mutability of capitalist relations. These coincided with both a new militancy among craftsmen and the elimination of the property requirement for voting in many American states. Interest in cooperatives became central to this movement. The most prominent of Philadelphia's philanthropists such as Maclure and his associates had yet to form New Harmony. Warren's new "Labor-for-Labor" or "Time Store" won considerable interest in the new Workingmen's movement at Philadelphia.[11]

So, too, Langdon Byllesby drew similarly cooperative solutions from his own *Observations on the Sources and Effects of Unequal Wealth*. The orphan of Lincolnshire immigrants who had settled at Philadelphia, he had been raised by Thomas Ryerson, a veteran of Pennsylvania's Revolutionary movement who raised Byllesby at Easton and in the South. After tinkering on a flying machine and writing an anonymous 1813 satire on *Patent Rights Oppression Exposed*, Byllesby published his own newspaper at Easton. When it failed, he moved his family to New York City, where he lauded Owen's critique of capitalism while proposing a cooperative rather than a communitarian strategy.[12]

New York freethinkers and Owenites readily embraced the emergence of a workers' movement at Philadelphia. George Henry Evans's *Correspondent* greeted the *Mechanics' Free Press* of Philadelphia with the declaration that it "ought to be in the hands of every mechanic in the United States," and Henry Fay became its local agent. Ephraim Conrad's press, meanwhile, sought to replicate the Philadelphia movement locally with tracts like that by the "Loaf-Bread Maker," probably Jonas Humbert of that craft, an individual later prominent in the movement.[13]

At New York City, a crisis in the building trades similar to that in Philadelphia erupted in the spring of 1829, just before the busy season for construction. The building trades there had actually won a shorter workday years earlier, but the conditions of an economic depression encouraged employers to plan to extend the working day or reduce wages. The previous year had seen a broad movement against the "auction monopoly." The New York Anti-Auction Committee briefly mobilized considerable support among the small shopkeepers and artisans of the city and ultimately collapsed before the imperatives of an election year.

Emerging from that movement, Thomas Skidmore, who also participated in the fall 1828 campaign of the National Republicans—soon to be called the Whigs, attended a mass meeting of their committee of the "friends of the protection of American Industry, and the determined opponents of British influence and Auction monopolies."[14]

The Idea of Expropriation

At this point, the term "Agrarianism" entered the American political lexicon, as an effort to revive ancient Roman Agrarian Law with a radical and democratic redistribution of land. Thomas Skidmore, a Yankee tinkerer persuaded a large solidarity meeting for the building trades to adopt "Agrarian Resolves." Robert Dale Owen later recalled "the eager and impassioned manner in which that sturdy Agrarian, after dropping his coat and neckcloth (quite a revolutionary scene it was!) thundered out, to my great astonishment, the sentiments it contained." Perhaps to his greater astonishment, the mass meeting cheered and adopted them. The approach won the active support of Paine's old friend Ming, whose son, Alexander Ming, Jr., subsequently published Skidmore's *Rights of Man to Property.*[15] The employers soon disclaimed any such desire to lengthen the workday and the final mass meeting charged a Committee of Fifty to maintain vigilance against any threats to the rights of local workingmen.

Skidmore had come to the city almost a decade earlier, in June 1819. He had spent most of his early life in an isolated southwest corner of Connecticut, and learned carpentry from his father. However, he worked as an itinerant schoolteacher in New Jersey, Virginia, and North Carolina, where he served in the militia during the War of 1812. He had tinkered about in the new industries of Wilmington, Delaware for several years, before rejoining his family, which had relocated to New York City.[16]

Likely working periodically in the building trades with his father, Skidmore also tinkered with various inventions. Reflecting his visionary side, he wrote such figures as Thomas Jefferson and DeWitt Clinton, soliciting support for a massive telescope that might demonstrate the "existence or non-existence on the surface of the moon and other Heavenly bodies, of animate beings, similar or dissimilar to ourselves," crowing the "electrical, optical and chemical advances of the past two centuries" with a transformation of humanity's view of itself.[17] Increasingly, though, Skidmore saw such a change in increasingly political terms. This reflected a particularly acute tension with the Owenites. The collapse of New Harmony, Nashoba and kindred Owenite efforts left Robert Dale Owen and Frances Wright in the city. Renting and renaming lecture rooms on the Bowery as a "Hall of Science," they plunged into the efforts to establish reason as the guide to religion and social organization. When they revived the *New Harmony Gazette* as the *Free Enquirer*, they had naturally turned for its printing to George Henry Evans.

He had followed the development of socialist ideas and understood the impasse of communitarianism. He regarded Raymond as having failed to recognize the egalitarian imperatives of his own political economy. He read—and must have personally known—Blatchley, but remained skeptical of Owenism. He charged that leading communitarians profited "from the labor of those whose welfare they consulted." Like Paul Brown, he saw "no actual experiment made of the community system at New Harmony—everything being in the proprietorship and under the dictation of a few Aristocratic theorists."[18] The plebeian critics of capitalism recognized what many contemporaries did not: the distance between utopian community and company town—between New Harmony and Pullman—was not so great as it might seem.

Through the summer of 1829, Skidmore urged New York City's workingmen to follow the example of their peers at Philadelphia, though there were several important innovations. At New York, the rise of the political movement became inseparable from the formulation of a distinct and uncompromising "Agrarianism." Through those weeks, Skidmore worked on his own argument for *The Rights of Man to Property!* His book appeared in August under the imprint of Alexander Ming, Jr., the son of one of Skidmore's earliest supporters and one of Paine's old friends. Its goals included: a state convention to displace the constitution and its institutionalized "checks and balances" on democratic self-rule; the full political, social and economic equality of women, blacks and Indians; and the confiscation and redistribution of the wealth of the state. In its pages, the author merged the discontent of the rural Housatonic Valley with an Enlightenment secularism.

Under his influence the Committee of Fifty reorganized in the fall, as elections for the state assembly approached. Based on the successes achieved elsewhere and a mounting frustration with the employers' control of the political system, they sponsored a meeting on October 19 that launched a Workingmen's party. Four days later, Evans issued the first number of his *Working Man's Advocate*, a weekly paper to promote the movement. Its masthead proclaimed Skidmore's call for expropriation.

By this point, those reactionaries who had warned against dropping the property requirements for voting saw their worst nightmares begin to take form. An independent Workingmen's party grew out of a series of meetings at the old Military Hall on Broome Street. Its titular head advocated a program of systematic expropriation of large estates. The "Workies" showed surprising strength in the election, particularly in the Lower East Side wards. Then, when the ballots came in—even with their opponents in charge of the count—almost all of their candidates came very close to winning election to the state assembly, one of them actually being sent to Albany.

The freethinkers became so prominent that its critics began to call it "the Fanny Wright party." It ran such figures as Dr. Blatchley, a socialist then living with two nephews active in the Antimasonic movement and eager to unite disaffected elements capable of actually winning power. The party's appearance also inspired electoral activities by individual plebeian critics of the social order. Shortly after the party took the field, Russell Comstock, the anti-alcohol "Ciderist" who denounced the kindred evils of alcohol, slavery, capitalism from the steps of the City Hall before the authorities carted him off.[19]

The 1829 campaign actually proved quite successful as an initial venture. In a matter of weeks, the unorganized labor movement of the city had combined to challenge the expertise of professional politicians on their own ground. Skidmore, Ming and other Agrarians on the ticket canvassed the working-class neighborhoods of the city. The first of the three days of the election seemed to indicate an overwhelming victory which mobilized the party's enemies. Even so, the final, official results sent Ebenezer Ford, a carpenter to the state assembly. All of the other assembly candidates had come within sixty-five votes of Ford's total, with the single exception of Dr. Blatchley. In short, much of the enfranchised work force and an overwhelming majority of the organized working class had struck out on an astonishing political course of their own with leaders who made no secret of their revolutionary project of Agrarian transformation. Interestingly enough, the yet enfranchised black voters in New York City departed from their usual Whig predispositions to support the Workies, some likely responded to the unusually egalitarian views of leaders like Skidmore and Evans.[20]

In the end, though, it somehow went terribly wrong. After the Workingmen's party's limited successes in the election of 1829, various forces combined to reorganize the party, to exclude Skidmore from any direct influence in its leadership, and to place the party on a course to its disintegration. The historical literature on the subject tends to follow the contemporary sources into an oversimplification of the process. Working at the turn of the century, during the heyday of the AFL's business unionism, the pioneering generation of labor historians tended to see the collapse of party as the price for its unwitting adoption of Skidmore's improvident political radicalism. More recently, scholars have tended to accept Skidmore's charge that the party's radicalism was betrayed by politicians from the older parties.

There is considerable evidence for the latter conclusion. Skidmore's Agrarianism focused on the results of the American republican experiment with greater clarity than had the communitarian or Ricardian socialists. After the election, the Workingmen's party did face the unenviable task of assimilating new members who had shared little of the party's experience. Cast adrift by the disintegration of the National Republicans, supporters of the *Evening Journal* did seek tactical allies against Tammany, and most of the politicians who led it certainly had few concerns more important than office-seeking. However, leaders of the *Journal* faction also included veteran trade unionists like Robert Townsend, a politically connected leader of the local carpenters for a generation may well have viewed Skidmore as an ambitious upstart that had led his craft into the dangerous waters of politics.[21] As in any event, the complex motives of many diverse individual participants can support a wide variety of interpretations.

In a sense, Skidmore's proposed social transformation shared some of the shortcomings of Owenism. To be sure, his Agrarian reconstruction depended upon the reasoned self-interest of the propertyless and near-propertlyess majority rather than a further enlightenment of the educated elite. Despite Owen's secularism, though, his vision of the future turned on a strategy salvaged from pietistic sectarians. In the same way, Skidmore's critique seemed to demand more than the old faith in the compelling power of reason and the imperatives of a rational blueprint.

Many of Skidmore's followers sought measures to bridge that gap between an Agrarian ideal and the existing realities of working-class life. Evans gave voice to such doubts in his *Sentinel*, a new daily edition of the *Working Man's Advocate*. Through it, veteran Owenites and free-thinkers criticized Skidmore's Agrarian blueprint down to detailing the technical problems about its implementation. Beneath such conflicts lay the realization of many in the *Sentinel* current that the movement needed some immediately practical reforms that might simultaneously provide the wedge for a broader program for radical social change.

Perhaps for lack of a better alternative, Evans adopted Robert Dale Owen's plan of "state guardianship," a proposal that society assume the responsibility for educating children. Owen's reform would make society, through the agency of its government, responsible for the education and raising of children. They hoped that such a reform could win widespread support from those immediately assisted, be put into place quickly, and ultimately—they believed—undermine the premises of the established order. The weaknesses in the proposal for state guardianship need not detract from our realization that the motives of the freethinkers and former Owenites who advocated it could remain as iconoclastic and radical as Skidmore's. Meanwhile, anti-Jacksonian forces around the *Evening Journal* emerged in the party to challenge "state guardianship."

In short order, the party began to fly apart, though neither Agrarianism nor state guardianship brought matters to a head. Rather, the proposed reorganization of the party polarized its ranks. Both the *Evening Journal* and the *Daily Sentinel* factions wanted to replace regular public meetings called by the Committee of Fifty with permanent ward committees. Writing as "Marcus," Skidmore counterattacked, in the columns of the *Journal*, with his own "Plan of Organization." He did not oppose permanent ward organizations, he explained, but wanted the ultimate authority to remain in the hands of mass meetings. When the date of the big vote arrived, the *Journal* adherents shouted Skidmore down, while Evans and the *Sentinel* faction struggled without success to maintain the unity of the party.

The refocusing of the Workingmen's party from Skidmore's Agrarianism did not necessarily repudiate it as an ultimate goal. Certainly, some of his critics were self-seeking politicos and others feared the taint of his radicalism, but most seemed to recognize what he had not, the need for a strategic mechanism to establish policies that would move society towards such goals. In general, the struggle was not a simplistic (and thoroughly anachronistic) battle between "reform" and "revolution," nor between a "middle class" and "working class" program.

Still, Skidmore, Ming, Frederick Freund and a handful of allies launched what they hoped would be the first revolutionary workers' party in American history. In mid-January 1830, a few "original workingmen" met at the Military Hall in the Bowery to call a larger meeting for January 27 of those who "hold fast to the principles of free, equal, and open nominations" by mass convention. Determined to reconstruct the former Workingmen's party, Skidmore delivered a series of lectures at the Military Hall on Wooster Street that led to "a numerous meeting of Mechanics and other Workingmen Men" on February 23. It nullified the December proceedings, and filled the vacancies on the Committee of Fifty. That spring, Skidmore and his followers launched their own daily *Friend of Equal Rights*.[22] Their "Poor Man's party" made only episodic appearances, those during the elections of 1830 and 1831.

Within weeks of Skidmore's departure, the *Journal* faction made clear that it cared no more for "state guardianship" than "Agrarianism."[23] Elections for the new General Executive Committee polarized what was left of the Workingmen into hardened factions. Although the *Sentinel* forces elected Simon Clannon, a painter and original Worky, as its corresponding secretary, the *Journal* faction had no more patience with state guardianship than it had with Skidmore's Agrarianism. By the summer of 1830, the *Journal* faction forced the General Executive Committee into a closed session, and won a narrow vote of twenty-five to twenty against state guardianship and denying the *Sentinel* faction's right to a minority report. A July special election in the Fifth Ward pitted competing Workies against each other.

That August also saw rival state conventions. Disaffected National Republicans unwilling to become Antimasons dominated the "Workingmen's" parties at Albany, Troy, Utica and other towns upstate, so any moves towards a state party tended to strengthen the hand of the *Journal*. General Erastus Root, a renegade Democrat headed the state ticket of the *Journal* faction, while the *Sentinel* teamed Auburn manu-facturer Ezekiel Williams with Buffalo merchant Isaac S. Smith. Not surprisingly, neither ticket made a strong showing. As Owen and Wright left the city, Evans tried to hold together the remnants of the party. He spent the winter of 1830–31 arguing for the formation of Workingmen's Political Associations around written con-stitutions with subsidiary political clubs in the wards, in preparation for the municipal elections in April. Thereafter, the *Sentinel* party began to discuss the possibilities of transforming an existing party. Evans hoped that a broad coalition in opposition to Tammany might force the advocacy of reforms upon a reluctant Democratic party. However, neither the National Republicans nor Antimasons expressed much interest in the project, and the Democrats triumphed at the polls.

1832 destroyed what was left. Skidmore's largely moribund faction left no indication that it had even made it through the summer. Skidmore had hoped to inspire "a permanent, increasing party." As that expectation dissolved before his eyes, he renewed efforts to secure a livelihood. That midsummer, he perfected a new technique for casting globes, which he hoped would bring economic security to him and his household. Within a few weeks, though, the cholera epidemic swept through the city, took him from a world he had not recast. Evans, in hindsight acknowledged that Skidmore had been "grossly misrepresented and cried down, as every Radical Reformer ... during his lifetime," but expected his book would be "admired, in spite of its errors, when thousands of the popular publications of the day shall be forgotten."[24]

The presidential election dealt the Workingmen's party its *coup de grâce*. The *Journal* faction all but disappeared into the anti-Jackson coalition. The *Sentinel* Workies expressed no enthusiasm for Henry Clay or the most likely Democratic nominee, General Andrew Jackson. Evans, for one, had never been a Jacksonian but, like other Workies had some admiration for the secularism of his probable running mate, Richard M. Johnson, an advocate of Sunday mail and critic of impris-onment for debt. The *Sentinel* leaders generally declared that Jackson, sugar-coated by Johnson's presence on the ticket, might be palatable. Although Martin Van Buren, the upstate politician won the vice pres-idential nomination, the faction generally folded into the Democratic organization. What was left of the Workingmen's party which had taken the field three years before with such promise had simply disappeared.

The Persistence of a Class Movement and Class Radicalism

The presidential campaign that demolished the Workingmen's movement elected Jackson. A Democrat legendarily described as an advocate of "the common man," Old Hickory marked a generational departure from the Revolution and reflected a geographic shift of power to lands that had been only coveted from the Indians by his predecessors. Most importantly, he and his new Democratic Party institutionalized white supremacism more than any of their predecessors.

Even as the builders of the first labor parties in world history watched their creations disintegrate, the son of Benjamin Turner and one of his slaves emerged from a long and ultimately unsuccessful process of reconciling himself to his enslavement. In the plantation country of Southampton County, Virginia, African slaves constituted the majority of the population, and lived enough of their lives beyond the immediate supervision of the whites for Nat Turner to have learned to read and write. For years, he had been an active lay preacher to his fellow slaves, sharing his revelations with them and with some whites.[25]

The rebellion began on August 21 with a small number of slaves living near Turner, though it moved quickly from house to house. Armed with knives, hatchets, axes, and clubs to avoid gunfire that might alert the whites, the rebels told the slaves that the time for their freedom had come and killed any whites they had encountered. Before the militia could respond, the slave rebels numbered at least 70, who had killed almost as many whites. Turner's force sometimes spared poor whites who they recognized as being looked down on by the white planters. Still, once the authorities responded, though, it took them only two days to crush the rebellion.

Turner himself remained at large until October 30. While awaiting trial, he reportedly shared his view of the rebellion with an attorney who compiled what he called Turner's confession. "The Prophet" faced trial on November 5 and quickly found himself convicted, and sentenced to death. On November 11, they hanged Turner, after which they flayed and beheaded the corpse as an example to anyone tempted to follow his path. In total, the government tried forty-four other slaves and five free blacks were tried for insurrection and the criminal rampage through the country. They hanged eighteen slaves and one free man of color, selling another dozen of the slaves out of state. Over the next twenty years, free blacks in the North, such as Henry Highland Garnet—as well as whites such as Thomas Wentworth Higginson—took up the memory of Nat Turner as a hero and patriot.

However, the white elite—particularly the dominant Democratic Party of Jackson and the Southern faction among them—seized upon Turner's rebellion to end the debate over emancipation that had been fading across the lower South with the rise of cotton and its rebirth of the American commitment to African slavery. Thereafter, they described slavery as a "positive good" that kept civilized whites from being murdered in their homes by savage blacks. This further racialized assumptions about civilization. Any whites who offered even the most mild and abstract criticisms of slavery in the South found themselves assaulted and driven out of their communities.

Those white supremacist assumptions became even more evident in the official treatment of the native populations. Across the southeast, state and local authorities sought to clear the Indians out to make way for more plantations in the service of that increasingly lucrative cotton crop. In the process, they sought to round up entire nations and remove them to an "Indian Territory" (present Oklahoma). Paradoxically, white authorities targeted the so-called "Five Civilized Nations"—the Cherokee, Creek, Choctaw, Chickasaw, and Seminole. The Cherokee proved to be civilized enough to hire a legal team and win its lawsuit against the state of Georgia, being sustained all the way through the U.S. Supreme Court. In the end, though, President Jackson ignored the courts and sent the U.S. Army to herd these large human populations on a forced march across the South that lost as much as half of their charges along the "Trail of Tears."

The Seminoles, who had provided a regular refuge for runaway slaves since colonial times, threatened the viability of the plantation system as it spread into southern Georgia, inspiring Andrew Jackson's controversial military seizure of Spanish Florida. Ultimately, the security of slavery required a series of wars to remove the Seminoles to the west, along with the other four of the "Five Civilized Nations." Indian removal proved very costly not only in terms of money and lives but of faith in American institutions. Disgusted, future anarchist William B. Greene resigned his commission in the U.S. Army, and disaffection with Indian policy led to the later court martial of the Gen. Ethan Allen Hitchcock.

Abolitionists, moreover, became increasingly convinced in the justice of the Indian cause. Interestingly, even after removal, Seminoles like Wild Cat, Alligator, and John Horse sought to assist former slaves through establishing communities on the Mexican border.[26]

With or without explicit proposals, the maroons influenced the history of the United States. At the same time, though, Indians, Africans and Europeans met and mingled, particularly beyond the frontiers of settlement for the white authority. Visions of a genuinely multicultural, multiracial society shimmered periodically, just beyond the clear reach. John Dunn Hunter's vision of a joint Indian and white rebellion against Mexico was hardly unique.

By the 1830s, the mixed-blood Eleazer Williams urged a similarly autonomous colony in the Green Bay area in Wisconsin. Born and raised among the Mohawks, Williams attended school in Massachusetts, served in the War of 1812, and became a missionary to the Oneida, who lived alongside the Munsees and Brothertowns, and dreamed of moving far enough to the west to escape the whites. By 1818, Williams proposed that these peoples unite related groups in Canada and the Seneca in the Sandusky area, to join the Menominee, Winnebago, and sympathetic whites already in the Green Bay area. Over the next six or seven years, he gathered those inspired by his hopes for a grand confederacy blending white and Indian values. Locally, he came to be remembered largely for his claim to have been the lost son of Louis XVI and Marie Antoinette than for his visionary plans to reconstruct race relations. Unlike Priber, Lewis, Hunter, and others, Williams died a natural death, in 1858 on New York's St. Regis Indian Reservation.[27]

In the end, the equality of rights for which the Workies contended may have been real enough, though they did not explicitly transcend the restrictions the dominant classes had imposed on them. Then, too, the New York movement included such figures as Fitzwilliam Byrdsall, the Floridian admirer of John C. Calhoun.[28] Too, one can always cherry-pick anomalies.

Leaders of the movement, however, remained clear, if sometimes abstractly so, on issues of race. Skidmore's time in the South provided him an exposure to slavery denied most young New Englanders to the most visible social injustices. The distaste he acquired for slavery there proved to be anything but a quite belief in an abstraction. Evans—in his *Working Man's Advocate*—brushed aside the lurid stories about how Nat

Turner's rebellion had massacred white Virginians, adding that they may have been "deluded" as to means, but they hoped to gain freedom and "no doubt thought that their only hope of doing so was to put to death indiscriminately, the whole race of those who held them in bondage."[29] Viewing slavery through the eyes of the slaves and publicly asserting their right of revolution began to define what radicalism had to be.

Working-class radicals in the antebellum American city expressed a deep affinity for Wild Cat, Alligator, and other maroon leaders. The first movement of Workingmen in the U.S. denounced Indian removal, and Seth Luther, their buckskin-clad spokesman for the ten-hour day launched the agitation after experiencing a less intense working life among the Indians. Later radicals studied life among the native peoples, and, when Evans later revived his paper, he quoted Black Hawk, the leader of the Sauk and Fox resistance in the papers and tracts of the land reformers. The abolitionists' "Modern Dictionary" satirically redefined "democracy," "liberty," and the "republic," demonstrating their new definitions with the observation that "Northern troops" of the republic made "Glorious War" on a few poor Indians for the purpose of catching a handful of free and equal, "liberty loving, runaway democrats."[30]

The new radicalism of the "workingmen" also began to face the serious problems of gender. However, the movement's close relationship with Frances Wright indicated that it reached far beyond the usual lines of gender expectations. In the generation after the American Revolution, women assumed an increasingly public role. Certainly, in the evangelical nature of the so-called "Second Great Awakening," women had been playing an expanding role in religious pursuits. Lay preaching opened the door to women.

However, Wright's career offered a particularly secular assault on gender roles. She only took to the platform on her own authority, not claiming the inspiration of the Holy Ghost or the spirit world. Moreover, like Owen, she explicitly defined marriage as a human rather than divinely ordained institution. She became the first of a long line of often forgotten women to do so, running through Ernestine L. Rose to Victoria Woodhull and beyond.

The dynamic tended to make the "workingmen" increasingly supportive as the changing economy needed more and more a work force of "hired hands" that could be of either gender or any age. The new industries particularly employed disproportionate numbers of women (and children). By 1824, several hundred walked out of the textile mills at Pawtucket and stayed out for a week. Four years later, "factory girls" waged a strike of similar size at Dover, New Hampshire.[31] These developments made the perceptions of a workers' movement change with its very composition and nature.

* * *

"What a season of deep interest is the present!" declared Frances Wright, who pondered the scene in 1830 with her particularly cosmopolitan vision. "What distinguishes the present from every other struggle in which the human race has been engaged, is that the present is, evidently, openly and acknowledgedly, a war of class, and that this war is universal."[32]

She continued:

[E]very where the oppressed millions are making common cause against oppression; it is the ridden people of the earth who are struggling to throw from their backs the "booted and spurred" riders whose legitimate title to starve as well as to work them to death will no longer pass current; it is labor rising up against idleness, industry against money, justice against raw and against privilege. ... Truly there hath been oppression and outrage enough on the one side, and suffering and endurance enough on the other, to render the millions rather chargeable with excess of patience and over abundance of good nature than with too eager a spirit for the redress of injury, not to speak of recourse to vengeance.[33]

Wright's coining of the concept of "class war" anticipated massive and radical change. However, it would not come because of the character of "the present." Rather, it would turn on a more genuinely deeper understanding of what "class" meant, which ran far beyond the skilled white workingmen who could vote and had a plausible chance of being allowed to organize. It would depend upon the scope and seriousness of mass mobilizations of the class around what they not only wanted but would insist upon.

The next fifteen or twenty years would test the extent to which a movement could meet Wright's expectations.

PART TWO

Working Citizens Towards a Working Class: From Organization to a Movement

The Communists do not form a separate party opposed to the other working-class parties ... the existing working-class parties, such as the Chartists in England and the Agrarian Reformers in America.

—*Manifesto of the Communist Party*

From the earliest to the latest times, the whole history of republican communities will be found to consist in the struggle between these two classes—on the part of the industrious, producing citizens a struggle to retain control of the society which they themselves have created and which owes all its prosperity and all its greatness to them; a struggle on the part of the aristocratic class to gain the administration of affairs, to reduce the laboring citizens to an inferior position, finally to deprive them of their political rights, and to quarter themselves in the shape of office holders, civil or military, on the community for support.

—*New York Tribune*, June 17, 1856

4

The Movement Party:
Beyond the Failures of Civic Ritual

Half a century beyond its founding, the white republic had largely abandoned the more expansive expectations of its promise. It had cultivated political and economic power structures rarely even considering more than their own self-interested and legalistic version. It sustained the freedom of all to profit from the ownership of persons, places and things, and to buy and sell. And, for what it was worth, it would sustain that freedom for any and all. This meant little for those who lacked the capital to share in this liberty. By 1837—five years after the demolition of the workingmen's parties—it left its working citizens so desperate and hungry as to storm through the streets of New York's Lower East Side in a flour riot that recalled those of the disenfranchised and impoverished under the monarchies of the Old World. The responses of the authorities ran from arrests to government inquiries into the politics of "the dangerous classes." That same year, armed citizens murdered an Illinois newspaperman for challenging the extent to which that right to property should be accepted, which would be treated as something like an act of God. Pointing out the intellectual inconsistencies and injustices would likely change very little.

This Old World version of liberty, equality and community hardly satisfied those working citizens aspiring to something of a republican utopia in America. Through the 1830s, radicals of all sorts grappled with the utility of politics in that effort, dramatically so in the case of the residual forces of the movement for working-class politics. During those same years, a growing antislavery sentiment inspired a genuine abolitionism, part of which veered towards the ballot, as did a socialism revived by the followers of Charles Fourier. By 1844, veteran Workies sought to construct a new sense of solidarity that would draw these currents into a common political movement around the idea of democratic land ownership, a goal that seemed most likely to inspire a united "movement party" of all interested in "labor reform."

New York: the Locofoco and Trades Union Shadows of the Workies

Maintaining an ongoing movement for fundamental change remained uncertain after the 1832 collapse of the Workies. The reelection of Andrew Jackson that year confirmed the national ascendancy of the new Democratic Party. Although never as universally popular among workers as the older scholarship tended to portray him, Jackson articulated a distrust of the banks and a hostility to existing monopolies that struck a responsive chord, at least among workers at New York City. However, George Henry Evans and other veteran Workies remained ready to mount another effort.

In February 1834, New York bankers called a rally in City Hall park to protest the president's policies, but found a large number of hostile plebeian citizens present. They overwhelmed the meeting. They passed antimonopolist resolutions, after electing former *Sentinel* Workies as presiding officers. In response, the *Courier and Enquirer*—allied with the anti-Jacksonians, who began calling themselves "Whigs"—suggested that employers fire workers favorable to Jackson, and actually blacklisting some of the more prominent, such as John Windt, the freethinker and president of the New York Typographical Association. The city's first popular vote for mayor that came later that spring brought troops from Governor's Island into the city to maintain order.[1] In the end, the Whigs won.

That result left the Democrats out of power and desperate to secure the help of trades unionists and former Workies, though many wanted concessions. Evans and William Leggett of the *Evening Post* publicly criticized Northern Democrats for their acceptance of Southern slavery but focused the bipartisan support for the state charter of monopolies. "With us 'Democratic Republicanism' is something more than a *name*," warned Evans, who insisted that antimonopolist Workies still "belong to no *party*."[2] At one point, Ely Moore, a printer who also presided over the local General Trades Union (GTU), presided over a meeting of these radicals at Tammany Hall itself.

The GTU represented a serious new force that united dozens of small craft unions in the city. Windt, along with Samuel Huestis of the old

Society for Promoting Communities had reorganized the union in 1831, and it called a city-wide convention of the trades in the spring of 1833. By the end of the year, representatives of some twenty-one societies with over four thousand members in the city, Brooklyn and Newark acted as a union of the trades or a "trades' union." By June 1834, the GTU coordinated citywide support for a strike by the Journeymen Loaf Bread Bakers in hopes of coordinating and supporting such constituent bodies.[3] However, as the fall elections approached in New York, the Democrats nominated Moore for the U.S. House—he came to be called "Labor's First Congressman"—and Job Haskell, a former Workie for the assembly, their entire slate signing a pledge to oppose chartered monopolies and winning the help of Evans and his old comrades.

The New York born John Commerford succeeded Moore as president of the GTU. He had been a leader of the local cabinet- and chair-makers, and the former organizer of the Brooklyn Workies, identified with Evans and the *Sentinel* faction. Commerford, like Moore, claimed to be a loyal Democrat, but his practical loyalty always rested with what he perceived to be best for his labor constituency.[4] Based on its successes, Commerford's GTU drew similar bodies from across the country into a short-lived National Trades' Union (NTU).

The New England Association of Farmers, Mechanics and Other Workingmen provided one of the most interesting of these, being a remarkable forerunner of the Knights of Labor. Josiah Mendum and Horace Seaver—editors of the Boston freethinkers' *Investigator*—anchored the association, along with Dr. Charles Douglass and the carpenter Seth Luther in Connecticut, where they launched the *New England Artisan*. Luther and others had issued a "Ten Hour Circular" for the first city-wide general strike in 1835 over the issue by the Philadelphia crafts.[5]

Then, through the spring and summer of 1835, however, those newly elected Democratic assemblymen blithely continued to charter monopolies. The Democratic Workingmen's General Committee, Evans's *Man* and Leggett's *Post* made their protests. The Washington *Globe*, Jackson's quasi-official mouthpiece effectively read Leggett out of the party, and refused to pay Evans the $6000 bill for campaign printing. This forced Evans to abandon the high rents and prices of the city for a farm with "a poor worn out soil," he had bought for $500 two years before along the Waycake Creek in Monmouth county, New

Jersey. Still, Evans re-established his small printing operation on the farm and returned episodically to the city.

Then actively courted by the Democrats, the veteran Workies agreed only to block strategically the nomination of the five most flagrant "monopoly Democrats" at the upcoming October 29 convention. Party leaders responded with a well-worn tactic, keeping the hall locked until they had snuck up the back stairs to occupy the platform. Then, after the insurgents named and elected Joel Curtis, a former Workie to preside, the clearly outnumbered regulars turned off the gas and plunged the hall into darkness. To their surprise, the antimonopolists pulled hundreds of candles from their coats and lit them with the new "lucifer" or "locofoco" matches, allowing the enlightened convention to continue. Later, critics used "Locofocos" to imply a rabble of dubious legitimacy, while supporters embraced the term as indicative of a resourceful determination.

The Locofocos postponed launching a permanent Equal Rights party into February 1836. They literally occupied the same ground as had the Workies, meeting at the same place on Broome street, and appealing to the same disaffected craftsmen on the Lower East Side. As treasurer, they picked Dr. Moses Jaques, who, as a boy had ridden with his father in the Continental army as their treasurer, and, for mayor, they ran Alexander Ming, Jr., one of Thomas Skidmore's former adherents. When the local authorities brought legal action against the Union Trade Society of Journeymen Tailors, Commerford and other GTU leaders publicly turned to the Locofocos.

Nevertheless, the problems proved insurmountable. 1836, like 1828 marked a presidential election, over which Locofoco Evans—without enthusiasm, he wrote—raised Van Buren's name to the masthead of his paper. Indeed, the Locofocos found organization at the state level elusive enough. A September convention at Utica nominated for governor Isaac S. Smith—a *Sentinel* candidate six years earlier—and placed Jaques on the ticket for lieutenant governor. Astute Whigs later endorsed the Locofoco assembly nominations of Clinton Roosevelt and Robert Townsend, Jr. Both major parties began leisurely to pull the Equal Rights party to pieces.

More importantly, the Panic of 1837 began to send retail prices spiraling and trade collapsing. In February, the Locofocos tried to reach beyond politics to protest the rising cost of living with a mass meeting in City Hall Park. As Ming condemned the banking system from the speaker's platform, impromptu speeches at the edges of the crowd announced that wheat and flour had been hoarded at warehouses on the Lower East Side. Hundreds rushed off into an old-fashioned Flour Riot. Although none of the fifty-three arrested in the riot had any documented association with the party, the state assembly opened a formal investigation of the Locofocos. Democrats renewed their efforts after Jaques took four thousand votes for mayor, largely a popular protest against "hard times."[6]

In October 1837, a handful of Locofocos protested reunion with the Democrats and continued stubbornly to meet as a "rump" faction of the Locofocos. Windt and Florida-born Fitzwilliam Byrdsall signed a defense of the insurgency, joined by Egbert S. Manning, a blacksmith, and Robert Hogbin, a former Workie. For years thereafter, Hogbin went to the Military and Civic Hotel on Broome Street at the times mandated by the party constitution to sit there alone in an empty hall.[7]

The legacy of the party came quickly into dispute. Just entering his forties in age, Windt had already spent nearly twenty years with Evans and the city's radicals. As Fanny Wright's proofreader, the president of the New York Typographical Association, and a prominent Locofoco, he had found himself blacklisted. Rather than leaving the city, Windt began eking out a living as a movement printer in his own little shop.[8]

The veteran freethinkers persisted, as they had for years. John Fellows, Thomas Herttell, Henry Fay and other old Paineites had been celebrating the birthday of Common Sense since 1824, and their organization of "Moral Philanthropists" survived the implosion of the Locofocos to inspire a rising generation of secularists such as Walt Whitman. By 1840, none bore a greater burden of this than the veteran Chartist and freethinker Gilbert Vale with *The Diamond* and his *The Life of Paine* and raising money to turn Paine's old New Rochelle home into a shrine, to which John Frazee, a former Workie donated his skill as a sculptor to raise a Grecian slab at New Rochelle. Evans saluted "The Author of *Common Sense* and *the Crisis*—His *Rights of Man*, effective artillery for tearing down Rotten Despotism, his *Agrarian Justice* excellent material for building up Democratic and Social Republics."[9]

One of the most neglected figures in early American radicals began her career among them. Then in her mid-twenties, Ernestine Louise

Potowska, the daughter of a rabbi at Piotrków in Poland, had already waged a long personal struggle for her own freedom. An innate scholar, she rebelled against an arranged marriage, and wound up briefly in Berlin, the Low Countries, and France, where she witnessed the Revolutionary upheavals of 1830. Moving on to England, she taught languages, and made room deodorizers, a first step towards a profitable business as a maker of cologne and perfumes. There, she met Robert Owen, and took to public platform to promote his ideas, despite her limited English. As the two collaborated on the organization of the "Association of All Classes of All Nations," she met and married the Owenite jeweler William Ella Rose. The two of them set off for America with a group hoping to establish a new community.[10] On the way, the couple decided instead to go their own way, but for decades, Ernestine L. Rose became a prominent speaker at gatherings for abolitionism, women's rights, or radical labor reform.

Among the ruins of the labor movement, Commerford managed to salvage a core of the old trades' unions leaders to form a new secret society to sustain the lessons won through open mass action. The largely upstate Mechanics Mutual Protection Association survived through the entire 1840s and into the next decade. However, it seems, in many places, to have harkened back to the days when "mechanics" of all sorts—employer as well as worker—combined for common purposes of mutual aid.[11]

The depressed economy exacerbated the newly awakened sense of class grievances. The manors upstate continued to demand rents from tenant farmers, regardless of the devaluation of the value of their crops by the markets. This ignited tensions over longstanding grievances over the nature of the farming system. In 1839, the tenants rose up in a series of open, sometimes violent, revolts known as the Antirent War.[12] None of the state authorities handled the situation very well.

Then, too, radical Democrats challenged the old constitution of Rhode Island, urging expanded suffrage. With dispute over which constitution prevailed, the followers of Thomas W. Dorr claimed victory for universal white manhood suffrage, elected him governor and launched their own state government. The effort included local labor figures such as Luther. Armed repression broke the insurgency in the so-called "Dorr War," but those who remembered the conflict remained active for decades.

New Perspectives: Abolitionism and Socialism

A decade after efforts to lead a localized Workingmen's movement, Evans, Commerford, Windt and other veteran radicals still aspired to construct a national movement. However, they knew that such projects could not be organized from scratch but had to build from the materials at hand. Two currents provided such materials in the aftermath of the 1837 crash of the erratic, uneven, and inequitable nature of that economic boom fired by rise of "King Cotton." One challenged the boom-and-bust character of the emergent national economic structure and the other to the realities that cotton had gained its primacy in that structure on the backs of African slavery, dissolving the old hope that it would prove to be a residual colonial practice that would naturally dissipate.

The rise of cotton mandated an intensification and expansion of slavery that inspired a wider African American resistance to slavery, which set the preconditions for the emergence of practical abolitionism. Some among the communities of free blacks in the North staunchly opposed slavery, and even those who gave it less thought could not remain uninterested. The arrival of a runaway among them left free blacks no choice to comply with the law to cover noncompliance by moving the runaways to another, safer location. In fact, unenslaved African Americans knew that even their compliance could not serve their most selfish personal interests because it would acknowledge that their very existence would be a magnet to escaped slaves. This created an immediate practical consensus about assisting fugitives among free blacks, who became increasingly adept at it.[13] This made it very difficult for white abolitionists to denounce the institution on moral grounds and not become involved in law-breaking themselves when the circumstances called for it.

Abolition—an insistence that the laws sustaining slavery had no moral weight—began a decade earlier, but became overtly political after the Panic. In an age of intense religious revivals and a growing thirst for justice, William Lloyd Garrison had launched his *Liberator* in 1831, repudiating older, gradualist schemes of emancipation in favor of an "immediatist" stance on the issue. Joined by such figures such as Frederick Douglass—who had "stole" himself out of slavery—Garrison's views inspired the American Anti-Slavery Society. While

Garrison and those closest to him favored petitioning of the government over the issue, they opposed any abolitionist electoral bid to take and exercise power within a system that sustained slavery.[14]

Nevertheless, in November 1839, those who wanted political action formed the Liberty Party, which fielded a national ticket of James G. Birney of Kentucky and Thomas Earle of Pennsylvania. This coincided with a growing radical interest in electoral politics. Government power had thwarted the Locofocos, the Antirenters and the Dorr rebels, inviting a political challenge.[15] Even groups that balked at politics—the trades unionists, cooperationists, and communitarians—began seeing the advantages of confronting the political authorities.

What made this issue political was the reality that abolitionists confronted the weight of law. Determined efforts to assist runaway slaves knit together a series of local networks. Late in the eighteenth century, Isaac T. Hopper and other black Philadelphians pioneered organizing efforts to assist runaway slaves. In the 1820s, other Quakers, Vestal and Levi Coffin established the first long distance route from North Carolina into Indiana, sometimes secreting fugitives in false-bottomed wagons or hidden rooms. Late in the decade, Hopper and David Ruggles constituted an association at New York City that would eventually assist over a thousand slaves.

Ultimately, genuine abolitionists of all sorts united to resist enforcement of the Fugitive Slave Law. In the 1840s, the home of Reverend John Rankin on a hill over Ripley, Ohio towered over the river just across from slaveholding Kentucky. Meanwhile, Josiah Henson and others formed the Dawn institute near Dresden in Ontario as one of the most important centers to retrain fugitives in the safety of Canada, educating and training them for life as free people. In 1844, Zebina Eastman's Liberty Party newspaper, the *Western Citizen* at Chicago, introduced the language of railroads into the process, referring to "stations" and "station masters," moving "cars" with "passengers" along the way to freedom.[16]

Modern scholarship has sought to demystify the scale of organization, the importance of whites within it and the role of that supporting network in the plans of individual slaves to make their bid for freedom. The implication that one could generalize about the network implied a more formal national organization with regular meetings among dues-paying membership with fixed abodes. Whether in the legendary view or the revisionist corrective, perhaps the greatest problem disallows the very great variations in where, when and how escapes from slavery took place. The actual numbers of those who successfully escaped slavery remains hotly debated. Some, on both sides of the issue had interests in both exaggerating and minimizing the numbers, and offered widely different estimates. Estimates range from 25,000 to 100,000, with the census numbers for blacks in Canada West officially showing only 11,000 in 1860. One of the organizers of the escape network on the northern border offered very specific estimates that "nearly 40,000" gained freedom crossing "into Canada over Detroit and St. Clair rivers between the years 1829 and 1862," with a total of 50,000 reaching Canada overall, with thousands more hiding in communities in the non-slaveholding states of the North.[17] Reliance on the official numbers in Canada, of course, assume runaways took up residence openly there or did not drift back into the northern U.S., as they thought it was safe

Certainly, slaveowners saw abolitionism as an attempt to expropriate their wealth in pursuit of some abstract notions of human liberty, a position they shared with the American elite generally in response to a revitalized socialism. Years before, as a well-heeled nineteen-year-old from Batavia, New York, Albert Brisbane had headed to Europe where he studied under such thinkers as Georg Wilhelm Friedrich Hegel, and became acquainted with such diverse figures as Karl Ludwig Michelet, Heinrich Heine, Felix Mendelssohn and Franz Liszt. When classes were out, he wandered far afield. In 1832, after four years of this intellectual vagabondage, Brisbane had gone to Paris, where thinkers such as Henri Saint-Simon (who had fought with our French allies in the War for Independence), Victor Considerant and, later, Auguste Comte proposed a new science of society.[18]

None impressed Brisbane as thoroughly as had the elderly Charles Fourier. In 1801, Fourier's *Les Quatres Mouvements* announced what he called his great discovery of the vast organic and mystical universe in which the existing material status quo of the western world would be transient. Owen had hoped to persuade governments to take appropriate measures to make its subjects happy, clean and industrious. St. Simon had even looked to an autocracy of talent to make this transition. The tailor Fourier, however, anticipated a democratic mingling of all classes in *phalanstères*, huge apartment buildings that would provide residents their food, heat, laundry and other necessities.

As the U.S. economy collapsed, Brisbane returned and set to work gingerly publicizing Fourier's perspectives. With his former tutor, he launched a Fourienne Society, composed mostly of French speakers around New York City. Persistent effort over the next three years enabled them to publish Brisbane's *Social Destiny of Man*, followed by a weekly paper, the *Phalanx*. They called their Americanized version of Fourier's blueprint *Associationism*. Early allies included Osborne Macdaniel, Parke Godwin, and Horace Greeley, the eccentric young country printer who had just gained control of the *New York Tribune*, which he built into what became, for a while, the most widely read paper in the nation.

George Ripley, William Henry Channing, Charles A. Dana, John Dwight and other members and associates of the Transcendentalist Club at Boston had already formed their own community at Brook Farm in West Roxbury. They launched one of the prominent reform publications of the day, the *Harbinger*, proclaiming Fourierism a fuller expression of their concerns and hopes. Over the next few years, dozens of new phalanxes popped up not only across the northeast, but in Ohio, Michigan, Illinois and Wisconsin, and as far south as Virginia. As new *phalanstères* began to form, they created the American Union of Associationists.[19]

Fourierism remained vague—or flexible—enough to appeal to an immense range of figures with criticisms of capitalism, functioning under the rubric of the American Union of Associationists (AUA). It had close ties to other communitary currents with A. D. Wright, J. J. Franks, R. S. De Latre, Henry J. Seymour, and others leaving to join the Perfectionists' community of evangelical Christians at Oneida. The descendant of Hicksite settlers in Vermont, John Orvis had dropped out of Oberlin and studied mutual insurance and antislavery under Elizur Wright. The middle-aged New York shoemaker Lewis W. Ryckman resurrected cooperation as a variation, as had Josiah Warren among the Owenites.[20] Indeed, Ryckman may well have had earlier experience among the Owenites and Workies.

The Longley clan demonstrated the complex interconnections of radicalism in the Ohio Valley. From Yankee roots, the family moved through New York, settling in Butler County, Ohio. There, the cabinet-maker Abner Longley pursued his education under William H. McGuffey—yet to win fame for his readers—at Miami University, founded in part by the old Owenite James M. Dorsey. Longley emerged as a "New Light" Universalist, an early settler at Lebanon, Indiana, and going into the legislature as a Jackson Democrat (though he later became a Republican). By the time he moved to Cincinnati, he had taken up Fourierism, becoming involved in the socialist community at what would later be Utopia, along with Josiah Warren and the Wattles brothers—John O. and Augustus Wattles. Abner's sons followed his example, Elias becoming a printer, who promoted phonetic and phonographic spelling. His brothers—Servetus, Septimius, Cyrenius, Alcander, Albert and Abner—followed him into the trade, and their two sisters—Salome and Mary A.—married printers or editors.[21]

Young Alcander Longley spent a lifetime synthesizing radical impulses in the region. He took up Fourierism, land reform, cooperation, and spelling reform with alacrity. Other local radicals, such as Lucius A. Hine, William McDiarmid, and William Haller shared the breadth of Longley's interests and the first two the noteworthy longevity of his career.[22] Longley lived long enough to play a role in the Socialistic Labor Party after the Civil War and died while trying to organize a cooperative project in Chicago in the wake of the 1917 Russian Revolution.

Up the river at Marietta, Edward P. Page continued to pursue his own projects. After the Federal government declined to give him Florida, he headed for St. Domingo, returning to report South America "a paradise for communities." Afterwards, he passed on his mantel to local followers and died the following spring.[23] They buried him in the local Mound Cemetery, alongside town founders, Revolutionary veterans, and beneath the large ancient burial mound of the original inhabitants, which lent its name to the grounds.

Racism may have obscured and minimized the impact of those Fourierist "intentional communities," but its course became inseparable from that of abolitionism, particularly those involved in the Liberty Party. Although the party had gained only small and localized support in 1840, it held another national convention at Buffalo in August 1843 to renominate Birney for president. When the Fourierists held their own convention the following December, they invited the abolitionists. Conversely, even the anti-electoral abolitionists around Garrison found themselves following the Libertymen towards a "broad platform."

The New York agent of Garrison's organization, John A. Collins, for example, publicly embraced Owenism and Fourierism, organizing the Skaneateles Community upstate himself.[24]

Amid the remnants of a workers movement in the New York City area, Evans and his circle followed all of this with a certain guarded sympathy. The freethinking secularist Locofoco workingmen had difficulty grasping the evangelical insistence on the conscious, individual rejection of sin. It seemed as though a great social gulf divided the middle-class clergy and professionals who shaped abolitionism from craftsmen who led the National Reform Association (NRA) and the middle-class clergymen, though recent scholars have rightly argued for greater similarity than expected.[25] So, too, Fourierism—like Owenism—seemed to be an insufficient, abstract retreat from politics.

Evans addressed the problems posed by the various personal styles of social reform sketched by the abolitionist *National Era*. The "hot blooded and hasty" radical of "an irascible temper" denounced anything or anybody, in or out of the movement for deviations from its principles, producing "the little clique" sensing the destiny of the human race in its hands and combining a "narrow mind and honest purpose" in a leader "who feels, but does not reason." The "constitutional declaimer" and the kindred "metaphysical reformer" had facts and figures at his fingertips to "display his skill in exhibiting its numerous phases" before the public and to hold the organization to the straight and narrow. "More anxious to be right and useful than conspicuous and in authority," the "true reformer" hoped to be "practical as well as speculative," suspected "a wisdom he has not reached," and realized that "a bitter fountain cannot send forth sweet waters."[26] Evans sought a movement with room for all three, but denied to the "hot blooded and hasty" a self-destructive prominence and to the "constitutional declaimer" a special doctrine.

By the winter of 1840–41, Evans launched his own periodical, the title of which reflected what he thought should be the focus of a broad, united movement—*The Radical: Devoted to the Abolition of the Land Monopoly and Other Democratic Reforms*. By the fall of 1841, he proposed electoral action around nonpartisan electoral strategy. Participants would agree not to support any candidate "who will not pledge himself to exercise all the proper influence of his situation to restore to the people, in some equitable manner, the Equal Right to Land.[27]

In particular, Evans urged political action for land reform around three fundamental measures. First, he urged that legislatures exempt the seizure and resale of homesteads themselves for debts. On purely economic grounds, prevailing practices left creditors unable to get more than a fraction of the debt. His argument assumed the social, political and cultural value of the family farm and its importance in keeping food production and land from further concentrations and speculation.

Second, he extended the professions of American republicanism into practice with Federal Homestead Bill. This would permit the free settlement upon the public domain by landless Americans and those declaring their intention of becoming citizens. The United States government, which claimed to belong to its citizens, owned vast tracts of land while most of these citizens had none. Here, too, officeholders had already raised such legislation, in part, perhaps, to foster the more rapid development of their region. Evans, however, saw the measure as the fulcrum for shifting American life.

The final proposal limited the amount of land any individual could own. Evans correctly viewed this as both his most radical measure, and that most essential to his complete program. Although often denounced as an attack on private property, proponents pointed out that the measure would increase the number of landholders. Coupled to a homestead bill, it would keep western development egalitarian and ultimately re-establish the social foundations elsewhere for a genuine republic.

Some of his comrades later described Evans as "the first" to address the fundamental grounds of social inequality, but his real contribution synthesized much that had gone before. He reviewed various social critiques and attributed many of his ideas to John Gray and Thomas Spence of Britain, as well as Saint-Simon and Fourier of France, even citing individuals of color. He lifted the name for his proposed movement—*National Reform*—from evangelical Christianity.[28]

Their radicalism clearly grew within the dominant American culture, for all its confusions and clarities. Some would certainly trace their tradition to the Democratic Party, which—in New York, at least— claimed a direct continuity from Jefferson's old party. These spoke of land reform as rooted in the views of Jefferson, as opposed to the Federalist perspective of Alexander Hamilton. While Jeriel Root, a self-described life-long Jeffersonian Democrat in central Illinois, concluded that his party had adopted "the principles of the old federalism." Indeed, Jaques pointed out that he had discussed inequalities in the land in an 1835 letter to Andrew Jackson. Citations of Jefferson became ubiquitous in the early writings of Evans and other National Reformers.[29] Appeals to Jefferson or even Jackson seem ubiquitous in early movement literature, though they faded rather quickly. Jefferson did have some claim on them. He responded cordially to Skidmore's speculations about life beyond the Earth, though he annotated those of Edward P. Page with "Mad" or "Lunatic." He responded favorably to the Society for Promoting Communities, and to William Ludlow of the Rational Brethren. He met Frances Wright, and acknowledged her plans for Nashoba had inspired "certain portions of our white brethren, under the care of a Rapp and an Owen; and why may it not succeed with the man of colour?"[30] Nevertheless, while forward-thinking enough to be lionized by generations of radicals, Jefferson never really superseded the limited social vision of a slave-holding Virginia patriarch.

Most fittingly, radicals claimed the legacy of Tom Paine. Long the hero of secularists, land reformers regularly participated in the annual festivities around Paine's birthday. Too, when radicals launched their own celebrations of the Fourth of July, they sometimes chartered steamboats to nearby locations, like Paine's old farm at New Rochelle. Gilbert Vale campaigned to rehabilitate Paine's reputation with a solid little biography and the transformation of his old home into a shrine to his memory. At an 1846 NRA "ball," Evans saluted "The Author of *Common Sense* and *the Crisis*—his *Rights of Man*, effective artillery for tearing down Rotten Despotism, his *Agrarian Justice*, excellent material for building up Democratic and Social Republics."[31]

Personal associations to that plebeian dimension of the Revolutionary tradition were essential. The old Minuteman John Fellows, who died in early 1844, merits consideration as a vital pioneer of the land reform idea. One old Continental veteran assured Thomas A. Devyr "that neither Land Monopoly nor Bank Monopoly was ever contemplated" by those who had won independence. An octogenarian Revolutionary veteran attended meetings in the city. Somewhat later, "a Patriarch 99 years old, strong in health, clear in intellect" showed up to declare himself a National Reformer. The local Veterans Corps of the War of 1812 included a spate of other local radicals who had been active in the war, including Samuel Huestis of the old Society for Promoting Communities endorsed the NRA plan.[32]

National Reformers sought to root themselves in the American experience, even as they grappled with the peculiarities of their national experience. In the process, they regularly brushed aside the social restrictions and limitations on the American political system. Conceding the validity of communitarian withdrawal by the disenfranchised of Europe, Commerford thought that, in America, the ballot meant that what was "socially wrong can be politically righted." With an eye to the contemporary Chartist efforts to secure electoral rights in Britain, Evans agreed that Americans enjoyed "those means of progress," which obligated them to fight for "something more *ultimate* than they." This made Evans's approach "the most truly American measure," and "the greatest idea" since the attainment of independence.[33]

Even more paradoxical perhaps, National Reform alternately presented itself a simple common sense solution to social problems—measures easily adopted by governmental bodies—while regularly discussing its long term social implications. Moreover, the involvement of the Libertymen in politics would make it ultimately impossible for the old Locofocos to avoid slavery. So, too, the more general the insurgency became, the more difficult it would be to avoid the general critique of capitalism posed by the Owenists and Fourierists.

Also, land reform seemed to be the simplest kind of measure. If a thousand carpenters jostled for 950 jobs in the city, explained Commerford, the opening of the public lands would enable them to raise money to move fifty of their number and their families to the west, leaving reduced hours and full employment for those who remained. In no immediate sense, as Henry H. Van Amringe explained, would such a law "invade *what are called* vested rights in land" or "invalidate existing vested titles to land."[34] The reaction in the streets to the NRA's message bolstered their faith in this strategy.

National Reform and Revolution

By late February 1844, Evans and Windt recruited Devyr. A thirty-nine-year-old veteran of the "physical force" wing of the British and Irish movements, and implicated in its insurrectionary plans. He fled to New York where he edited a Democratic campaign paper before turning to the seemingly familiar struggle of the tenant farmers upstate. On Tuesday, March 8, they gathered a handful of others in the back room of Windt's print shop, and "projected *The National Reform Party*," a movement Devyr said "eventually led to the Great Civil War."[35]

Land reform had particular appeal to a distinct strata of the work force, but that was exactly what the NRA had, at least to start. Not only were they all white, male and skilled, but they were close to Evans's age, thirty-nine. Several recalled the pioneering days of organized free-thought and the Workingmens' Party of fifteen years before; more had participated in the Locofoco revolt, a few simultaneously leading unions of the local craft and efforts at national labor federations. Aside from the émigrés—Devyr and émigré Canadian revolutionary William Lyon Mackenzie—they had been born or raised in the U.S. [36]

Evans and his core group shared an ability to see society through the eyes of the enfranchised workingmen he hoped to reach. Skilled craftsmen defined themselves by self-sufficiency, personal liberty, and willingness to accept social responsibility. Radicals further realized that the same concerns about home, family, personal autonomy and economic security that drove the engines of competitive industry and industrial development would also be thwarted in most cases by the emerging social order.[37] They understood that such aspirations, when denied, provided a spur to radicalization.

The initial point of unity for the NRA was something like the temperance pledge in which signers promised to swear off voting for the enemies of land reform. That is, those who refused to give their written promise to work for homestead exemption, land limitation, and an end to "all further traffic in the Public Lands of the states and of the United States, and to cause them to be laid out in Farms and Lots for the free and exclusive use of actual settlers." The core of the NRA understood that it could successfully magnify its influence by mobilizing the broader Agrarian and democratic concerns of their fellow citizens.

The NRA left no official records beyond what found their way into the press. Too, it sometimes functioned under the name of the "Agrarian League" or "Young America," an explicit echo of the "Young Europe" organizations—not to be confused with the expansionist Democratic literary circle. From its inception, the NRA projected formation of affiliates at Brooklyn, Albany, Troy, Lowell, Philadelphia and Boston, and planned a "Missionary system" to send paid spokespeople to form auxiliary groups elsewhere. It established affiliates from New England south to Philadelphia, Wilmington, and Baltimore, and as far west as Chicago and Milwaukee.

Reasonable estimates of the NRA's strength could run from a mostly artisan base of several hundred, mostly in the eastern cities, to well into tens of thousands with over two hundred papers supporting their measures. However, the social composition and the perception of political openings made for a fluctuating level of organization and activity. The New York City group met weekly until organized and then tended to gather monthly, though these evolved to be monthly meetings, and, later, more infrequent assemblies. While strong in places, a very lax organization sufficed in places such as New Harmony, where the association often hibernated until going into intense periods of activities when relevant legislation pended.[38]

The NRA provided no doctrinaire blueprint to which the masses might be won. Evans took a particularly pragmatic and open-ended course, placing him at odds with other freethinkers who wanted to make an issue of religion. To him, whether one viewed the earth as a manifestation of Nature's bounty or divine benevolence mattered little to the achievement of these measures. Notwithstanding their Locofoco roots, the new movement drew upon Whigs, Libertymen and even nonvoting opponents of government into its ranks.

Land reform successfully solicited the support of experienced activists. Most organizations through the history of the movement have found it easier to focus on the recruitment of people generally inexperienced in radical politics. They ask more basic questions, express fewer doubts and those more easily addressed. While eager to draw such members and supporters, land reform hoped to persuade experienced radicals and even aspired to regroup entire organizations behind its efforts.

After months of preliminary efforts, it sought to draw other radicals in a national convention in May 1845. It also participated in Robert Owen's "World Congress," and assisted a largely Fourierist coalition in an Industrial Congress that year. By 1846, the NRA essentially abandoned its earlier plans for regular annual conventions in favor of these broader National Industrial Congresses (NIC) in June. Certainly, it successfully involved in its ranks—or those of allied currents— Workies of ten and fifteen years before, such as William Heighton and

John Ferral in Pennsylvania, or Seth Luther and Dr. Charles Douglass in New England.

So, too, the NRA proved remarkably accommodating to local conditions and the political predispositions in particular crafts and localities, which involved it in a network of organizations, such as the Mechanics Mutual Protective Associations or the cooperative Workingmen's Protective Unions. When it encountered interest in secret societies, such as the Industrial Brotherhood, it participated and even launched its own society, Young America, eventually inspiring a Brotherhood of the Union.[39]

Most importantly, it swept into action those Fourierists eager to find a practical political application of their socialism. These included leading Brook Farmers, such as Lewis Ryckman and John Orvis. Ultimately, they even brought Albert Brisbane into their efforts. This politicization of what had been communitarian socialism also represented a socialist transformation of land reform.

From the outset, Evans and the core group of the National Reformers expressed a class consciousness, albeit one that had to develop quickly if it would avoid slumping back into Locofocoisms. They thought capitalists demanded that their private concerns had the power to remake the nation's economic life and social structure. The existence of such things always belied the fairy tale assumptions of a "free market," because it ceded some investors the special power to control prices, levy fees, and exact financial tribute from others, including other businesses.

Capitalist rule in America echoed conditions in the Old World monarchies because of what John H. Klippart called "singular anomalies in a Republican form of Government." So, too, William Heighton wrote Evans with shock of judges who labeled "the great moral and political truths" of the founding documents to be "mere lifeless forms! 'indefinite abstractions,' intended by their Great Author for show, humbug—anything but practice." Joshua King Ingalls warned that what democratic standards existed in the United States "could be reversed tomorrow."[40] Driven back from their repeated efforts to extend the fundamental premises of the American republic, mid-nineteenth century social radicals found themselves defending those premises and principles—and attacking the hypocrisies in their implementation.

From the beginning, the founders of the NRA aspired to a broad social reconstruction. Too, land reformers had always expected to take up other "corollary" concerns. Most immediately, they sought concrete practical reforms that would materially undermine exploitation and oppression in any form. Ultimately, Evans wrote of these as "such sliding measures as will take society out ... of the present erroneous institutions." It officially took up the demand for a legislated ten-hour workday, labor cooperation, women's rights, and a wide range of other measures. In this sense, the NRA became something of a political foster parent of what Thomas Wentworth Higginson called the "sisterhood of reforms."[41]

This reflected their ultimately pragmatic sense of the world they wanted. Evans never offered a doctrine on how land ownership might ultimately be viewed. As a group, they did not look back nostalgically to a world of small farmers. Some of his followers argued that, land should be "never owned, bought or sold." Very few envisioned a human destiny forever tied to family farms. Evans and the core of his organization consigned such issues to the future deliberations of the people, such questions required no division of effort among social reformers in the present.[42]

With each citizen assured of the option of becoming a small farmer, a social equality essential to a truly representative government would emerge. Further, it would provide the basis for an ongoing decentralization of power into township democracies. In economic terms, any large-scale industrial projects would become possible only with cooperation and accountability. Such an Agrarian future assumed the due regard for future generations and a respect for the equality of citizens. On the one hand, the logic of Evans's measures could "convince those who work on the surface of things" who had not considered the numberless social ills created where "there is no limit to the acquisition of property." On the other, the operation of such measures would "deny the right of a man to use his capital in any way he pleases."[43]

Maintaining equality had priority over economic and industrial development. While favoring veterans benefits, the NRA opposed granting bounty lands, largely because experience indicated that most veterans would likely not occupy such lands themselves and wind up selling them to investors. However, the NRA declared for the gradual development of industry within a democratic and cooperative context.[44]

How these radicals sought to create that society was also innovative. Their language often echoed Skidmore's desire for "pulling down the present edifice of society," building "a new one in its stead," and remodeling "the political structure of our State" into something "essentially different from anything of the kind heretofore known." They could also agree with his assessment of failed revolutions in which a monarch "might have been dethroned, but the throne itself, would in all probability, have remained, and been occupied by another." Then, too, they shared Skidmore's fears that "every artifice will be resorted to, to defeat or delay" his measures, "the most likely" being "the proposition to adopt the system *in part*."[45] Skidmore had called for a sweeping social revolution achieved by the election of a constitutional convention by the "working classes" mandated to supersede the existing state government and restructure the political, social and economic order in New York.

NRA leaders remained much more flexible about how that social transformation would take place. Elizur Wright asserted the "right" of the poor "to rise in one universal STRIKE" and Lucius A. Hine made "the severest condemnation of the whole system of plunder—I take no half way steps." Unlike Skidmore, though, these NRA figures believed that "a good many things must be done first."[46]

Their first efforts—and failures—to make effective the old Locofoco idea of questioning of candidates and soliciting pledges moved beyond towards the idea of independent action. The *Voice of Industry* early anticipated "a new party," arguing that movement had begun to function as one whether or not one preferred to label it "the Workingmen's Party. Some call it the National Reform Party. We call it the Humanitarian party, which represents the tendency of this age to Mutual Guaranties." Brisbane spoke of "the whole Movement Party of this country.[47]

As these working-class land reformers followed its agenda into running their own insurgent candidates, they also moved towards coalition work with other radicals. Most importantly, they regularly talked of their faith in the liberty and equality of people of color, however the discussion remained abstract and reflected more the logic of their intellectual positions rather than their experience and practice.

The determination of the land reformers to abolish what they regularly called "wages slavery" and to secure "free labor" through what they called "free soil" created a dynamic that, in turn, would shape its own history.

*   *   *

Even as the depression had unraveled the Locofocos at New York City, a St. Louis newspaperman waged a persistent battle for labor reform in slaveholding St. Louis, though Democratic mobs destroyed his business three times. In response, Elijah Lovejoy moved to nearby Alton, Illinois and resumed his attacks on the institution. On November 7, 1837, an armed force from Missouri crossed over and attempted once more to destroy the paper. When Lovejoy tried to protect his press, they murdered him.

The news that the defenders of slavery were ready to kill other whites to sustain their institution—and the authorities allowing them to do so—had an immense impact. The event cast new light on the efforts of former President John Quincy Adams to fight against the gag rule to introduce antislavery petitions into Congress, but the effects rumbled beneath the surface of life in the North. It moved the seventeen-year-old Susan Brownell Anthony to begin circulating some of those petitions. In a tiny congregation at Franklin Mills (now Kent), Ohio, the thirty-nine-year-old Connecticut-born John Brown brought new meaning to his long personal struggle to establish his security. "Here, before God, in the presence of these witnesses," he told them, "from this time, I consecrate my life to the destruction of slavery!"

That mob from St. Louis had no idea what they had unleashed.

5

Confronting Race and Empire: Slavery and Mexico

On May Day 1848, National Reformers at Cincinnati hosted an estimated thousand supporters at an open air celebration. Most leaders of the movement there had, from its inception, embraced abolitionism. Moreover, it is quite likely that African Americans celebrated the traditional workers' holiday alongside whites. The veteran socialist John Allen, visiting from Indiana, reminded them that "Working men, as Reformers, had not always been just to labor. The cause of labor was one." He continued, "The time had come when the laborers of the North must make common cause with the laborers of the South; and the prejudices of color be done away with. Land reformers were especially called on at this juncture to give the weight of their influence on the side of freedom." Allen with an appeal for "Universal freedom and homes for all—for the colored man no less than the white!" The crowd applauded, despite "some slight sounds of displeasure."[1] The course of a serious "movement party" permitted no further detour around the issue.

Intelligent, strategic, and heroic, the efforts of enslaved, fugitive and free African Americans had an impact on the development of radicalism in the antebellum country that far outreached their numbers. The very fact of black self-organization made ignoring their concerns virtually impossible for the antislavery movement among whites. More importantly, the fugitive issue shaped everything, inspiring an unprecedented reliance on direct action to assist runaways. This—together with white working-class antislavery—moved much of the Liberty party to take their program beyond the "one idea" of abolition, which drew them into expanding electoral coalitions with the land reformers at the local and state level. By 1847, the additional factor of the U.S. War with Mexico effectively built this into a national strategy.

Brothers of Color

Although largely overlooked, the documented people in the society organized themselves, creating a dynamic that forced larger and larger circles to respond. Repressed or ignored, organizations that contributed immensely to shaping black identity in America followed a course similar to that of the European revolutionaries who applied the standards of fraternalism to national purposes. Context made black associations more overtly political and their most fundamental idea of labor reform shaped a leadership described as bound in "the triple chord of Masonry, Church fellowship and Anti-Slavery association."[2]

Freemasonry provided a ubiquitous model of organization among African Americans as among others in western societies. The English order in the colonies admitted fifteen applicants of color before the Revolution, including a mulatto from the Indies named Prince Hall. Later, after securing independence, white masons declined fellowship with blacks, so the excluded obtained a charter for their African Lodge from England in 1784. What happened later remains uncertain, but the 1820s found African American masons struggling to recruit and build their organization. Later, Peter Ogden, a ship steward faced a similarly racial exclusion from the Odd Fellows, and organized black members of that body to bypass the whites in America by establishing direct ties to England. As among other Americans, blacks interested in fraternal concerns and mutual aid gave rise to a series of such orders.[3]

Yet, Prince Hall masonry provided the most visible source of leadership among free blacks, which had a major role in the organization of abolitionist sentiment among them. Membership meant a great deal to such prominent antebellum African American leaders as Dr. James McCune Smith, Martin R. Delany, William Wells Brown, and others. One newcomer celebrated his arrival in New York by joining the freemasons even as he took membership in a church. Remarkably, the order in the South formed a natural secular body that rose alongside the African Methodist Episcopal Church. Despite escalating repression through the years leading to secession, blacks at New Orleans sustained five AME congregations and three lodges of the Prince Hall masons.[4]

The order's usual identification with the "middle-class respectability" naturally meant something different among African Americans.

More than among whites, perhaps, membership included workers, such as William Cooper Nell, a printer who well understood the contradiction between the racism of white society and its appreciation of church memberships, fraternalism, and self-improvement. "To make me a sectarian, Odd Fellow, Good Samaritan, Son of Temperance, or Free Mason, before you make me a man and a citizen," he wrote, "is to mock my heart and insult my head; liberty, first, names, societies and conventionalism afterwards." Then, too, while a George Washington Dupee of Louisville might have been remembered as a clergyman, that career began as a slave engaged in manual labor, and, after his manumission, he continued to earn his bread as a brickmaker.[5]

Finally, even where the concept of "middle class" might indicate black ministers, schoolteachers, and professionals, it hardly celebrated and sustained respectability. The son of a freed woman and an unknown white or mixed race father, Dr. Smith had been a star pupil in the New York African Free School on Mulberry Street, being selected to represent the school in greeting Lafayette on his visit. Denied admission to Columbia College and Geneva Medical School because of his race, he ventured abroad, to the University of Glasgow. Funded by his church, he set up his medical practice on West Broadway, treating patients of both races, and serving as the chief physician at the New York City Colored Orphan Asylum.[6] Writing for the public as "Communipaw," Smith also became a "race man" in his fraternal sensibilities.

Furthermore, black laboring people and their concerns naturally formed a more central feature of fraternal concerns. As among Italians or Germans, nationalist concerns among African Americans addressed the social conditions of their people as essential to their goals. Moreover, no blacks in the U.S. could long ignore the realities of slavery, which would almost invariably be an all-consuming focus of labor reform among them.

Too, workingmen such as Dupee, then, played a disproportionately greater role in black fraternal orders, as in the black community generally. As capitalism fueled the development of the wider economy and society, it left blacks occupying distinct niches requiring less capital and avoiding direct competition with whites. George DeBaptiste, who settled elsewhere along the river than Dupee had been born in Virginia to free parents and became a barber and servant to such prominent figures as General William Henry Harrison who he served through his 1840 presidential campaign and into the White House. After Harrison's death, DeBaptiste returned to establish a freighting business based at Madison, Indiana—on the Ohio River between Louisville and Cincinnati. He used this work to advise and move Kentucky slaves north of the river through Cincinnati to safety. By 1849, the Kentucky authorities offered a reward for his capture and kidnapping to their state for "nigger-stealing," so he moved to Detroit.[7] There, DeBaptiste rebuilt a shipping operation, this one to get runaways not merely into the non-slaveholding Northern states but into the safety of Canada.

The plebeian character of this underground work is obvious on both ends of DeBaptiste's career. His association with fraternal networks along the Ohio involved, on one end, some highly respected and relatively prosperous ship stewards, who traveled from one river town to another. At the other, this network reached beyond free blacks into what one scholar described as "slave societies." Once relocated to Detroit, DeBaptiste partnered with the tailor William Lambert, who later admirers described as a "philanthropist," though his standing as an artisan might have made such a description peculiar among whites.[8]

Throughout, the Ohio River had been a remarkably permeable barrier between states that accepted and rejected human slavery. The work of African Americans often moved them from one community to the other, and required the mingling of free and slave workers. Encouraged by Prince Hall Masons at Cincinnati, some Louisville blacks were discussing whether to form a lodge as early as 1850. The Methodist schoolteacher William H. Gibson had been initiated three years before at Baltimore and served with the majority of the group, which favored discretely locating the new Mount Moriah lodge across the river at New Albany. For three years they crossed the river in skiffs at midnight and hiked the five miles to the city. In the end, they relocated their lodge to Louisville, and remained quite active, even after the police raid of 1859.[9] Although responsible for this state of affairs, white slaveholders had every reason to fear an organization that could regularly and repeatedly slip blacks back and forth across the Ohio in the middle of the night.

Organizations less well documented than freemasonry also provided even more suggestive possibilities. Louisville's Benevolent Society—composed of slaves as well as free blacks—came to be documented only because it later enlisted Gibson's help in its postwar reorganization as the "United Brothers of Friendship and Sisters of the Mysterious Ten."[10]

Remarkably, fraternal organizations among slaves including Gibson, were involved in secretly crossing the Ohio at night.

At St. Louis, a similar border community, Moses Dickson, a barber and AME minister started an antebellum Knights of Liberty, upon which the postwar International Order of Twelve of the Knights and Daughters of Tabor grew. Born in Cincinnati to Virginia parents, Dickson served an apprenticeship and attended school before going south. There, "he witnessed such scenes of monstrous cruelty as caused his African blood to boil with suppressed indignation at the sight of the outrageous suffering of his people." With some like-minded young men, he reviewed plans for an antislavery secret society. He found other sympathizers in Iowa, Illinois and Wisconsin before the group formally organized.[11] Like DeBaptiste, Lambert, and Gibson, Dickson demonstrated the connection between antislavery resistance and fraternal organization.

DeBaptiste and Lambert launched their own secret society, the "African-American Mysteries, the Order of the Man of Oppression." A newspaper reporter who later interviewed Lambert described him as a "philanthropist and tailor." The "son of a slave father and free mother; a man of education, wide reading, rare argumentative power," Lambert became not only a local spokesman for the black community, but a widely known and respected associate of some of the greatest figures in the national agitation. Until the declaration of emancipation as a Federal war goal, Lambert and DeBaptiste spirited refugees into the safety of Canada.[12]

By 1849, Frederick Douglass himself begun calling for a national organization around these goals that would have an open and public existence. He proposed a "Union of the Oppressed for the sake of Freedom." Henry O. Wagoner, a black abolitionist from Chicago wrote to declare "No people have ever achieved anything favorable to their united or general prosperity, without harmony, union of sentiment, and concert of action." He hoped "that every colored man who has the least spark of public spirit about him, will give you every encouragement to push this plan forward, and to bring it into practical operation as speedily as can be done."[13]

As in European revolutionary circles, tradition and precedent obscured in the shadow of freemasonry played their role among African American secret societies. When Baltimore blacks formed an Independent Order of St. Luke, they took the name of a degree in "the Antient and Primitive Rite" of freemasonry. This was ascribed to an older Brotherhood of Light, the *Frates Lucis*, which included mystic versions, such as Cagliostro's Egyptian rite. St. Luke was also the patron of Iatric freemasonry, that of the healers, indicating that the order may have foreshadowed Dr. Harvey Johnson's later Mutual United Brotherhood of Liberty, popular among medical and teaching professions.[14] Such suggestive associations took substance in the shadow of freemasonry.

Ideologically, black participants in these Masonic and quasi-Masonic traditions found themselves naturally drawn to claims of ancient roots in Egypt that celebrated the African origins of the order and its civilizing influences. In 1853, Delany—perhaps most famous for his foray into fiction with *Blake; or, the Huts of America*—made explicit arguments based on *The Origin and Objects of Ancient Freemasonry: Its Introduction into the United States and Legitimacy Among Colored Men*. Later, Albert L. Rawson, the multi-faceted bohemian socialist and Orientalist, reminded students of the Bible that, in dim antiquity,

the descendants of Ham, in Egypt and Babylon, led the way as the pioneers in art, literature, and science. Mankind at the present day lies under infinite obligations to the genius and industry of those early ages, more especially for alphabetic writing, weaving cloth, architecture, astronomy, plastic art, sculpture, navigation and agriculture. The art of painting is also represented, and music indirectly, by drawings of instruments.[15]

This became institutionalized with the advent of Egyptian rite masonry, claiming to be rooted in those origins. On November 9, 1856, its head, Jacques Étienne Marconis de Négre brought the order to New York. Interestingly, he ignored the white Masonic taboos by attending to his business at the "United Grand Lodge of New York"—the Prince Hall Masons. Later, the black masons described this remarkable visitor himself as a black representative of the Grand Orient. Whatever the case, radical internationalism inspired those who extended their hands across the color bar.[16] Whites, however, could and would engage in no such activism without the initial black drive to self-organization and race solidarity.

It is also noteworthy that Native Americans had their own secret society traditions. Circumstances in the wake of the mass dispossessions in the southeast politicized these, even beyond the officially permissible margins of U.S. life. Among the Cherokee, the Keetowah enforced the blood oaths among the tribal leaders never to accede to further cessions of land to the whites. It found itself at the center of an ongoing civil strife that eventually merged into a broad antislavery and Unionist current at the time of the Civil War.

The sheer weight of such efforts had a long-term pervasive influence on the entire society.

Black Resistance, the Liberty Party
"Broad Platform" and the Origins of Free Soil

Black self-organization reflected the proto-nationalist drive for self-reliance and the hope of self-emancipation. Perhaps these premises probably made more sense to people, black and white, against the backdrop of African slavery and in a less pretentious age. These aspirations, of course, grew from the black experience rather than organization. A group captured a boat, and a Virginia slave shipped himself north in a crate. After Harriet Tubman's escape in Maryland, she worked closely with Thomas Garrett at Wilmington and others to establish a regular system to move escapees from jeopardy.

Increasing organization lay behind such memorably dramatic incidents. The African Mysteries made their goals clear as it put recruits through the three degrees of Captive, Redeemed, and Chosen. Initiates originally appeared blindfolded "in rough and ragged garments" with a chain about the neck, pleading for "Deliverance." Asked how he expected to get it, the applicant was to reply "By his own efforts." The member lost the chain when he attained the degree of Redeemed, but became Chosen only by learning "the full intention of the order," that "the general plan was freedom." The Chosen incorporated other ranks, including: Rulers, Judges, Princes, Chevaliers of Ethiopia, and Sterling Black Knight. They incorporated the legacy of the slave rebellions with the Knight of St. Domingo. That required attaining a mastery over "the principles of freedom and the authorities on revolution; revolt, rebellion, government—in short a digest of the best authorities."[17] Enjoying no more freedom in the U.S. than Italian nationalists under the Austrians or the French, African Americans responded with similar associations. The goal of that organization had been to ensure that fugitives would be "never left unprotected in their journeys." Hardships the escapees endured "were not only shared with them by their conductors, but repeated time after time by the hundred or so of men who cheerfully assumed this arduous duty." They hid the fugitives "in barns and all sorts of retreats," until dark, after which they slipped to a home at the foot of Eighth Street belonging to a worker on the Michigan Central railway. Once "concealed under the docks," the fugitives crossed the mile of water into Canada. "We never lost a man by capture at this point," boasted Lambert, "so careful were we, and we took over as high as 1,600 in one year."[18] At times, they claimed to average getting four to five across in a day.

Another network labored along the Mississippi. Members of the Prince Hall lodges at New Orleans confirmed contact with an AME minister from Missouri, working on a steamboat. This most likely was Dickson, and his St. Louis-based Knights of Liberty. A later raid on a Masonic celebration at New Orleans netted about thirty free blacks and slave members, indicating that in New Orleans, as in Louisville, the order took slaves into fellowship. That free blacks assumed fraternal obligations to assist their enslaved brothers posed obvious implications, in terms of slavery.[19]

Resistance circles organized well in the east as well. A Vigilance Committee formed at Boston in 1841 had to be reorganized nine years later. In upstate New York, Douglass addressed an August convention of former slaves at Cazenovia, who pooled their efforts for the same purposes.[20] Despite a dramatic and escalating series of confrontations and clashes with the authorities, most of their efforts avoided detection.

By 1848, participants engaged in efforts that began to terrorize the slaveholders. That April, abolitionists tried to organize the use of the schooner *Pearl* to get nearly eighty slaves from their owners at Washington, DC. The scale alone demonstrated the extent of organization and planning among abolitionists.[21] Partly in response to this, Southern leaders insisted upon the inclusion of a much more demanding Fugitive Slave Act in the Compromise of 1850.

While limited and later exaggerated, white allies played an important role. Lewis Hayden shaped much of Boston's resistance to that Fugitive

Slave Act. He himself had escaped slavery from his native Kentucky into Ohio, then to Detroit before moving on to Boston, where he became one of the leading members of the Prince Hall masons. Based on the reality that whites and blacks could more easily accomplish specific tasks, he seems to have been one of the supervisors of the division of labor that developed. Whites such as James N. Buffum and John C. Cluer entered the courthouses to thwart the efforts of the courts to return runaways, while Hayden or Nell mobilized a menacing black street presence around the building. Later, as resistance stiffened, whites such as Cluer and Dick Hinton showed up among those essentially African American crowds.[22]

Like Buffum and Hinton, Cluer brought a strong labor background to his abolitionist work. A Glasgow-born Chartist who had come to the U.S. in 1839, he became as committed as Seth Luther to the mill women, agitating among them for the ten-hour day. By the 1830s, women workers began elbowing their way into their own, particularly in factory towns such as Lowell. In 1834, 700 of them went on strike and twice that number walked out two years later. Women at Pittsburgh earned the label of "the Amazons" after a month-long 1845 textile strike. The position of these "factory girls" also invited analogies to slavery, which—like the rhetorical use of "wages slavery"—could either deepen resentments or fostered a sense of solidarity.

An increasing flight of slaves across the Ohio valley also inspired an "antislavery league." One participant recalled a body of "hundreds of men who were willing to engage in any enterprise which would defeat the swaggering negro hunter." They boasted "a detective and spy system that was far superior to anything the slaveholder or the United States had," a plausible claim north of the river. At times, "as many as fifty educated and intelligent young and middle-aged men" scouted the river for runaways while ten others worked regularly south of the river.[23]

The numbers organized into this kind of work seem to merit skepticism. With disarming specificity, Dickson described his Knights of Liberty as an "army of true and trusty men" numbering 47,240 across the country, but he included in this local associations, such as the Order of Twelve at Galena. Lambert's interviewer reported his claim "that over 60,000 took the highest degree" in the African American Mysteries. Later, members of a secret society at Richmond claimed to be "composed almost exclusively of colored men" with branches "over the entire South."[24] Surely, though, these different estimates of 47,000–60,000 organized members of some of these organizations seems excessive for activities that, at any given point, might be involving no more than hundreds. However, these were not membership audits in organizational reports. While developments at any point may have mobilized only hundreds—or even dozens—but those ready and willing to violate the federal Fugitive Slave laws over the years might well have run into the thousands. Moreover, as Dickson explicitly stated, what he discussed included local societies working under different names. He, DeBaptiste and Lambert at Detroit and the unnamed brothers in Richmond actually seem to have been discussing estimates of a common loose national network.

More importantly, the large numbers of initiates claimed would have surely included the tens of thousands of fugitives themselves. As abroad, those involved in such underground resistance groups as the African Mysteries used secret passwords and signs to avoid the authorities. One of the hunted found help by using a memorable phrase such as "Cross over." The applicant asked "cross?" and waited for the reply, "over." Or a seemingly meaningless exchange about travel ended by mentioning "a place called Safety." "Have you a brother there? I think I know him," said one. "I know you now. You traveled on the road." The fugitive could also make an inquiry by "pulling the knuckle of the right forefinger over the knuckle of the same finger on the left hand." The response simply reversed the fingers with the same motion. Knowledge of these secrets is what defined "membership,"[25] In this sense, counting the legions estimated to have been able to find freedom in this way would certainly have made the claims of 47,000–60,000 members much more plausible.

This background of a remarkably successful largely African American resistance made the fate of the runaways after slavery a question that demanded growing attention among antislavery people of all sorts. Prominent leaders, including the presidential candidate James Birney of the Libertymen urged his cothinkers to take up a "broad platform" that would address questions beyond slavery. In New York, figures such as William Goodell, Gerrit Smith and Beriah Green became key advocates of this course. Goodell, a veteran of the American Anti-Slavery Society also edited the journal of its state affiliate, the *Friend of Man*, which increasingly had an expansive view of social reconstruction in mind.

Almost as soon as the NRA appeared at New York City, it began a rigorous effort to get Smith, Birney and other political abolitionists to embrace land reform as a part of this. Hardly used to finding themselves courted, the Libertymen balked, even as Garrison and the non-electoral wing of the movement, which opposed any move towards a political movement around a "broad platform," saw the NRA as latter-day Locofoco Democrats. At times, he and other abolitionists had sharp verbal skirmishes with some land reformers.

Individually, most of the leading National Reformers had actually always been individually hostile to slavery. Some, such as John H. Keyser even ignored the ill-advised 1844 endorsement of the Democratic ticket by their organization to vote for Birney, for which Democrats physically assaulted him at the polls. After the election, the well-educated, widely travelled multilingual Fourierist Albert Brisbane not only endorsed the NRA platform but expressed confidence that slavery "must cease, for a great truth cannot be lost." Then, too, land reformers wondered "how can abolitionists form a political party without *landless* men?"[26]

Conversely, abolitionist such as Benjamin W. Dyer saw a link between the Libertymen and land reformers as essential to the future of a broad radicalism. A forty-year-old native of Vermont, a local history remembered him as one of that "class of earnest reformers, who … had the faith and patience to labor and wait for time to bring forth the fruition of their hopes. Beginning with temperance and antislavery, he became a regular collaborator of Garrison and Wendell Phillips, as well as Goodell and Gerrit Smith. He also worked with Elihu Burrit, the "learned blacksmith" active internationally for the abolition of war, and the close ally of Henry Clapp, the famous New York "bohemian." Dyer's interest expanded to education and land reform by 1847, when he moved to Randolph and attended the NIC.[27]

More fundamentally, though, radical workers in the North described their lot as a wage slavery that "leaves man to perish in the midst of sur-rounding wealth." Capitalism forced the landless to "hire out or starve." As Evans put it, the slaveholder "has inherited other people's *bodies*, and the Landholders has inherited other people's *land*; and thereby *holds* their bodies." Evans spoke of "different grades of slavery" imposed on American workers, all of which needed abolition. In part, such absurdity reflected the pragmatic sense that Evans expressed in writing his Chartist correspondents, "the white slave states have no more to do with the black slave states on this question, than they have with England."[28]

Some claimed that wages slavery represented something worse than chattel slavery, and that the abolition of the former should have priority. Part of this clearly reflected a reluctance to burn bridges with the Democrats, but it also represented more of an exaggerated rhetorical device than a well-reasoned analysis. Radicals on both sides of the Atlantic sometimes argued that nineteenth century capitalism involved a "more extensive" and "worse" oppression than feudalism. Too, Brisbane "found less aristocracy" in Germany than America, which would have flabbergasted the Germans in his audience had they taken him literally.[29]

Moreover, many land reformers never described the lot of "chattel slaves" as worse than "wages slaves." Horace Greeley thought "Hireling Labor ... in spite of the evils" would, in the long run, be more "progressive," leading "more rapidly and surely toward a better condition," while Southern slavery "tends towards decline, bankruptcy, dissolution." In fact, the same NRA leaders who declared "wages slavery" a greater evil at one point could, in another time and place, describe "the Chattel system" in the South as "the worst degree of Slavery that exists," disclaiming "any desire whatever to represent Southern Slavery in any other light than that in which our Anti-Slavery friends have placed it." "Making a man's body a chattel is the most heinous crime to that of murder," insisted Lewis Masquerier.[30]

Libertymen also pushed back over these inconsistencies. One pointed out that the NRA wanted an explicit legal ban on the seizure of land for nonpayment of debts without insisting on the same ban against placing human beings on the market. The NRA, he argued, would limit land ownership while permitting an "unlimited property in human flesh," "in the bodies and souls of millions of your countrymen." Goodell, Smith and others conceded that the abolition of land monopoly would also eliminate slavery. They had "no doubt it would abolish slavery at the South, to make the slaves proprietors of land. And so it would, to give them access to the ballot box, or to concede to them the rights of marriage, and the family relation, or the right to claim wages. This is only saying that the abolition of slavery would abolish it!"[31]

Increasingly land reformers agreed that, while slavery might be an outgrowth of land monopoly, strictly abolitionist measures should not be set aside. J. E. Thompson thought it "remains to be seen" which form of slavery would be first abolished, and William West dismissed the entire debate over priorities as "ridiculous." "We would not apologize for Slavery in any form," insisted an Ohio Agrarian, "but would be glad to strike the manacles from every slave whether white or black." Jeriel Root wisely suggested that "if we saw the magnitude and power of these evils, we could not stand isolated, contending about the greatest, for all of them are deadly enemies to Christianity and Liberty" and "either of them if left alive, will consume our Republic."[32]

Tensions between white plebeian land reformers and the more elite leaders of abolitionism did not long survive systemic contact, particularly with working-class African Americans and abolitionists. This began to take place almost as soon as the NRA had begun to reach beyond the city. As early as September 1844, "a colored man who had been a slave" attended a workingmen's meeting at Milford, Massachusetts, where he "gave an account of the oppression he had been subject to." Evans reported this as what he clearly believed to be a hopeful and positive sign.[33]

By early 1846, the Maine NRA ascribed its gains to "the help of the Abolitionists" who were "rather friendly." That same year in Ohio, Salmon P. Chase readily embraced the NRA's goal to be "an object of great importance in a republican government." He only doubted "the practicality of effecting and permanently establishing these and kindred reforms, until freedom for all laborers, and just wages for all labor, shall have been secured by an impartial and resolute application of the fundamental maxims of genuine democracy—which demand equal and exact justice and equal rights for all men."[34] By that time, Evans also complained bitterly about New York's disenfranchisement of black voters.

The convergence allied the NRA and the Liberty party in the first "Free Soil" state convention, held at Albany in October 1846. This radical coalition first introduced the term into politics. To its questioning, Henry Bradley, gubernatorial candidate of the Liberty party declared for all NRA measures but land limitation on which, he wrote frankly that "had I thought as much as you have done ... I should perhaps agree with you fully." He suggested trying a homestead law and exemption, resorting to limitation only "if these measures should not have the effect to prevent Land Monopoly," and urging any methods short of "anarchy and its accompanying violence and bloodshed." "I am aware," responded another abolitionist candidate, "that this rule would produce an amazing change in the business and order of society, yet I must conclude it would be for the better, and if any evils resulted it would be because of the wrong so long indulged!"[35] In the end, the impressed militants adopted a ticket largely overlapping with that of the Libertymen.

This initial "Free Soil" effort took the field, with a mix of exclusively NRA or Liberty candidates. The colorful Irish street agitator, Mike Walsh was among the few endorsers of Democratic candidates. Of course, neither National Reformers nor Libertymen expected an outright electoral victory but sought a balance of power that would deny either major party a majority. In other words, radicals in the Fourth Congressional District did not expect the 4,749 votes they would have needed to win but the 712 that separated the major parties. In that case, John Commerford and the two other independents won nearly 1500 votes, which denied the victor of majority. The insurgents knew that, if united, they could hold the balance of power.[36]

This approach marked a major break from the NRA's Locofoco roots. From its inception, the movement proposed a political strategy focused on questioning candidates of the existing parties prior and requesting their written pledge to promote reform. The practice would resurface periodically, and provided a useful tool for fostering coalitions. However, the general experience turned them increasingly to the construction of an independent political coalition and its own transformation from an organization into a social movement. In the process, the NRA formulated practices like the Industrial Congress and expressed hopes for a "Movement Party" with a maximum influence through minimal organization.

The National Convergence

After the 1846 campaign, Smith spoke for many Radical Abolitionists in declaring National Reform "the greatest of all Anti-Slavery measures. Abolish Slavery to-morrow, and Land Monopoly would pave the way for its re-establishment. But abolish Land Monopoly—make every American citizen the owner of a farm adequate to his necessity—and there will be no room for the return of slavery." Libertymen in Smith's district ran as the "Poor Man's Party." Within the NRA, even Devyr—

that cantankerous émigré openly predisposed to the Democrats and mistrustful of abolitionists described Gerrit Smith "as politically pure as Greeley was politically villainous." On the other hand, land reformers, such as Joshua K. Ingalls realized that, "when the merely political issues were not involved, the discussions were profitable, spirited and harmonious."[37]

At the same time, experience with the major parties became increasingly disheartening. In the spring of 1847 municipal elections at New York City, the NRA sought to translate the some four thousand New Yorkers who had signed their petitions to the Federal Congress into ballots. The numbers drew some pledges, such as the Tammany candidate for Almshouse Commissioner. More importantly, a dramatic eleventh-hour pledge came from Whig mayoral candidate William V. Brady, and the movement hurriedly printed a special edition of *Young America* to announce the withdrawal of Dennis Lyons, the NRA candidate. However, the Whig *Express* labeled Brady's pledge a forgery and the veteran Locofoco Levi D. Slamm of the Democratic *Globe* derided the gullibility of the radicals.[38]

The results certainly hinted at genuinely stronger support. Despite Lyons's withdrawal, 1600 and 2000 voters voted for him, and land reformers likely supplied Brady's 1500-vote margin of victory. Indeed, Leonard the NRA-pledged Democrat ran so far ahead of his ticket that he won by a margin of almost 2100 votes, despite the Whig victory in the mayoral race. After three years, then, the city NRA had a plausible voting strength of between three and four thousand, more than an electoral balance of power.[39]

Against this backdrop, the New York NRA prepared to host the second annual National Industrial Congress. Lewis Ryckman urged a "Union of All Reformers, For One Great Reform," and Masquerier defined its core as a "mighty Abolition national Reform." Their papers reprinted the earlier resolutions, adding a stronger antislavery presentation. Lowell's "Industrial Reform Lyceum" provided Garrison a platform within a movement he still denounced, and it also described slavery in Garrisonian terms as "a crime against Humanity" that "ought to be abolished immediately." Increasingly, NRA spokesmen described themselves "true abolitionists," aspiring "to abolish all Slavery, North, South, East and West." "Do our anti-slavery friends ever discuss the merits of the Labor question? the Peace question? or the abolition of capital punishment?" asked one, adding that "we discuss all of these, and Slavery, South and North, besides; and are 'National Reformers'."[40] The Congress assembled on Wednesday June 2 at the Military Hall on the Bowery, the meeting place of the old Workies from 1829. On the fourth day, they left this to reconvene *gratis* in the Chatham street lecture rooms of Dr. Edward Newberry, a thirty-four-year-old dentist later associated with the circle around the Modern Times community on Long Island. The Congress reaffirmed the original three NRA demands, but added support for both ten-hour legislation and cooperation to the pledges required of candidates. Trade unionism was also on the agenda, although only a few had begun to reorganize publically and some, such as the new Louisville Typographical Society formally adopted NRA measures. The body significantly tabled a motion by the Owenite émigré, Benjamin Timms "to inquire into the results of Trades' Unions, in order to ... convince them of the inutility of the Trades' Unions," immediately inspiring a countermotion urging "the propriety of Trade Union Societies for temporary relief."[41]

Opposition to the U.S. War with Mexico and to expansionism generally preoccupied them. They denounced the conflict as "waged at the insistence and behalf of Southern Slavery and Northern Capital; it is fit that they bear the expense thereof," for its cost entailed "a direct tax upon the property of the country." U.S. soldiers, they argued, "should no longer be sent by 'Peace makers' to convert fertile fields to desolation and populous cities to heaps of ruins." The Congress favored the disbanding of the army and the navy, urging workers "never to fight for despots who enslave you, for territory which without a change in our governmental policy, you will only be permitted to occupy as serfs or slaves." "Defeat would be more profitable to us. Retreat would be more honorable," declared Elizur Wright, Jr. in his *Chronotype*. "The whole organization of society, as at present existing, is a *State* of War," proclaimed the Industrial Congress.[42]

The intensity of this antiwar stance clearly drew the land reformers and abolitionists closer. Rev. William H. Channing had planned to write the body, but West ably expressed the abolitionist concern that war "must inevitably result in the conquest of new territory which must fall into the hands of speculators and monopolists, thereby extending and perpetuating wages and chattel slavery, with all their religious, moral and political evils, and it is therefore desirable to bring it to a speedy and honorable termination." West proposed adding another corollary measure to the NRA platform. He urged the group to recommend "to National and all other Labor Reformers throughout the nation, to nominate no candidates who are not pledged to use the influence of their stations, if elected, to withhold supplies from the U.S. Army now in Mexico, and to cause said Army to be withdrawn thence as soon as possible."

This growing association with abolitionism provided a major source for the shift of the NRA from its militantly anti-clerical roots. West denounced the clergy as "tools of the capitalists and "instruments of the slave owners" and proposed "a government and church of our own," but Ingalls—himself a former Universalist minister—objected. Agreeing with Ingalls, Evans urged a movement open to all regardless of their religious belief or disbelief. This shift particularly annoyed the veteran Dorrite, the Fannie Lee Townsend's proposal to condemn the clergy because they realized it would be a needless offense to some anti-slavery radicals.

In the end, the prospect of presidential nomination provided a unifying, national issue. For at least a year, Evans had urged an independent radical ticket. Based in his newspaper office on Chatham Square, now described as "the Free Soil building," he urged the nomination of Sen. John P. Hale of New Hampshire, who, quipped Evans, had been excluded by the Democrats "on a strong suspicion of being favorable to Human Rights." He had subsequently won reelection to his seat in the U.S. House of Representatives with backing from the Liberty party.[43] Hale had already become one of the loudest voices in government for a break with the Democrats.

At the NIC, Appleton Fay of Massachusetts pointed out that the national Liberty convention was deliberating upstate at Macedon Lock. By then, Wendell Phillips and others had been discussing antislavery as a way to get a "thorough and complete" reordering of party politics in the U.S. In short order, the NIC jettisoned the old practice of pledges, in order to act "as an independent party" with the Libertymen, hoping to rise above "mere party purposes." Finally, Alvan E. Bovay suggested that the body send Hugh T. Brooks—one of their former liaison to the upstate Antirenters—to the Liberty convention.[44]

The NIC not only accepted Fay's suggestion for joint electoral action but came within a single vote of endorsing his resolution to advocate abandonment of the existing political order. He advocated adoption of a "Pure Democraty" around a "free state" constitution that would incorporate mechanisms for "direct legislation"—the plebiscite—as a substitute for ongoing government. West and others advocated this explicit goal as a further means of uniting land reform and antislavery.[45] Disagreements centered more on the tactic of advocating direct legislation than the ultimate goal of abolishing government.

That fall, the question of long-term goals dominated the concerns of the Massachusetts movement. On October 13, Fay and his Worcester group urged "the necessity and importance of the immediate ABOLITION (in due form) of the Representative system of Legislation, and the benefits and *practicability* of establishing a pure Democraty in its stead, by the peaceful adoption of a Constitution by the People that shall secure *to them* the opportunity and means of enacting, by direct vote, *all the Laws* by which they shall be governed!" A "UNION OF ALL THE FRIENDS OF HUMANITY of every political party and of every religious caste, and of *no* party and of no caste," they suggested, could "establish a *Righteous Government* by 'political action' upon the broad platform of Human Equality and Humanity's Rights." On October 23, Boston radicals, led by Horace Seaver and Josiah Mendum of the *Investigator* met at the hall of the Protective Union to defend the ideas of advocating "certain political measures that would be beneficial to the working classes."[46]

The convention assembled on October 30.[47] Joined by abolitionists such as Cluer and D. S. Grandin, they expanded the platform of land reform and took ten hours to declare slavery "a crime against Humanity" that "ought to be abolished immediately." They suggested common action with the Liberty Party to "secure to every disenthralled slave, whatever their complexion ... the peaceable and immediate possession of a sufficient quantity of Land to enable them to procure the necessary means of subsistence whenever their liberation is achieved." After "unanimously and enthusiastically" endorsing Samuel E. Sewall, the abolitionist gubernatorial candidate, it initially seems to have named Amasa Walker as a distinct land reform candidate for lieutenant governor. However, the same issue of the *Voice of Industry* that reported Walker's nomination also stated that the movement had thoroughly embraced the "LIBERTY TICKET," including John M. Brewster rather than Walker.[48]

The Massachusetts results in 1847 hardly proved encouraging. The *Voice of Industry* took some solace in the "healthy and permanent increase" of the Liberty vote, especially in the Third Congressional District and the NRA vote at Worcester "ran as high as 72 which speaks well for a beginning," but the paper could not "give a statement of the National Reform vote of this State ... as the 'powers that be' have been very careful that all deserters from the old Dynasties, be put down *"Scattering."* The *Voice* further fumed that "a more mongrel, conformatory, conscience-elastic, set of voters than Massachusetts contains, we do not know where to look for. They have swallowed Texas, the Mexican war, and the whole of *Cottondom* with all their abominations, without a single shudder."[49] Such conclusions left them an even greater affinity for the Radical Abolitionists.

By this time, the old rationalizations faded quickly. Earlier, working citizens—that is, white working-class men—could complain bitterly about the inattention abolitionists seemed to accord their concerns while focused on those enslaved African American workers living at a distance. Grandin, an abolitionist supporter of both land reform and the cooperative Protective Unions responded with an oft repeated anecdote about a runaway slave who stopped by to attend a meeting of Northern white workers. Realizing what he had done, the whites asked why he had decided to escape. Under close questioning, the fugitive admitted to having had no personal complaint about his former condition other than being a slave. Pressed further, the African American simply informed them that his old position now stood vacant, should any of those present wish to apply.[50] None ever did.

Meanwhile, the New York radicals tried to replicate in 1847 their "Free Soil" experiment of making joint nominations for some state offices. Exclusively NRA candidates got statewide totals ranging from 1729 for State Engineer and Surveyor through 1929 for state inspector. Brooks, the NRA's former liaison with the Antirenters and the Libertymen got 1845 for lieutenant governor. Results in New York county indicated that the NRA's alliance with the Libertymen carried a measurable price in terms of the working-class voters with old Locofoco predispositions. The ticket there had fallen off to between 343 and 423 votes.[51] Nevertheless, the independent campaigns of the Liberty, Antirent and National Reform tickets won a total of over 15,000 votes, again enough to deny either party a majority in some races.

* * *

At the start of 1848, a new kind of radicalism began to emerge as elements of political abolitionists folded into the core of the land reform movement and those communitarian socialists interested in politics. "We are aware that the paths of the Liberty League ... and of the National Reformers converge," wrote the NRA national secretary Bovay to their new comrades upstate. "We believe they must soon meet." They aspired "to act in good faith and consistency towards all races of man" and, as events unfolded, this led them along a "natural and inevitable" path to make common cause with the abolitionists.[52]

Such seemingly abstract appeals to equality had become explicit. Masquerier sought to tell African Americans held in slavery that they not only had "an inalienable right to your bodies, but also to that domain which you have for ages cultivated for the use of your masters. You have more right to colonize your masters than they have you." Van Amringe described National Reform as demanding land for "any landless actual settler, man or woman," Lest his meaning be unclear, he continued:

We do not say free to native citizen only. For red men, and persons of African descent, although domesticated among us, are not, under our national laws, recognized as citizens. Yet they are the children of the same God, as ourselves, and entitled equally with ourselves to freedom and a home on the earth.[53]

This dynamic remained part and parcel of a broader political crisis in American society, and its resolution would elevate the importance of this relatively small current to a point where it could leverage the entire course of the country.

6

Free Soil: The Electoral Distillation of Radicalism, 1847–8

By 1848, both National Reformers and Radical Abolitionists pursued a "broad platform," the planks of which became increasingly intermingled. Early in that year, Morris S. Barrett and Dana Lamb organized their "National Reform Club" out of the schoolhouse at Rosedale, Wisconsin. It required pledges from candidates not only to promote the three original land reform measures with the ten-hour day, but the promise "to abolish all laws regulating upholding or sustaining the institution of slavery" and discrimination "on account of birth-place or color."[1]

For many advocates of land reform, socialism, abolitionism, and women's rights, the election of 1848 seemed to combine their aspirations into a broad, sweeping statement of mass discontent. This reflected the increasing complexities in each of these movements, and, invariably, predisposed radicals to the creation of a common network around a broad spectrum of issues. The Liberty-National Reform "Free Soil" state tickets of 1846 and 1847 contributed to the decision of the Barnburner Democrats to launch their own national Free Soil Party in 1848, albeit with only the most watered and general antislavery positions and nothing of land reform. After drawing most radicals into the effort, the politicians leading the Free Soil campaign sought to dissolve it. Thereafter, the annual National Industrial Congresses of the land reformers embraced increasingly radical measures, overtly hostile to slavery and advocating equal rights for women.

The Free Soil Insurgency

Conflict over the U.S. territorial acquisition from Mexico shattered a party system that had prevailed for a generation. After having abandoned

Martin Van Buren, Southern Democratic leaders had gotten James K. Polk into the White House and a war with Mexico that threatened theoretically to extend slavery all the way to the Pacific coast. The conflict exposed the depths of the divisions in both of the major parties, with "Conscience Whigs" such as William Henry Seward opposing the old school "Silver Grays." Tension between Van Buren's "Barnburners" and the "Hunker" faction in New York led to a decisive break eager to launch a new party focused on the exclusion of slavery from those acquired western territories. This process began in New York through late 1847 and early 1848 with Barnburner conventions at Herkimer and Utica.[2]

Among its major achievements, it simply appropriated the name "Free Soil." While taking the title of the earlier NRA–Liberty tickets, it assimilated neither the radical land reform advocacy of "free soil" nor a universal hostility to slavery. On one level, this represented what historian Laurence Goodwyn's study of American Populism called a "shadow movement" within the elite. In contrast to its preoccupation with the Homestead Bill and the future of the western territories, the radicals within NRA elaborated a full program for social reconstruction.

The Libertymen and National Reformers responded somewhat differently. The Radical Abolitionists led by Gerrit Smith and William Goodell convened as "friends of Impartial Freedom and Comprehensive Reform" at Macedon Lock. Endorsed by the NRA, they called a mid-January racially mixed national convention at Auburn that endorsed a "broad platform." At that conference, not only did the presence of Hugh T. Brooks and William Eldar personify the connection of these currents, but the black abolitionist Samuel R. Ward raised land reform to be an integral feature of slave liberation.[3]

The radicals reacted differently to the rise of Free Soil. Those Libertymen who had not participated in the Macedon Lock convention met independently in hopes of negotiating an alliance with the "Barnburners," preferably around the nomination of a long-standing abolitionist such as John P. Hale with every apparent intention of negotiating with the "Barnburner." The NRA leaders, however, recalled the duplicity of Van Buren and the Barnburners in the earlier Antirent struggle and remained deeply suspicious.[4]

Early in the summer of 1848, the third NIC gathered as "Friends of Industry and Equal Rights." It met at the Willow Fisk Hall on the corner of Sixth and Haines Streets in Philadelphia from June 7 through June 15. The NRA had already enlisted veterans of earlier movements, such as John Speakman the Owenite druggist or John Ashton the former Worky-turned-Fourierist. Other leaders—and presumably members—of those movements had moved on, such had William Heighton and John Ferral to, respectively, rural New Jersey and Pittsburgh.[5]

Not only were New York, New Jersey and Pennsylvania represented, but also Massachusetts, Maryland and Delaware had delegates, with letters arriving from as far away as Illinois. New organizations and leaders that brought to bear experience earned elsewhere. The Fourierist AUA, the local "Daughters and Sons of Toil," led by exiled Dorrites like J. Sidney Jones and Fannie Lee Townsend and the quasi-socialist *Soẑial Reform Association*, among German émigrés endorsed land reform measures. Theophilus Fisk, an émigré Chartist had been a leader of Philadelphia GTU over ten years earlier. Other Chartists included John Mills, the shoemaker Thomas Phillips, and John Sheddon, a thirty-one-year-old Yorkshire tailor who had been urging a general convention of American workers to encourage cooperatives.[6] They reappointed the veteran Fourierist Henry H. Van Amringe as a traveling national lecturer, and suggested that supporters organize "an *Industrial Legislature*" in their states.

Perhaps the single most famous American writer of the day came to the fore in the proceedings. Born on a Chester country farm, the twenty-six-year-old George Lippard grew up at Germantown near the Wissahickon, with its colonial and Revolutionary associations. Periodically forced to live as a squatter in the city, he studied for the ministry and the law, as had his literary hero, Charles Brockden Brown before getting work on the *Spirit of the Times*. He wrote Eugene Sue's gothic sensibilities into American letters. In 1845, his scandalous, muckraking novel *The Monks of Monk Hall* divided Philadelphia, with the "laborers, the mechanics, the great body of the people" on the side of the author.[7]

Many hoped to carry the NIC farther into what John Greig, the Rochester Fourierist called "other collateral measures as shall appear to be dictated by wisdom and experience for the immediate relief of the toiling millions." In particular, they looked to Ira Davis's translation of Fourierism into cooperative Protective Unions, opposition to Asa Whitney plan for a transcontinental railroad subsidized by government land grants, and the compilation of "full particulars of the Prices and

Hours of Labor." They also adopted a version of Appleton Fay's proposal from the previous year that all legislation should be published and submitted to a plebiscite before becoming law. It also devoted a day to discussing the revolutionary situation in Europe.[8]

In the face of an impending presidential election, Townsend pressed for an ongoing independent party and the NIC agreed that the movement should start to make its own nominations before questioning other candidates. Some hoped to nudge the Democrats, but Van Amringe, fresh from the west, made a strong case for the Liberty ticket of Gerrit Smith and Elihu Burritt. Joshua K. Ingalls thought that he—with Evans, Windt and "several of the Pennsylvania, Western and other delegates," described as "true abolitionists"—carried the day. In the end, the NIC endorsed Smith, while making William S. Waite of Illinois their vice presidential candidate.[9]

Because both Waite and Burritt had declined to run for vice-president, they named Charles C. Foote, a thirty-eight-year-old New York-born Presbyterian minister, Foote studied medicine with the idea of doing foreign missionary work, but instead worked between pastorates in New York and Michigan. An abolitionist noisily concerned about land reform, temperance and other issues, Foote also became involved at Detroit with George DeBaptiste and William Lambert in practical efforts to resettle "landless refugees from American Slavery" into Canada.[10]

In reality, the radical nominations gained almost no traction. Lippard's *Legends of Mexico* had already cast the Whig candidate, General Zachary Taylor as thoroughly as his earlier work had done with George Washington. For Lippard, the Whig "American System" provided a first step towards the organization of a vast national "Army of Industry" to build a "Palestine of Redeemed Labor."[11]

Even during the NIC, the Democrats tried to derail the movement's momentum, aided by such leaders of the local Chartist Club as Edward Powers and John Campbell. When Evans got an invitation ostensibly from the factory workers on the southwest side, he showed up to find himself on a platform with local Democrats. When the meeting passed resolutions supporting the governor, the Democratic press reported it as the action of the NIC.[12] Afterwards, Campbell headed right to the Democrats, brandishing his *Negromania*, a collection of pseudoscientific racist selections aimed at convincing literate voters against the "mania" over slavery.

However, Van Buren's Free Soil insurgency swept away most of the movement. Land reformers and Libertymen faced the problem, the latter meeting at Buffalo in preparation for the national Free Soil convention, which came to order on August 9. Attending on behalf of the NIC, Van Amringe found so many observers present that it looked more like a mass meeting than a partisan convention. The recorded participants included one Russell Comstock of New York, likely the "Ciderist" driven from the City Hall years before, William E. Stevenson, the Pittsburgh cabinet-maker and future governor of West Virginia, and a series of Midwestern abolitionists, such as Charles Volney Dyer, Owen Lovejoy and Joseph K.C. Forrest from Illinois with George W. Julian of Indiana, and Sherman Miller Booth of Wisconsin.[13] In general, though, the Van Buren organization steered the convention away from radicalism.

In hindsight, Van Buren might have still won the core NRA–Liberty group to the Free Soil coalition. When Alvan E. Bovay questioned him on behalf of the NIC, Van Buren stalled into late July, and his eighteen-page response meandered past any clear definition of what his "Free Soil" campaign meant. John Greig and Rochester NRA badgered Van Buren until it got an unprecedented second reply from the candidate. In it, Van Buren repeated the Democratic preference for selling public lands and insisting that this response be kept confidential.[14]

The common rejection of their radicalism by the new party pushed the more intransigent Liberty Leaguers and National Reformers even closer. In September 1848, those in New York held their own convention at Canastota. Later, at Peterborough, Ingalls "attended a public meeting of the friends of the movement for Anti-Slavery, in the interest of their candidate, but as a Land Reformer, for they had a Land Reform plank in their platform." While upstate Ingalls spoke before a black congregation at Little Falls on "land and freedom." Veteran abolitionists such as Arnold Buffum, Benjamin Timms, and Stephen Pearl Andrews—who had pursued these activities in Texas at great personal risk—embraced land reform. Enough Radical Abolitionist sentiment existed beyond New York to sustain some independent Libertymen, including Charles V. Dyer, who ran for governor of Illinois.[15]

The abolitionist press reflected a similar openness to this. Some, such as the *Aurora* at Centre, Indiana had long supported land reform, but more strictly abolitionist papers from Nathaniel P. Rogers's *Herald of Freedom* in New Hampshire to Booth's *Wisconsin Freeman* began

FREE SOIL

blending land reform concerns. Soon, Evans reported his "shaking the
hand of that true friend of freedom, William L. Chaplin," the editor of
the *Albany Patriot* and defender of the upstate Antirenters. In Ohio, the
Anti-Slavery Bugle of Aaron Hinchman and George W. Keen declared,
"We wish that every Land Reformer were an Abolitionist and every
Abolitionist a Land Reformer." [16]

In the end, official returns trickled into the Smith-Foote column
to a paltry total of 5,239 votes, which Greeley simply reported as a
"scattering." New Hampshire and Iowa contributed about a thousand
votes each with 2,545 from New York, almost half from Greene,
Madison, Oswego and Oneida counties. Nevertheless, the returns
credited NRA Congressional candidates with 1,035 and 2,765 votes in
the Fourth and Fifth Districts, while the entire city officially credited
only 159 votes to Smith with another fifty in Kings county. [17]

Nevertheless, every leader of the land reform movement acknowledged that almost all of the ranks went to Van Buren, "cajoled by the
false cry of 'Free Soil, Free Men,' and other designing catch words." In
the end, though, the Free Soilers got nearly 300,000 votes, a bit over 1
in 10 voters nationally, despite the fact that thirteen states did not even
offer the option. They won well over a quarter of the electorate in Massachusetts, New York, Vermont, and Wisconsin, and the unevenness
of this meant that they won pluralities—even majorities—in selected
places. Jeriel Root looked west from Peoria to "the effect of the free soil
movement upon the newly acquired territory, for which so much of the
people's money has been expended." [18]

Significantly, those radicals who had joined the Free Soil effort had a
major impact on it. Founders of the Free Soil party in Boston included
Horace Seaver, John Cluer, Elizur Wright, John Orvis, James N. Buffum,
and Henry P. Trask, as well as abolitionist friendly to the NRA like
Samuel G. Howe, William H. Channing, and John M. Spear. They sent
John Turner, an old "Worky" as an alternate to the national convention.
At nearby Worcester, the NRA dominated the "primary assemblies" of
Free Soilers. Philadelphia National Reformers appeared on the citywide
Free Soil committee, and the Baltimore Free Soil Party had been "made
up in no inconsiderable proportion of National Reformers," who sent
Dr. J. E. Snodgrass to the national convention. Even in upstate New
York, the new party enlisted such radicals, such as Henry Waterman a

veteran of every phase of labor reform activity since the trades' union movement at Albany over a dozen years before.[19]

With or without Van Buren, the Free Soil party nevertheless expressed and encouraged the discontent, particularly among officeholders. Hale, the stalwart Libertyman of Vermont had been in the government, joined by Horace Greeley who briefly replaced a Democratic Congressman removed for election fraud. The movement could directly claim several members of Congress, notably Joseph Cable of Ohio and Robert Smith from downstate Illinois.[20]

However, the more amorphous sentiment for land reform and against slavery moved many Free Soilers headed to Washington in 1849. These included Charles Sumner, Henry Wilson, David Wilmot, Galusha Grow, and William S. Holman from the northeast. More importantly, the Midwesterners provided: Benjamin F. Wade, Joshua R. Giddings, and Salmon P. Chase of Ohio; George W. Julian of Indiana; Isaac P. Walker and Charles Durkee of Wisconsin; and John Wentworth of Illinois. Julian frankly ascribed the subsequent course of American politics to "the Free Soil platform of 1848 and the Land Reformers of New York."[21]

The Radicalization of Free Soil

After the election, Van Buren and his people abandoned the Free Soil coalition leaving the remnants of the insurgency in the hands of radicals. Local parties, such as that at Worcester, moved towards an even more radical platform. Those who stuck with the Vermont Free Soilers adopted homestead exemption, which Elizur Wright, Jr. called the first radical step beyond a homestead bill. When the Free Soil politicians returned to the Democrats in Wisconsin, the remaining Free Democrats nominated the socialist Warren Chase for governor.[22]

The aftermath of the campaign left intransigent Libertymen and land reformers to address their relationship to the broader antislavery movement together. Gerrit Smith took Ingalls, Van Amringe, Evans and William V. Barr to Canastota for a Free Church convention. At Smith's home, National Reformers mingled with Theodore Weld, Angela and Sarah Grimke, Ingalls entertaining them with a rendition of August J. H. Duganne's song "Acres and Hands." Later, at the Weld's, he met more such "progressive people" among the abolitionists who "had considerable thought for the wrongs of the industrious poor."[23] Particularly given the betrayal of the movement by the leadership of Van Buren's short-lived bolt from the Democrats, the NRA even began a positive reassessment of the anti-electoral abolitionists such as William Lloyd Garrison. Lucius A. Hine of Cincinnati had always found Garrison "the most pleasant" when "the most denunciatory" of social wrong. He admitted that he admired Garrison for his enemies and his followers, who included "the best friends of all the reforms," including radical land redistribution. Nevertheless, Hine's *Garrisonian Politics* took that wing of the movement to task for its blanket abstention from elections and their unwillingness to see the antislavery potential of the Constitution.[24] That is, it rather reasonably aligned itself in the slavery debate with the positions of the old Liberty Party.

This established the foundations in New York and Pennsylvania for a united radical point of view. In November 1848, the Philadelphia NRA attended the state convention of Garrison's organization and introduced and discussed land reform resolutions until a general consensus emerged both as to their value and the inappropriateness of their formal adoption, after which the land reformers withdrew them. By 1849, Elijah M. K. Glenn, the upstate lecturer for the New York Antislavery Society— Garrison's body—gave talks on land reform as well as abolition.[25] Others, such as John M. Spear and John A. Collins also had strong credentials in that wing of the movement, as well as advocating socialist and land reform measures.

The movement also took on a distinctly anti-electoral, anti-institutional stance that provided more common ground with the Garrisonians. Citing Appleton Fay's resolutions at the previous NIC on behalf of "direct legislation," William West had urged the May 9 convention of the Garrisonians at New York's Broadway Tabernacle to unite with the NRA, since both movements favored abolitionism, land reform, and non-resistance. When Evans pointed out that the NIC had actually not adopted Fay's resolutions, West conceded that, in fact, the resolution had failed but by only one vote, indicating that land reformers were "nearly equally divided" on the abolition of government.[26]

Moreover, the 1848 NIC actually adopted the kind of non-resistance position Garrison had long favored. It recommended "a general law, securing to the people the means and opportunity to vote *directly*" for or against proposed laws. In the end, William West could, without fear of contradiction, portray the NRA to the non-resister abolitionists as similarly anti-institutional. "Perhaps," he wondered, "some professed National Reformers among hitherto non-voting Abolitionists will assist us *now?*" He thereafter urged abolitionist-NRA unity around "*a government of* ALL for *the benefit of* EACH, in itself the PERFECTION OF SELF-GOVERNMENT" by which he essentially meant no specially designated governing bodies.[27]

Then, too, the arrival of growing numbers of émigrés from the continent encouraged the radicalization of the American movement. Étienne Cabet brought a large number of working-class French radicals to the communitarian cause, but small numbers of German thinkers had been drifting across the Atlantic since the repressive measures of 1830–33. Peter Eckler, one of Evans friends not only republished the iconoclastic fiction of John Lithgow, but printed the writings of Johann Adolphus Etzler, the German-born prophet of environmental technologies, and Masquerier wrote his own popularized version of Etzler's vision. Johann August Röbling, later famed as a bridge builder—his own demonstration of the Hegelian dialectic—had emigrated to America in 1831, joining a communist society, "Germania," in which Peter Kaufmann participated. He became the earliest of a core of "Ohio Hegelians"— John Bernhard Stallo, Moncure Daniel Conway and August Willich.[28] However, new repressions in the wake of 1848–9 would send a larger, even more militant new wave of European revolutionaries.

The movement certainly took a broad spectrum of forms across the Midwest. In places, local iconoclasts ran for public office, registering only a handful of votes. Elsewhere, well-known local figures launched circles of the Brotherhood of the Union. The Owenite John Harmon and Daniel A. Robertson, a transplanted New York Locofoco ran the *Lancaster Eagle*, the most important Democratic paper in Fairfield County, Ohio, the latter moving on to become a pioneering newspaperman in Minnesota. The few known members of the local Brotherhood accounted for two of the five founders of Bloomfield, Iowa, influencing, among others, James Baird Weaver, the future presidential candidate of the Greenback–Labor and Populist parties.

The association between a visionary radicalism and an entrepreneurial spirit became very evident in Midwestern cities such as Milwaukee and Chicago. There, the local NRA not only included many radicals and workers, but also William B. Ogden and Wentworth, proprietor of the *Democrat* and a major power in his party. "The time has come when the voice of Labor must be heard," declared Wentworth's Chicago *Daily Democrat.*[29] The sentiment did not keep sometimes Congressman and Mayor Wentworth, like Ogden, from becoming one of the city's foremost real estate speculators and leaving their names memorialized in two of the city's major thoroughfares.

In the Midwest, self-interest drew some imaginative entrepreneurs, local boosters and politicians to radicalism. A land speculator with large tracts hoped to see adjacent lands settled as quickly as possible. Some of the associations of self-labeled squatters or settlers that cropped up across the region actually served as lobbies for real estate interests. Too, a Homestead Law—stripped of land limitation—could more effectively privatize public lands where the competition would naturally favor the larger landholders over time. Too, lead mine owners in Galena, Illinois or Mineral Point, Wisconsin interested in privatizing mineral rights more clearly saw benefits in homestead legislation designed with agriculture in mind.

To the left of these more prominent Free Soilers, radicalism remained broad almost from its inception as an organized force. Roughly forty miles northwest of Chicago, Seth Paine—the founder of a community at Lake Zurich—took up abolition, land reform, socialism, and spiritualism. He published Owen Lovejoy's *Western Citizen* and slowed the willingness of the Liberty party in Illinois to take up those questions. In short order, though, that paper embraced just such a "broad platform." "Free trade, direct taxation as a consequence, the abolition of the army, the dismantling of the navy and the 'Murder School at West Point' and a dozen other things as further consequences," wrote Lovejoy, belonged in the Libertymen's platform. Charles V. Dyer, the acknowledged spokesman of the state's "Underground Railroad" hosted Van Amringe, and James H. Collins, a prominent legal voice for the fugitive slaves helped to found the Chicago NRA. More silently, figures such as Allan Pinkerton labored systematically for the Liberty Party.[30]

The 1848 campaign had demonstrated that radicals hardly remained isolated. That year, the Libertymen ran Dyer for governor and placed the *Chicago Times* in the hands of Chauncey T. Gaston, the British born NRA printer with some ties to Wentworth's *Chicago Daily Democrat*. Gaston's former collaborator on the literary *Gem of the Prairie*, John

Locke Scripps called himself a "Free Soiler with Democratic proclivities" even after taking over the Whig *Chicago Tribune*. The émigré German radical Dr. Carl A. Helmuth of the influential *Illinois Staats-Zeitung* not only helped to launch the Chicago NRA, but embraced Free Soil and sympathies for the Democrats.[31]

Downstate, the radical insurgency had a serious impact among the Whigs. Jesse W. Fell, the Pennsylvania cabinet-maker transplanted to Bloomington, Illinois alternately speculated in McLean county land and agitated for what amounted to its more rapid settlement and development. A close advisor and ally of Whig Congressman Abraham Lincoln, Fell and his cothinkers successfully used their advocacy of such measures to challenge the Democratic coalition downstate.[32]

Wisconsin provides the clearest measure of how these diverse currents interacted. Only 973 voted for the Liberty Party in 1846, but nearly 7,700—over a third of the total—voted for Negro suffrage. By the beginning of 1848, a "Free Democratic State Convention" took form under sponsorship of Durkee and Samuel D. Hastings as well as Chase and Booth who had reported on the Barnburners for the *Freeman*, attended the founding national convention of the Free Soil party, and returned an ardent supporter of the party, despite misgivings about Van Buren. Wisconsin Democrats replicated the schism in New York, led by Andrew E. Elmore. In the end, 10,500 Wisconsin voters—well over a quarter of the state's total—cast Free Soil ballots.[33]

In that state, the Yankee Warren B. Chase spearheaded the radical drive. After a New England childhood plagued by his illegitimacy and orphanage, the self-described "Lone One" had worked his way west as a farmhand, eventually settling at Southport (later Kenosha) in the Wisconsin Territory. Earlier, he had drawn nearly two hundred into the Wisconsin Phalanx at Ceresco, the second longest-lived of any Fourierist project. As a delegate sent to the 1846 constitutional convention, he advocated abolishing the militia, capital punishment, imprisonment for debt, gender and racial barriers on the suffrage, and private ownership of unoccupied lands. Elected to the state senate in 1848, Chase agitated for various reform measures, including the introduction of Protective Unions into the state.[34] Ceresco provided Van Amringe with a ready base for his work.

The pioneer of land reform there, Andrew E. Elmore had been one of the first white settlers at Mukwonago. The local postmaster and an organizer of Waukesha County, he also served on its Board of Supervisors and won election as a Whig in a Democratic district to the territorial legislature and the 1846 constitutional convention where his insistence on an elected judiciary moved one of his conservative friends to label him "the Sage of Mukwonago."[35] After switching to the Democrats, Elmore organized a powerful faction within the party favorable to land reform.

After being dispatched to the west, Van Amringe focused his efforts on Wisconsin. There he found Chase the socialist, Booth the abolitionist and Elmore the reform Democrat, as well as German radicals like Dr. F. Huebschman and Frederick Fratney of Milwaukee's *Volksfreund* united behind a radical agenda. Despite his personal misgivings about wintering there, the aging radical launched his initial tour of the state at Mineral Point in October 1847 and remained in the state until March 1848 after speaking at Dodgeville, Ceresco, Waukesha, Milwaukee, Racine, Rochester, Southport and other towns. Then, in the fall of 1848, Van Amringe returned to settle in Wisconsin. An observer of his talk on land limitation and women's rights at Madison found him "a man of reading and research." Locals later credited him with "the healthy condition of Land Reform in our State."[36] Its version of Free Soil politics had always inclined towards radicalism.

When Van Buren and the Barnburners abandoned Free Soil to return to the Democratic Party the "friends" of reform in the Midwest also sought to win Democratic adoption of the Free Soil platform. Robert Smith of Illinois, who had never wavered from his Democratic allegiance, saw the chance to push that party for some modest reform measures. Such concessions convinced Elmore as well as Wentworth that radicals might find the Democrats to be "One Line in one grand party of progress."[37] The challenge for them was to demonstrate that the Democratic Party could be that "one grand party of progress."

In Wisconsin, at least, Elmore and other radical Free Soilers adopted the "Madison platform," with positions far to the left of the national Free Soil party. So did Wisconsin Congressman Durkee. When William Pitt Lynde, a Milwaukee Congressional candidate vacillated on land reform and initially opposed a ten-hour measure, Elmore and his allies withheld its support. Only after his eleventh hour commitments did Elmore dispatch riders across the state with radical endorsements (as in the East, though, such pledges meant nothing after the election). Congressman Moses M. Strong at Mineral Point posed similar problems.

As this broader statewide current seemed to take up more radical positions, those groups to their left sought to draw them further. The socialists L. M. Parsons and Lester Rounds reported the progress of the Ceresco experiment for the abolitionist readership of the *Freeman*. C. J. Allen, associated with both the Fourierists and the NRA, also presided over state as well as county conventions of the Anti-Slavery Society.[38] In the end, those Rosedale National Reformers began as critics of the time-honored exclusions of Americans from citizenship based on race or gender.

Still, the convergence of these transformative measures shaped a new leadership in the Midwest with a new kind of radicalism. Van Amringe, the NRA and NIC national lecturer, stumped the region talking about land reform, socialism, woman's rights and other issues, regularly declaring himself an abolitionist. Although he defined slavery as hostile to Christianity and the Declaration of Independence, he urged skepticism about the antislavery pretensions of the "Factory lords, Land lords, Banks, Speculators and usurers in the North."[39]

The Sectional Dynamic of the Radicalization

The sectional character of this radicalization of the movement became more pronounced with the crisis Free Soil had imposed on the core of the movement back in New York City. In the aftermath of the election, Ingalls returned to the city to find the core of the NRA "completely disorganized." Greeley's increasingly moderate *New York Tribune* squeezed *Young America* out of business. He had earlier loaned Evans $200 and now called in the debt. Evans had scraped together half the amount, sold $75 worth of his New Jersey farmland and got the balance as a small loan without security or interest from a wealthy benefactor (probably Gerrit Smith). In mid-1849, Evans acknowledged that he could no longer maintain the paper. Horace Seaver of the *Investigator* warned the movement against allowing *Young America* to go under, but Evans was eventually, in Thomas A. Devyr's words, "literally starved back" to his farm.[40]

It seemed to Ingalls that the American movement, like that in Europe, faded before "the reactionary tendency of things." Unable to sustain his own *Landmark*, Ingalls turned it over to William Haddock, an NRA leader who kept it going for a few months until he left town. Across the East river, Devyr turned his retrieved Antirent press to a succession of printers eventually lured away by local Democrats. Moreover, the Fourierist *Harbinger* and the spiritualist *Univercoelum* merged into the *Spirit of the Age*, which, as Ingalls recalled, "succumbed after a short life." Even the *Voice of Industry*, renamed the *New Era of Industry* began to teeter; faltering as editor D. H. Jacque withdrew into the Lowell Water Cure House, leaving John Orvis to nurse the paper into 1848, before it finally folded.[41]

What was left of the NRA pulled itself together to mount a spring mayoral campaign for the militant abolitionist land reformer David Marsh. Four days before the April 10 election, the Democratic candidate gave his pledge to the NRA and Marsh withdrew, but the Whig, Caleb S. Woodhull won. Masquerier again resurrected his call for independent political action.[42] Indeed, the NRA seemed spent as a distinct force.

New organizations filled the void. Gilbert Vale and his son, Gilbert, Jr. started the "Independent Order of Liberals," recalling the old free-thought organizations of nearly a quarter of century earlier. Inspired by the hardships and poverty of "aged or infirm Liberals" like William Carver, Ben Offen "and other less known" skeptics, they established mutual aid functions and planned an asylum and infirmary, a meeting hall, free library, boarding house, a cooperative housing association and a freethinkers cemetery out on the old Paine farm at New Rochelle.[43]

More importantly over the long run, George Lippard's Brotherhood of the Union drew in many land reformers. Planned at the time of the 1848 NIC, Elizur Wright announced its existence in November 1849 and Greeley reported its spread through New York in 1850. Members swore to sustain the "Holy Flame" kindled on "the altar erected by Paine, Franklin, Jefferson and Adams." It traced its origins through the Illuminati, Freemasons, Rosicrucians and Druids driven "to the shadows of the cavern and forest" by the rise of tyranny. The order also hoped to combat "the degradation of Labor, whether manifested in the form of Wages, Slavery, Land Monopoly, or Machine Monopoly, as the great Evil which tramples into the dust the holiest Rights of Humanity."[44]

The clearest contemporary organizational expression of working-class land reform at New York City, the Brotherhood recruited Evans, Ingalls, John Commerford, John H. Keyser, Ira B. Davis, Egbert Manning,

Marsh, Parsons E. Day and other old radicals. They met at Davis's cooperative bakery, and explicitly identified as the problem "that the present wages-system is only a piece of vassalage." They marched in local parades wearing a virtually paramilitary association, "dressed in handsome blouses and regalia. They were a fine company of men and attracted marked attention." Starting as the Nazarene Circle, the local Brothers embraced the legacy of the French revolutionaries, renaming themselves as the Ouvrier Circle.[45] It represented an organizational history going back through the NRA and Locofocos to the Workies and articulated grievances and ideas stretching back to the previous century.

That the dynamic had clearly shifted west became evident in the annual sessions of the NIC convened in Cincinnati and Chicago in 1849 and 1850. The original body had scheduled later sessions for the Midwest, confident that workers there would take up similar concerns. In these cities—as at Milwaukee and—to lesser extent—at St. Louis— land reform did inspire to the same constituencies it had in the east. However, they tended to be far more explicitly antislavery.

The Cincinnati movement had long seen itself as part of a broad struggle against corruption, slavery and war. Even before Fourierism— or spiritualism—swept the northeast, Cincinnati had its own Spiritual Brotherhood that groped towards its own understandings, established secret societies, formed communities, organized pioneering coopera- tive ventures and agitated broadly for land reform and women's rights. The Brotherhood had enough support in Ohio to establish a statewide Grand Circle. Upriver, the town of Utopia provided a viable model of community with Josiah Warren having several of his cooperative "time stores" in the area.

Living on the outskirts of the city was Frances Wright. The notorious Scottish Owenite who had coined the idea of "a war of classes" abandoned none of her old radicalism when she married William Philquepal d'Arusmont, a Pestalozzian educator she had met in New Harmony. After living in Paris, they returned to America, settling at Mount Healthy. She regularly discussed and advised the movement in the city.

Moreover, the Cincinnati movement also long included blacks, as did the abolitionists. Thomas and Marie Varney, former Owenites operated a printing business in the city. Their eighteen-year-old black apprentice, Peter Humphries Clark became particularly close friends with the

Southern-born William Haller of the local NRA. Years later, as the leader of Cincinnati's black schoolteachers, Clark left the Republican party to rejoin Hine and Haller in a state-wide Workingmen's party and the socialist movement.[46]

In June 1849, Cincinnati hosted the NIC "pretty numerously attended" by representatives from half a dozen states. They discussed "Anti-Slavery, Temperance, Land Reform—the Rights of Labor, the abuses of Capital—abolition of capital punishment, etc., etc." Evening meetings showcased Fannie Lee Townsend and a Mrs. Burns lecturing on "phonography." Van Amringe talked of "a harmonious integral reform, and not a fragmentary one," and Lucius A. Hine about combining "all the fragmentary reforms of the day, genuine movements constituting the whole of progress, and he who introduces the widest range of inquiry in his philosophy is the noblest reformer." William McDiarmid, a Wheeling Fourierist urged them to write a document demonstrating the underlying interrelationship of all the various reform proposals, and the NIC assigned the laborious task to John Pickering, the local author of *Workingman's Political Economy*.[47] Regrettably, a serious cholera outbreak in the city scattered the participants.

The next NIC assembled at Chicago's City Hall on Wednesday, June 5, 1850 confirmed this dynamic. After B. H. Boynton of the Milwaukee NRA served as one of the two temporary officers, the Congress elected Chase, the socialist and Wisconsin's former Free Democratic gubernatorial candidate to preside with Boynton and Allen as secretaries. Andrew E. Elmore, represented the state's radical Democratic faction. Wisconsin and Illinois dominated the session, though Ingalls showed up from New York City, as did Hine from Cincinnati bearing Pickering's draft.[48]

Ingalls thought the Congress "not very numerously attended, but a marked degree of talent characterized the members." William Sampson the Chicago Free Soiler served as a vice president along with Jeriel Root, Ingalls and Hine. Seth Paine, Daniel S. Curtiss, and John Ludby, a transplanted old veteran of New York's Workingmen's party. William S. Waite from Greenville, Illinois sent a letter, as had Thomas Champion of Philadelphia, John Ferral the labor leader, John Otis Wattles the Indiana communitarian and abolitionist, "and others."

On other matters, the 1850 NIC set aside precedent. Upon convening, it immediately adjourned to participate in afternoon celebrations by the local Odd Fellows. It accorded "all persons favorable to the objects" standing as "honorary members" and its sessions blurred into public meetings in the City Hall "at early candle light," easing into "informal" evening discussions of land reform and talks by Hine, Van Amringe and others "on the religious features of the great humanitarian reforms, to good and very attentive audiences." Rev. M. Skinner's church hosted a social reform sermon by Ingalls. Mindful of the loss of the 1849 proceedings at Cincinnati, this session decided to publish their own as a pamphlet, and designated the site of the next year's gathering as Albany.

Most importantly, the 1850 NIC clearly relocated land reform within broader antebellum concerns, urging a "concert of action among reformers." It adopted the usual land reform resolutions and heard Chauncey Gaston's address on Land Limitation which still kept the NRA of the radical craftsmen distinct from the more prominent and moderate versions of land reform. They voted to "favorably commend" their proposals "to the approbation of ... existing popular agitations and movements" as a means to "strike the fetters from Ireland and Great Britain, from Germany, France, Italy and from the world." Ingalls also raised the old Worky demand for Free Schools, asserting "the right of every person to be educated at the public expense." He also proposed "a mutual system of Exchange and Finance, or Banking," which could ameliorate the exploitation of rural districts by urban centers and of Western and Southern states "Eastern and European Capitalists."

Back in 1848, the NIC talked about "such other collateral measures as shall appear to be dictated by wisdom and experience, for the immediate relief of the toiling millions." Bovay, had long warned of the need to distinguish between the "indispensable" and those "to postpone for the moment, except for purposes of discussion." He warned that "putting forward too many issues at once" without priorities invited politicians and aspiring power brokers within the movement to climb about the reform platform to stand on the less important planks of their own choosing. Over the next two years, though, those "collateral," "cognate," "secondary, subsidiary or auxiliary principles" formed a broad platform for radical social change.[49] "All truth whether social, religious, political, physiological, and psychological constitutes unity," it declared, "and no fragmentary reform can be carried out without going hand in hand with all other reforms."

Hine reported on auxiliary and affiliated associations, urging the "Friends of Universal Freedom" to establish "Industrial Reform Associations." Advocating universal education, universal homes, universal prosperity, universal labor and universal happiness, these would affiliate in county associations and statewide "Industrial Legislatures" that could both advise and implement the deliberations of the "National Industrial Congress." They also began discussing this expanded "National Reform" as "Industrial Reform."

Van Amringe, the NRA's national lecturer persuaded the NIC to set aside three days for special discussions of peace activism, antislavery and women's rights. Upon convening, the body had recognized land and labor issues. In these, he argued for an acknowledgment of human equality "without distinction of sex" and denied any special power "inherent in the husband, brother and son over the wife, sister and mother." The Congress agreed, resolving that women's rights were "the same as those of men" in terms of "liberty, property, self-government, the elective franchise and eligibility to office."

Slavery sparked "an animated discussion," but the NIC urged "a Free Land Proviso" as "the most sure proviso against Slavery Extension and all unjust servitude" and declaring that American slaveholders had "no better claim of humanity" than that of "Joseph's brethren who sold him into Egypt." So, too, it condemned "the further extension of Slavery" by the new national Compromise of 1850. This represented the old passive hostility to slavery. In addition, it declared slavery "a moral, social and political evil, repugnant to the law of God written in the constitution of man, to the law of love revealed in the gospel of Christ, and to the declaration of rights proclaimed in the American Declaration of Independence." Other resolutions touched upon free blacks, complaining of the "abridgment of the liberties of free American citizens."

The 1850 NIC balked at Pickering's full-blown social critique. The manifesto by John (also referred to as "Solon") Pickering simply exceeded its mandate by offering a sweeping declaration of primary human rights coupled to a series of related "secondary or auxiliary principles" and an impressive list of reforms that grew from them; he capped it with an analysis of contemporary American class formation. In the end, the NIC saw no way of its adoption being "of any service to the cause." However, as with Appleton Fay's 1847 "model constitution," they found the document thought provoking, individually expressed agreement, and voted to print it with the proceedings.

After the NIC, Ingalls visited Wisconsin. Warren Chase, Sherman M. Booth and some 8,800 Wisconsin voters still maintained the Free Democrats while the state's antislavery Whigs and Elmore's Democratic faction formed an even greater constituency for reform. That fall, the regular Whigs, for reasons of their own, assisted in the election of J. D. Doty as a Free Democrat in the Third Congressional district. The Whig state convention protested the Fugitive Slave Law and brought its leaders onto the same platform as Booth, Durkee and other radicals, including "General" J. H. Paine, recently arrived from Ohio with his abolitionist and NRA record. That year Bovay turned up at Ceresco to join the community only to find it dissolving.[50]

In the winter of 1850–51, the Wisconsin legislature—largely elected on such pledges—heard the governor's call for action on the land question. The NRA called due those pledges and the state legislature actually passed a bill limiting individual ownership of land to four city lots or 640 rural acres. However, the state required a bill's passage on three occasions, which permitted real estate interests, investors and manufacturers call due pledges of greater importance to the politicians. Claiming that they had fulfilled their pledge with the first vote, pledged legislators broke ranks, and men elected to promote land limitation voted directly against it.[51] The fate of radical land reform in Wisconsin had demonstrated that the shadow movement carried a substantial price.

* * *

Radicalism has very distinctive regional predispositions in the Midwest. With a less dense population and cheaper land, smaller networks of the discontented more readily established smaller communities that tended to be more pragmatic and willing to set aside the social blueprints. More inclined to cooperatives with very flexible and experimental features. In that context, they also had a greater influence on the world around them.

Nevertheless, the impact of further radicalization was national. And the engagement of the National Reformers was not merely with abolitionists but with African Americans engaged in the struggle for emancipation. By the aftermath of the election, a black congregation at Little Falls hosted Ingalls to speak on "land and freedom." More importantly, black leaders such as The *Voice of Industry* had long lauded the efforts of Frederick Douglass, who, in turn, praised his local Rochester land reform paper as "the poor man's friend, and every man's friend." William Wells Brown "wished success to the Land Reform movement," as did other black leaders. They tended to describe abolition as "the first step towards ensuring their [the land reformers'] ultimate success. Labour is degraded by Slavery. Its abolition will elevate labour, and secure to men their manhood." Despite earlier clashes with the NRA, Frederick Douglass, by 1851, praised Rochester's *National Reformer* and its "great cause" which had "engaged some of the noblest heads, and most philanthropic hearts of their age."[52]

Beyond electoral actions, the networks ready to win direct action against slavery had increasingly brought to the fore African American women, such as Harriet Tubman. Others, such as Isabella Baumfree, who took up the *nom de guerre* of Sojourner Truth bridged the gap between runaways, organized abolitionism, and the wider movements for social reform. A veteran of a socialist community in New England, she also spoke regularly at gatherings for spiritualism and women's rights.

However tentative, initial and partial, the focusing of black and white concerns around a common plebeian sense of liberty, equality and solidarity represented an explosive force.

PART THREE

An Unrelenting Radicalism: from Movement to Cadres

Had I interfered in the manner which I admit ... in behalf of the rich, the powerful, the intelligent, the so-called great, or in behalf of any of their friends, either father, mother, brother, sister, wife, or children, or any of that class, and suffered and sacrificed what I have in this interference, it would have been all right ... an act worthy of reward rather than punishment. I believe that to have interfered ... in behalf of His despised poor, was not wrong, but right.

—John Brown, last speech, November 2, 1859

7

Free Soil Radicalized:
The Rise and Course of the
Free Democrats, 1849–53

U.S. Senator John Parker Hale visited the local Free Democratic organization at New York City, after his national campaign for the presidency. Unblinkingly, he also addressed a meeting of the radical émigrés there, mounting a platform with the Stars and Stripes on one side and, on the other, "the French Red Republican flag" of the Union Socialiste. The events in the wake of 1848 on both sides of the Atlantic defined what participants understood of that red flag. At one of these, the shoemaker Bernard Paul Ernest "Honeste" Saint-Gaudens praised the red flag as "the symbol of the solidarity and fraternity of nations," and "the banner which had often been with the people against the power of feudality."[1] The recent presidential candidate of the Free Democratic Party and a member of the U.S. Senate, Hale had no qualms about sharing a platform decorated by such banners and the ideas of European revolutionary thinkers such as Auguste Blanqui, Pierre Joseph Proudhon as well as Karl Marx and Friedrich Engels.

The defeat of the revolutionary risings that erupted across the Old World and the sweeping American insurgency emboldened the conservative defenders of the old order. They moved to secure their power with militantly reactionary measures. Despite widespread verbal support in the past for a homestead bill, the Congress held fast against it, even as it helped impose a new Fugitive Slave Act mandating the cooperation of states and people that had chosen not to have slavery. Intransigent Free Soilers who still trusted neither party to be qualitatively better than the other stubbornly maintained their organization as Free Democrats. With abolitionists, land reformers, socialists, woman suffragists and others united, a coalition of internationalist radicals coalesced into a network of French anarchists, German socialists, black nationalists and other revolutionaries.

The New York City Industrial Congress and the Petition Campaigns

Towards the middle of the century, higher prices in the cities drove increasingly desperate workers to rebuild their unions and their city-wide federations. In 1849, a Boston printers' strike galvanized a general movement of the local trades. The attempt of Pittsburgh iron-mongers to slash wages provoked a united response by fourteen local crafts. John Sheddon, Isaac Rehm and other members of Philadelphia's Brotherhood of the Union fostered a cooperative Industrial Association among the women of the needle trades. Printers established cooperative labor papers. One historian wrote that "scarcely an industrial centre" escaped the movement "as far west as Illinois."[2]

The emphasis on women workers had been growing since their first job actions thirty years before. By the 1830s, women workers began elbowing their way into their own, particularly in factory times such as Lowell. In 1834, seven hundred of them went on strike, and twice that number walked out two years later. Women workers at Pittsburgh earned the label of "the Amazons" after a month-long 1845 textile strike. Over the next decade, large numbers of women struggled in the nation's largest cities trying to make ends meet.

For five years, the NRA at New York City had tried to get a local convention of the trades. John H. Keyser—back in the city from California—and Donald C. Henderson of the Tribune spearheaded the effort in May 1850. The hostile Democratic editor James Gordon Bennet also named K. Arthur Bailey of the Church of Humanity and Henry J. Crate, though reserving his special ire for Horace Greeley and his "organ of free soil whiggery and socialism." Keyser, Henderson and Bailey were also prominent members of the Brotherhood of the Union, and called their creation the New York City Industrial Congress (NYCIC). Its history as a broad-based movement with a wide spectrum of ideas unfolded in the columns of the Tribune.[3]

Through the summer and fall, the NYCIC battled for legitimacy. It proposed lien laws, debt reform, and the legislation of a ten- and, ultimately, an eight-hour workday. It also proposed municipal public works to employ the unemployed at a minimum wage set by law; the ward election of rent inspectors with the power to withhold rents from landlords providing substandard housing, and setting a ceiling on rents at 10 percent of one's income. The municipal authorities ceded none of this but, by August, granted the NYCIC use of a courtroom in the City Hall annex.

The Democrats made a particularly strong effort to court the NYCIC. Local Democratic leaders such as John Cochrane, Sanford E. Church, Theodore E. Tomlinson and Tenth Ward boss Elijah Purdy courted the body, which endorsed Fernando Wood for mayor simply because he pledged support. By the fall, Ira B. Davis and William V. Barr discussed organizing local committees to adjust the nominating process to reform the party. Given the twenty years of experience with such tinkering, it seems remarkable that some still retained hope in the party of Jackson. Yet the Free Soil bolt two years before had sparked a flurry of talk about Democratic reformism across the North.

Then, too, the earlier insurgency had placed in office a number of figures receptive to the movement. The 1851 NIC acknowledged allies in its "brother Congress," such as Greeley, Isaac P. Walker and Gerrit Smith. Back in Ohio, John H. Klippart "heartily rejoiced to see that our national legislators have, even at this late day, when, perhaps one third of the United States are permanently in the hands of Lords of lands, seen this error, and that such men as Walker of Wisconsin, [George W.] Julian of Indiana, thrill their council chamber with burning, truthful words in favor of the oppressed, landless, toiling millions." This is indicated by the discussion of the 1851 NIC of the need for "some concerted plan of action" to submit memorials to Congress "like the great petitions of the Massachusetts freemen and the English Chartists."[4]

The Thirty-First U.S. Congress got hundreds of these documents— some single pages of scrawled signatures and others glued into vast coiling scrolls, most going to the Committee on Public Lands. Perhaps 200,000 Americans signed these petitions, most of which called for the most radical measures of the NRA, such as land limitation. Some came directly from associations, such as the Ouvrier Circle of the New York City Brotherhood. New York produced seventeen petitions, New Jersey seven: and Pennsylvania fourteen, with only a handful coming from New England. From the Midwest came fourteen from Ohio (including one of three thousand from Cincinnati), nine from Indiana, eight from Illinois (at least half from Chicago), Wisconsin half a dozen, and two from Michigan. Few came from the South and the far west, with a dozen from St. Louis, Missouri, three from Maryland, and one each from Kanawha County in western Virginia and the squatters in Sonoma County, California.

Just as officeholders had appropriated the language of "Free Soil," some distilled "the land question" into something that could foster development. The city government of Milwaukee requested a homestead bill, as did the state legislatures of Illinois, Indiana and Missouri. In addition, related requests from legislatures included those of: Arkansas for a simple homestead bill (in non-NRA language); Ohio and Florida officials wanted to lower land prices to forestall a homestead bill; and, Wisconsin translated it into the Menominee Indians' lands. The encouragement of development trumped social justice.

The more pragmatic focused on Wisconsin Senator Isaac P. Walker, said to have a realistic shot at the Democratic nomination. When he gave a major address in the Senate for a Homestead Bill in early 1851, John Commerford praised it, while Dr. William J. Young added that Walker seemed to be the only one in government who understood land reform. Evans and Barr tried to get Greeley's *Tribune* to publish it. Keyser and others urged the NYCIC to call upon the local Democratic Party to "draw the line between the real and the spurious Democracy."[5] The NYCIC's identifiable trade unionists seemed particularly enthusiastic for Walker.

The prospect of a Walker nomination well served the local Democratic Party. Tammany Hall invited the NYCIC to a June 3 meeting to unite "all true Democrats" around the idea "of Land and other Industrial reforms." After a spirited debate, the NYCIC agreed to participate. The Democrats put their best foot forward, installing NRA leader William V. Barr as one of the meeting's officers, and Cochrane spoke for the party in offering to make "the land question" their key issue with Walker as their nominee. Regrettably, the partisan predispositions of the NIC survived the predictable fizzling of the Walker boom. Thereafter, the NYCIC went into decline with some national Reformers stubbornly trying to sustain the coalition.[6]

More generally and over time, the NRA current within the NYCIC resisted the drift towards the Democrats. H. H. Van Amringe expressed the prevailing sentiment when he insisted on once more nominating "a progressive candidate" for president. Evans continued to write about running Gerrit Smith again. As early as the spring of 1851, Lewis Masquerier's call for independent political action challenged the Democratic proclivities of the body. The more strategically conservative Dr. Young replied that the movement should "not want a party so much as the adoption of these principles." The 1851 NIC debated various nominations, including Samuel R. Ward, the black abolitionist.[7]

Indeed, one of the felicitous byproducts of the NYCIC had been the emergence of trade unions in those traditionally African American occupations. The suggestion at the NIC to run Ward for president surely reflected his role in organizing the American League of Colored Laborers back in the city. Around it, hotel waiters, coachmen and others established the first associations of black workers to improve wages and working conditions.[8]

The issue of race and the role of African Americans in a common movement came to a head at the June 1851 NIC in Albany. The national gatherings had grown increasingly radical, but this marked the first in three years east of the Alleghenies, and it came when the New York movement felt immense pressures to reach an accommodation with the Democrats. This time, though, the regularly worded NRA invitations to "all parties who are struggling in the cause of Human Rights and Universal Brotherhood" sparked an abolitionist and black response.[9]

John C. Bowers, "a colored gentleman from Philadelphia," presented his credentials and demanded a seat representing a "Building Society of colored men." A founding member of the Pennsylvania Antislavery Society, he had been prominent in the city's antislavery movement over the previous fifteen years. The Democratic *New York Herald* reported that "several white 'brethren' ... objected to his admission," one of them charging that Quakers from Philadelphia has deliberately sent a black man to disrupt the movement. Lucius A. Hine found that "the colored man in question possesses great fluency and accuracy of speech, a high intellectual and moral endowment" which left him unable to comprehend "why any one should object to sit with one whose genius can command respect ..." The Credentials Committee tabled the issue until assigning the uncontested seats, including that from the Cincinnati's Women's Rights Society.[10]

The sympathy for Bowers (and, conversely, the hostility to the racist Democrats present) reflected changes among militants in the local movement. Bernard Paul Ernest "Honeste" Saint-Gaudens openly insisted "on associating with the negro Freemasons and presiding at their initiations." When other white Freemasons accordingly blacklisted him, he "told them to go elsewhere, and, in the future, never attended any but negro lodge meetings, though he always explained to his children that Freemasonry was a sublime and impressive order." Then, too, back in Hine's Cincinnati, Peter Humphries Clark, a mixed race printer and schoolteacher worked in a movement shop and became a lifelong friend of the Virginia-born William Haller of the local NRA.[11]

The radicals clearly decided to make seating Bowers the unquestionable achievement of the gathering on the second day of the Congress. Evans added new members to the Credentials Committee, to ensure a minority report, but the *Herald* gleefully reported three hours of a bitter argument. When it came to the vote, only half a dozen of the twenty-eight delegates tried to block adoption of his credentials, and Bowers strolled to the front taking a seat directly before Evans, the presiding officer. While reading the correspondence, however, Evans came to the letter of John Campbell, the Democratic ex-Chartist who protested the presence of "a negro delegate—and when I say a negro, I include mulattoes, sambos, quadroons, mestizos, *et hoc genus omne* from a light buff or yellow, to sable dark, in fine all those with the taint of inferior blood in them—from this city is to be sent to your body."

For the only time on record, the even-tempered Evans sputtered that had he known of the contents he would not have even begun its reading it. This led to another two more hours of the "most violent, abusive, and intolerant harangues," during which one of Campbell's friends nearly came to blows with Bowers. The fight continued into a third day, establishing a clear and indisputable position that later congresses would welcome people of color. One unidentified NRA leaders—likely Evans himself—declared that they would dissolve the existing organization if it excluded African Americans and reorganize as a movement open to all.[12] In the end, the few walked out, but several new delegates joined, leaving the dynamics of radical land reform quite explicit.

In the aftermath of the NIC, the movement redoubled its petition efforts for the Thirty-Second Congress. Geographically, these later petitions marked a curious shift. From March through early August of 1852, the northeast produced even more than before—128 petitions from New York, including several for William Rees's Western Farm and Village Association with its plan for a colony in Iowa, 20 from

Pennsylvania, 4 from New Jersey, and 31 from New England. Support apparently grew considerably in the Midwest, where Ohio produced 103, with 30 from Wisconsin, over two dozen from Illinois, over a dozen from Indiana, 5 from Michigan and 4 from Iowa. Southern petitions had become even more rare. National Reformers had long described theirs as an abolitionist measure and, remarkably enough, expressed the naive hope this would prove no barrier to gaining political support in the South.[13]

In part, such networks that had not earlier felt an imperative to take positions on slavery or race felt compelled to do such given the new aggressiveness of the Southern political machines. They had insisted on a new Federal Fugitive Slave Act as part of the "Compromise of 1850," which imposed stringent national mandates on Northern communities to cooperate in the capture and return of runaway slaves to their masters. Isaac T. Hopper, "the father of the Underground Railroad," died shortly after these impositions inspired an even more open and serious defiance of slavery.

Such developments certainly roused the concerns of those remnants of the Liberty Party that convened at Buffalo on September 17 and 18, 1851. It frankly acknowledged the problems it had encountered in trying to function as an abolitionist-land reform current independent of the Free Soilers. By then, the party acknowledged the problems it faced. "The abolitionist is impatient with the Liberty Party, because it will not consent to be a mere abolition party; and the land reformer is impatient with it, because it will not consent to be a mere land reform party." The Liberty Party insisted on a "Civil Government must be just, equally just, ever just, toward all classes of its subjects. Civil Government, whilst it must suffer none of its subjects to be robbed of their liberty, must suffer none of them to be robbed of their land."[14] However, the passage of a fortified Fugitive Slave Act dropped their concerns right into the center of a national agenda.

Antislavery people now used direct action. When Boston officials arrested Shadrrach Minkins in February 1851, Lewis Hayden led other members of the vigilance committee and forcibly took Minkins from the Federal officials and secreted him into the city, an action later defended in court by Senator Hale. The following September saw a serious, armed clash near Christiana, Pennsylvania. The following month, at Syracuse, officials detained an escaped slave named William Henry, usually known simply as "Jerry," just down the street from a convention of Libertymen. Hundreds converged on the city jail and secured his release, though black leaders such as Samuel Ringgold Ward and Jermain Wesley "Jarm" Loguen had to head briefly to Canada themselves, for their own safety.[15] The authorities hardly quieted the resistance by taking reprisals. In particular, they arrested and tried a white neighbor, a miller named Castor Hanway for treason. The abolitionist movement successfully made it a cause célèbre. Congressman Thaddeus Stevens defended him while the radical feminist Lucretia Mott raised money. Violent encounters flared up periodically along the border.

The 1852 Election

On May 12, 1852, the U.S. House of Representatives passed a homestead bill 107 to 56, sending the measure to the Senate. There, Senators Salmon P. Chase of Ohio, Isaac P. Walker of Wisconsin and others brought the effort to the floor, swept by another wave of petitions. Nevertheless, within two weeks of the House action, Southern leaders of the Democratic caucus shuttled the bill and its petitions to the Committee on Public Lands, where it could be buried.

On June 2, the seventh annual NIC gathered at Washington, DC. The NRA had made some efforts to organize there over the previous six years. Most successfully, several circles of the Brotherhood of the Union formed there, and allied German socialists had cothinkers in the capital. Both the NRA and the Society of Iron Men sent delegates to the 1852 NIC from New York City, while Philadelphia delegates attended from the Sunday Institute, the Industrial Union, and the German Workingmen's Union. Washington's Brotherhood of the Union sent delegates, as did the Lowell NRA and other groups from Wilmington Delaware, Rhode Island, New Jersey and Wisconsin. After issuing its own memorial to the U.S. Senate, the NIC found itself drawn into matters more electoral.[16]

The session broke all precedent to call Congressman Charles Durkee of Wisconsin to chair. "General" J. Sidney Jones, the husband of Fanny Townsend, however, objected to the precedent of selecting a politician, and stormed out. With the abolitionist Durkee in the chair, the body got down to business. Eliab W. Capron the spiritualist proposed "a Circular to the Land Reformers of the United States." The NIC declared that "the contest of the parties is not the contest of interests." "The party of masses, the Labor Party, is a third party," it declared. "Organized or disjointed, unanimous or divided, conscious or unconscious of its own existence, *it is*." The NIC voted not to support any candidate not pledged in writing to land reform and authorized the questioning of candidates, retaining the option of "an independent nomination" should no party or candidate running offer a written pledge to the movement's goals.[17]

Soon, the Democratic presidential candidate Franklin Pierce began hearing much more than he wanted about land reform. The NIC contacted him, as did Benjamin F. Price for the New York NRA and Thomas A. Devyr wrote him privately at least twice. Still, Pierce remained silent. John Cochrane, the Tammany tactician, sent Pierce his own appeal through John A. Dix. He estimated the issue could shift some 6000 voters in the state, drawing equally from both the Democrats and Whigs. He offered to convey them a private response from Pierce.[18]

Faced with his silence, angry land reformers gathered once more at the Military Hall on Bowery and Spring, where some of them had been meeting for over twenty years. Commerford gaveled them to order on August 4, when the mainstays of the movement raged against the Democrats, feebly defended by E. P. Day, then printer of the *Democratic Free Press*. Devyr noted that they would have some sway with "a majority of the people of the west, and the workingmen throughout the country." Two days later, some participants also attended the city convention of "Independent Democrats" to select delegates to the national convention of the remaining Free Soilers at Pittsburgh. There, William West got passage of a mild land reform resolution and the body sent him, William J. Young and Lewis Masquerier to the national convention as part of the city's delegation under the leadership of Abraham Levy.[19]

Meanwhile, the U.S. Congress had once more distilled the sweeping proposals of the NRA into a mere Homestead Bill, which it consigned to the Committee on Public Lands. When Walker tried to get Senate to instruct the Committee to report the bill, sixteen Democrats and twelve Whigs thwarted the effort.[20] The bipartisan character of this action sparked another mass meeting.

The gathering of August 10 at the Military Hall was "very fully attended," it drew "from this and adjoining cities, notwithstanding the unfavorable weather." Self-identified Democrats officered the gathering, which should have made its denunciations of the Pierce campaign all the more stinging. Day, their earlier defender, suggested that leading Senate Democrats "be burnt in effigy." Some even toyed with the notion of endorsing Winfield Scott as vengeance on the Democrats, but the body postponed a decision until after the Free Democratic national convention.[21]

That national gathering began that same day, August 11 at Pittsburgh's Masonic Hall, later moving to Lafayette Hall. Identified with land reform as well as abolition, Samuel Lewis, of Ohio chaired the Executive Committee of the Free Democrats who seated delegates from Kentucky, Virginia, Delaware, and Maryland as well as representatives from all of the non-slaveholding states to prepare the national ticket. The platform echoed the old Liberty position that the Constitution gave "no more power to make a slave than to make a king, and no more power to establish slavery than to establish a monarchy, should at once proceed to relieve itself from all responsibility for the existence of slavery, wherever it possesses Constitutional power to legislate for its extinction." It also asserted that "a natural right to a portion of the soil; and that as the use of the soil is indispensable to life, the right of all men to the soil is as sacred as their right to life itself." Public land "should not be sold to individuals nor granted to corporations, but should be held as a sacred trust for the benefit of the people, and should be granted in limited quantities, free of cost, to landless settlers."[22] The convention also gave serious consideration to an even more radical minority report from Gerrit Smith.

The presidential nomination remained uncertain going into the convention. Those in the know spoke of Salmon P. Chase of Ohio and Hale of New Hampshire, though he had even publically declined to be put in nomination. In the end, though, the first ballot gave him 192 votes, with single digits going to Chase, Gerrit Smith and William Goodell, and one each to Durkee, Thomas H. Benton and Charles Francis Adams. The initial vote for the vice presidential nomination delivered 104 ballots to George Washington Julian of Indiana, 83 to Lewis, 16 to Giddings, with three votes each to land reformer-abolitionists James H. Collins of Indiana and George Henry Evans himself (likely from Masquerier, Young and probably Arnold Buffum), with Cassius M. Clay and Benton getting one each.[23]

On August 17, the land reformers at New York met again. Young began by noting that both Pierce and Scott had "already been questioned as to their views on Land Reform and refused to answer." The Democratic *Herald* implied deceptively that the meeting took the course of Devyr, West, and Lewis Ryckman, who wanted to back Scott. Other, surely more accurate accounts suggest a different outcome after Evans, Joshua K. Ingalls and K. Arthur Bailey urged supporting Hale.[24]

In the final analysis, radical unity behind the Free Democratic ticket was the logical outcome. Years earlier, John Commerford had told the abolitionists that the NRA would "not be humbugged by sounds to uphold Land Monopoly or Slavery in any form" and those wielding power in the South fully reciprocated by refusing to be "humbugged" by land reform "in any form." John C. Calhoun, noted Commerford, had repudiated land reform because the South Carolinian had understood that it "would make every man a freeman." The lesson of 1852 was that where "the master lives in opulence on the labor of his colored slaves," political leaders "look with disfavor on the movement, mainly because it portends change; and change, always desired by the victims of power, is always feared by its possessors."[25]

The old Liberty Leaguers held out, perhaps suspicious of a repeat of the Free Soil fiasco. They met on their own at Syracuse on September 30. After some debate, they nominated William Goodell and S. M. Bell, of Virginia—likely the Pennsylvania-born farmer in the Wheeling area, in what would become West Virginia. In the end, though, they seem to have quietly taken their place among the Free Democrats.

Eliphalet Kimball of Oxford, New Hampshire did not. He proposed demolishing the Capitol and White House as imperial rather than republican institutions, cutting the wages of Congressmen to $2 daily, that of a skilled artisan, and reducing the President's salary to $10,000 yearly. He wanted the laws "reduced to a few general ones," hoped the Congress would meet no more than every ten years, with the abolition of the navy and a "radical reorganization of the Army on democratic principles." He mistrusted the professional mercantile classes, corrupted by commerce and drink. This he did, reported the *Tribune*, on the basis of his military heroism, It said he advocated "the pure and simple reign of nature, without lawyers, doctors, parsons, dry goods retailers, or apothecaries." The newspaper added, "We bear Mr. Kimball no ill will, and hope it may not endanger his chances at the South for us to say that there are points about him and his platform which we rather like."[26]

In the end, Hale won over 155,000 votes, a bit under 5 percent of the total. This represented a falloff from the Van Buren-Adams count of four years earlier, but cast for a more clearly radical program. More importantly, the Free Democrats were not going to dissolve when the election ended.

Revolutionary Internationalism and the Free Democrats

A dedicated and coherent radical core emerged around the time of the election. The repression of the 1848–9 revolutions abroad sent thousands of revolutionary émigrés to the U.S. from many different nations but sharing a common desire to universalize democratic rights and social justice. Their new cosmopolitan radicalism drew together much of the broad spectrum of American dissent.

The Scottish-born Hugh Frederick Forbes became the principal organizer of the radicals in New York City during these years. A Scottish-born product of Eton and Oxford, he had held a commission in the Coldstream Guards. He resigned to run a silk business and, later, a mining company at Siena, Italy, where he joined the clandestine republican movement, operating in the teeth of the piecemeal occupation of Italy by Austrians, French, Papal and various local overlords. Deeply involved in the 1848 upheavals, he performed good service in the defense of Venice before heading for Sicily and, ultimately, joining Giuseppe Garibaldi's forces defending the new Roman Republic. Convinced that Europe's future would be "decided by the force of arms," Forbes began work on his *Manual for the Patriotic Volunteer*. When Rome fell, he joined Garibaldi's desperate race across Italy in an effort to run the Austrian blockade of Venice, the revolution's last holdout.[27] The Austrians kept them, but, with the August 1849 capitulation of Venice, Forbes's wife and the British government helped negotiate his release.

Eventually, Forbes accompanied the English republican William J. Linton, to Switzerland where he met Félix Pyat and other revolutionaries. There, Giuseppe Mazzini urged him to go to New York and work among the émigrés there. At Paris, he met the Catholic socialist Hugues-Félicité Robert de Lamennais, the Russian revolutionary Alexander Herzen and American abolitionist Maria Weston Chapman before continuing on to London, where he established associations that included the Fraternal Democrats and the most radical of the Chartists.[28] Forbes then crossed the Atlantic, settling in Boston.

There, Forbes found a very different situation than he had been led to expect. Italians and other immigrants not only found themselves isolated by language but Nativist hostility. When Archbishop John Hughes of New York denounced the upheavals of 1848–9, Forbes offered an *Answer to Archbishop Hughes*, followed by *A Few Words on Popery and Despotism*, and *Four Lectures upon Recent Events in Italy*. The *Tribune* noted that Forbes also toured the interior of New York "under the auspices of Mazzini and other friends of Italian Liberty." More significantly, though, the abolitionist *Independent* reviewed it positively, and Theodore Dwight described Forbes as "my esteemed friend, and the friend of America and of mankind, in my estimation."[29]

Forbes also found many Americans ready to work with thousands of European émigrés around a radical internationalist agenda. Abolitionists, land reformers and Fourierists had long declared their sympathies with the revolutionary movements abroad. Members of the Brotherhood of the Union regularly made such toasts as: "Kossuth, Louis Blanc, Ledru Rollin, Jules Lechevalier, Mazzini—the heroes and apostles of Brotherhood in the Old World." When the British Chartists made another effort at reorganization, they invited an American "mission of brotherhood" to a "World's Industrial Congress." In February 1851, the NYCIC assigned Parsons E. Day, a descendant of Joseph Warren, the Revolutionary hero of Bunker Hill.[30]

By the fall of 1853, Forbes had moved to New York, where he found émigré radicals of various nationalities ready for action. Earlier that summer, some Greeks kidnapped Martin Koszta, a Hungarian radical at the Ottoman city of Smyrna and turned him over to the Austrian navy, which clapped him in irons on their warship, the *Hussar*. On July 2, U.S. Naval Commander Duncan N. Ingraham moved his *St. Louis* alongside the Austrian ship, cleared his decks for action, and threatened to send a storming party should they not release Kosta, who had been in the U.S. and once declared his intention of becoming a citizen. After Ingraham forced his release and got him to safety, Forbes and others organized an "Ingraham Committee" to present the South Carolina-born naval officer with a medal of appreciation. Then, in early 1854, the French celebrated the anniversary of their February Revolution by hosting Americans, Germans, Italians, Hungarians, Cubans and Poles, as well as Ivan Golovin, "that rarity," a Russian revolutionary, along with a growing numbers of English Chartists. Among the latter, Wemyss Jobson, the former dentist to the royal family spoke on the "the Secret History and Policy of the English Government."[31]

Other fascinating Eastern Europeans also turned up. Ernestine L. Rose came into her own as a radical voice in these years. Too, one of the most singular, Andrej Bernard Smolnikar, was a self-defrocked Slovenian Benedictine priest. He brought his own kind of Catholic mysticism to spiritualism. A true eccentric, he continued to pass on the warnings of the spirits about the efforts of mystical *Secret Enemies of True Republicanism*. The Russian writer Ivan Golovin and the Turkish proprietor of an adjacent coffeehouse Christopher Bey Oscanyan hovered around the edges of the bohemian radicals clustered at Pfaff's Cellar on Broadway.[32]

However, in point of numbers and political weight, the French and Italians seem to have played the largest role in these early efforts. A veteran of the old *Sociéte des Droits de l'Homme*, Marc Caussidière had been sentenced to prison twenty years earlier, but the revolution of 1848 had made him Prefect of Police, in which capacity, he resisted the crackdown on the workers in the June Days, a decision that sent him into exile. Then, too, Garibaldi himself turned up in New York, attending political meetings with Forbes, though maintaining a low profile.[33]

Largely because of their importance in introducing the insights of Marx into the U.S., the Germans tended to remain the most well-remembered participant, four veterans of the Bund der Kommunisten (the Communist League) being particularly noteworthy. Most prominent at the time, Wilhelm Weitling had been among the earliest of the German artisans to step from democratic radicalism to anticapitalism. The son of a French father and a German mother, he had become a tailor at Magdeburg, and learned multiple languages before heading off as an iterant workman, where he encountered the ideas of Charles Fourier, Étienne Cabet, François-Noël Babeuf, and Robert Owen. In 1837, he joined the Bund der Gerechten (League of the Just), a group that had come out of the older Bund der Geaechteten (League of the Proscribed). The new organization became what Friedrich Engels later called an outrider of Auguste Blanqui's insurrectionist socialism. Weitling's influence helped move the group from a working-class radicalism to socialism. His *Die Menschheit, wie sie ist und wie sie sein sollte* represented a pioneering work that introduced socialist ideas to German workers, a reputation consolidated with his later *Evangelium eines armen Sünders* (Gospel of the Poor Sinners) and his *Garantien der Harmonie und Freiheit* (Guarantees of Harmony and Freedom). In 1846, it became closer to a Communist Corresponding Committee operated by Karl Marx and Engels at Brussels. By mid-1847, the groups converged as a new Communist League.[34]

One member of the League, Rudolf Hermann Kriege, had actually reached America before Weitling. Shortly after reaching New York, he made his first attempt to reach American workers with his *Die Väter unserer Republik in ihrem Leben und Wirken*, a biography of Tom Paine. Like many immigrants, though, Kriege responded to Nativist hostility by moving ever closer to the Democratic Party with his *Sozial-Reform-Assoziation*, and his paper, the *Volkstribun*.[35] By his early death in 1850, Kriege had virtually dissolved his organization into the party's base, though the local groups seem to have persisted.

By then, though, Weitling himself had come to the U.S. Near the start of 1850, he started his monthly *Die Republik der Arbeiter*, which quickly reached a circulation of several thousand. Weitling's publication and his Arbeiterbund had a much greater impact than Kriege's, but the wide open spaces of the New World quickly drew them into the efforts such as Communia in Iowa.

One of Weitling's followers, Friedrich Adolph Sorge began to assume a major role in the most important affiliate of Weitling's Arbeiterbund, that at New York City. The son of a freethinking Saxon vicar who often sheltered radicals hiding from the law, the twenty-one-year-old Sorge took up arms against the Prussians in Baden in 1849, after which he faced exile in Switzerland and Belgium, before seeking refuge at London and, in June 1852, taking passage to America. There, he became involved in Weitling's organization, but the young admirer of Marx and Engels soon became prominent in the education around their ideas.[36]

Other veterans of the Communist League came over about this time, notably two former Prussian officers who cast their fate with the workers' movement. Joseph Weydemeyer turned up and tried to launch a Proletarierbund and establish a newspaper, *Die Revolution*, which he used to launch an Allegemeine Arbeiterbund, or American Workers' League in March 1853.[37] Ira B. Davis and others associated with the

Ouvrier Circle and Forbes's coalition joined this group, which had an immense influence beyond its numbers.

The Freie Gemeide already had a loose national network among the freethinkers. It aimed at uniting relatively effective local circles of revolutionary veterans, who had clustered for years in cities from Boston to St. Louis, and New Orleans to Milwaukee. Figures such as Fritz and Mathilde Anneke in Wisconsin played a major role in shaping the movement in that state, she becoming a major national figure in the movement for women's rights. August Willich, convicted in the Cologne Communist Trials also came to America with considerable fame as a result. Individuals such as Joseph Dietzgen had little organizational role, but wrote continually to clarify the political tasks they faced.

The broad movement in New York took up the call of the Freie Gemeide and urged the new coalition to act publically through "a general union of Liberal Societies." By "liberal," the Germans meant philosophically free from the superstitions of religious dogma, people who would apply the standards of reason and science to the social world and politics. Only a few years before, the gymnastic republican Turners had reorganized as the Socialist Turner Leagues, with their own paper, the *Turn-Zeitung*. Forbes declared the Universal Democratic Republicans would "compare the platforms and candidates of all parties, without being the slave of any." This "Union of Liberal Societies" projected a national organization and anticipated "a radical reformation both in Government and Society in the interest of Liberty, which must lead to the enjoyment and happiness in life in which all are equally entitled." Affiliates had to have fifty members for two delegates and one more for every additional fifty.[38]

Operating through "the Convention of Liberals in America," the radicals had an impressive network. The Germans had not only the pre-existing organizations of the freethinkers and Turners, but groups identified as Social Reformers and an Arbeiterbund, likely associations reflecting the respective work of Kriege and Weydemeyer. The French and Italian affiliates of the UDR participated, along with groups of Cuban and Polish Democrats, and a broader Democratic Union of mixed immigrants, as was the general UDR as a propaganda body. American radicals participated fully in this coalition. Some—such as Ira B. Davis—participated in those bodies of émigrés, but it included two key American groups: the Free Democratic League ("Americans, opposed to the Extension of Slavery") and the Ouvrier Circle ("American workmen").[39]

The Free Democrats present in this internationalist coalition represented the insurgent forces for Hale who had chosen not to disband after the election. They held state conventions in February and September 1853. Participants included not only radical Democrats such as Sanford E. Church but radicals and innovators of all sorts, including Rev. Antoinette Brown, the first woman ordained by a major Christian denomination and Frederick Douglass, who closed one session by singing the Hutchinson Family song, "There's a Good Time a-Comin'." Out of state visitors included Hale and Henry Wilson.[40]

Within days of the September state convention, radicals in the city launched the Free Democratic League, as had some of their cothinkers upstate. After some planning meetings in a law office on Nassau street, it began holding public gatherings in the Stuyvesant Institute, a location shared with the spiritualists. Participants included bricklayer-turned-historian Henry B. Dawson, as well as George W. Rose, David Marsh, J. E. Snodgrass and William West—associates of the Ouvrier Circle or Forbes's coalition. The league adopted radical land reform measures, and planned to start their own newspaper. At different points, Hale, Wilson and Salmon P. Chase joined them when visiting. The state organization of the Free Democrats nominated Marsh for governor.[41]

To be sure, as with any secret society, messages are sometimes mixed and muddled, and some elements of any movement move far more slowly than others. In June 1853, the Brotherhood of the Union at Wilmington, Delaware hosted the 1853 NIC. With the New York City core of the land reformers conspicuous by their absence, fifty representatives turned up from Dover, Philadelphia and Wheatland, Pennsylvania; with letters from Lynn and Washington. The local NRA leader Robert B. McDonald had once built a current for land reform within the Democratic Party and persuaded the gathering to avoid "any matter that does not legitimately belong to the object of the organization" which remained "confined to the consideration of the subject of Land Reform." It was a noted attempt to reverse the trend evident over the entire history of these annual sessions, and was simply not up to the exigencies of the times.

More attuned to the changing conditions, Forbes and others had ties to a circle of African American abolitionists who remained aloof from a coalition with the whites. Dick Hinton described them as a "small coterie of clever colored men in New York City, revolving around a well-known physician of that race," surely Dr. James McCune Smith. Although Hinton thought the group cultivated "a counter race contempt, antagonism, and rage" against whites, Smith articulated the same kinds of social radicalism, declaring "that money is not that nobler idea; but liberty, equality, human brotherhood, in a word—manhood—is that nobler ideal ..." Indeed, as early in 1852, Smith wrote that it was "quite too late in the day to get up an association for the propagation of the pure African, or Irish, or any other breed."[42] Among these African American proto-nationalists, as surely as among other radicals, events seemed to demand internationalist concerns.

Aside from slavery, the immigrant character of these associations left them heavily predisposed to the Democrats in reaction to the Nativist associations of the Whigs. The liberation of Cuba had also always been the cause célèbre of the Southern Democratic and expansionists, and "the Cuban Junta" raised their own Lone Star flag. Their organization, the Order of the Lone Star had clear ties to the old school Democrats associated with Tammany Hall or the Irish-based Spartan Band, and the Democratic courtship of the local Industrial Congress.[43]

The new Trades' Assembly formed in New York City in the fall of 1853 reflected the fruits of that cooperation among English and German speakers. As committed as ever to land reform, Ben Price signed the call to found the Assembly and participated in it, knowing that the stronger unions might win the kinds of immediate concessions that the conquest of political power had failed to attain. Realizing that such a move would have to include the immigrant workers, they adopted the program of Weydemeyer's organization. These bodies, in turn, spread through many American cities over the next few years.

* * *

Goodell, Smith and the old Libertymen soon reappeared to lay claim to the rhetoric of liberty and equality as Radical Abolitionists. Lysander Spooner had long argued that the Founders had written a Constitution that had actually prohibited human slavery by specifying that nobody could be deprived of their liberty without due process. Goodell insisted:

All Nations and all National Governments are under an obligation and a necessity to protect the personal freedom of all their unoffending inhabitants. If the nation cannot protect him against despots and despotism, it cannot protect him at all. If it cannot protect him at home, under its own jurisdiction, it cannot protect him abroad. If it cannot protect him against his next door neighbor, it cannot protect him against foreign invaders. If it cannot protect all its inhabitants, it can protect none of them. If it has authority to protect one, it has authority to protect all.[44]

Government failure to protect African Americans legitimated direct citizen action to do so. The entire society shared the responsibility for slave emancipation.

Against this backdrop, abolitionists, Free Democrats, land reformers, and European revolutionists began to forge a coalition in the U.S. On one level, this represented the first efforts to establish something of a cadre organization aimed at a radical social transformation. Its platform would include the Stars and Stripes symbolic of American rhetoric alongside the red flag representing the means of making that rhetoric a reality.

8

The Pre-Revolutionary Tinderbox: Universal Democratic Republicans, Free Democrats and Radical Abolitionists, 1853–6

By the end of 1854, Americans in both the Ouvrier Circle of the Brotherhood of the Union and the Free Democratic League joined a city-wide federation of European émigrés in New York City, many still organized as they had been overseas. The *Liberator* noted the loose coalition and its composition, which included a general Democratic Union of naturalized citizens, organizations of Cuban and Polish Democrats, French and Italian sections of the Universal Democratic Republicans, and the German Arbeiterbund, Freie Gemeide and Turnerbund, that is, the overlapping organizations committed to socialism, freethought, and physical culture. At the fringes lurked the odd individual Russian and Turk. More remarkably though, through one of its key officers, "a small coterie of clever colored men" advocated the same goals, though one white thought them motivated by "a counter race contempt, antagonism, and rage" against Caucasians.[1]

Denied a redress of their grievances by the ballot or the courts, opponents of the Fugitive Slave Act took action on their own to resist its implementation. The same happened naturally enough when the same Southern-dominated Democrats who had passed that law sought to secure the institution by authorizing the organization of Kansas as a western annex of slaveholding, to which opponents again resisted actively. Facing armed enforcers backed by the Federal authorities, radicals began to take up arms in self-defense. Participants in those activities often hedged their bets about electoral politics by establishing ties to the new Republican Party, a broad new mass insurgency, though very watered in its concerns about slavery.

Radicalism Confronts the Slave Power Conspiracy

Triumphant in the wake of the Mexican War, the "Southern Rights" faction of the Democratic Party and its allies imposed a transparently self-interested agenda on the nation, and it did so ruthlessly. In the Compromise of 1850, the politicians had agreed to a Fugitive Slave Act requiring residents in any part of the county to help enforce the "right" of slaveholders to their human property which implied a plan to nationalize the institution. Later, they forced a Federal reconsideration of the ban on new slave states north of the old "Missouri Compromise Line."

More aggressive Federal efforts to return alleged runaways to slavery drove long-standing proponents of moral suasion to take forceful measures to defy the law and assist the runaways. On March 10, 1854, Milwaukee officials nabbed Joshua Glover, a St. Louis slave who had been living two years in Wisconsin. During his time there, he had toured antislavery societies as "Lewis Washington," hosted by, among others, Dr. Edward Galusha Dyer, who operated the station on the Underground Railroad at Burlington. Family stories recalled a visit from an "Uncle Benjamin" from Vermont, likely Benjamin W. Dyer. Like Benjamin, Dr. Dyer had joined the Liberty Party effort to take slavery into politics (and would eventually enter the state assembly as a Republican). Citing the threat of slavery to republican government, he asked, "What then is our duty as patriots, as philanthropists and as lovers of liberty? Which side shall we be on? Surely we will be for liberty." Such figures could not remain passive when the authorities seized Glover, and an estimated five thousand people followed Free Democratic editor Sherman Miller Booth in an assault on the jail and whisking Glover off towards Canada.[2]

When Federal authorities prosecuted Booth, Byron Paine, another associate of the local NRA defended Booth in a case that became a national cause célèbre as it dragged through the courts for the next five years. Booth and Paine argued persuasively that the Fugitive Slave Law violated the Constitution's protection of state self-government.[3] The defensive advocacy of "states' rights," then, became a two-edged sword in the sectional conflict.

Only weeks after the Glover rescue at Milwaukee, the authorities at Boston nabbed Anthony Burns off the streets. On May 26, a racially mixed crowd including Lewis Hayden and Thomas Wentworth Higginson stormed the court house, though thwarted by Federal forces, even as more abolitionists turned up. The next day, John C. Cluer showed up with Richard J. Hinton, prepared for trouble. Hinton's father had been a stonecutter working on the archaeology reconstructions at the British Museum and presided over a secret labor organization. Young Hinton had an apprenticeship in that trade, but also took up printing and drilled in the ranks of a seditious company of "physical-force" Chartists. He crossed the Atlantic a few years before joining the crowd at the courthouse. At one point, Hinton heard shots and turned to see the weapon "held in a dark-skinned fist and the face over it has remained forever engraved on my memory." Later estimates indicated that the government spent over $40,000 to return Burns to Virginia—well over forty times his value as a slave. The incident inspired William Lloyd Garrison to burn the Court decision, the Fugitive Slave Act and the U.S. Constitution, while the wealthy merchant Amos A. Lawrence recalled how he and his peers had gone to bed "old-fashioned, conservative, compromise Union Whigs" and woke up "stark mad Abolitionists."[4]

In late May, the Congress capped these atrocities with the Kansas-Nebraska Act which enabled settlers in those territories to organize a government in preparation for statehood. For years, Stephen Arnold Douglas and other Northern Democrats schemed to keep slavery off the national agenda by having "the people" of the territories decide for themselves whether to incorporate human slavery in their constitutions. Decorated in the democratic-sounding rhetoric of "squatter sovereignty," it conjured images of rough-hewn frontiersmen and farmers determining their own future. In reality, of course, the Federal authority would still have to manage the establishment of the territorial government, and the U.S. Congress would still have the ultimate decision whether to sanction statehood.

The implications of the legislation posed a dramatic alternative to the land reform vision of democratic equality. An Illinois NRA spokesman described it as an attempt to foster "the monopolies of land to make the rich richer, and to make the poor poorer (as all kings have done), and we will perpetuate and extend chattel slavery (until it shall become universal like serfdom in Russia) to maintain our glorious union!!" His comrades noted that the same legislators had also begun to publically disparage the goals of the Declaration of Independence.[5] Radicals wondered about the substance of any system of checks and balances that could not thwart the economic imperatives of the cotton interests.

The Free Democratic League sent John McMullen and former presidential candidate John P. Hale to assist in the deliberations of "a large and very enthusiastic meeting" of the "United Liberal Societies." Cuban revolutionaries—Miguel T. Tolen, Andres Poey, and Salvador Cisneros—attended, with representatives of European émigré associations. The meeting incidentally repudiated "the Maine liquor law," prohibiting alcohol in that state, but their focus centered increasingly on Kansas. By early summer, they discussed the plans of the Massachusetts Aid Society of Boston to send emigrants to Kansas, and Hugh Forbes announced that similar efforts were under way at New York.[6]

Shortly after, on June 12, Forbes conferred with Eli Thayer, the president of the Boston society. Thayer planned to subsidize part of the cost of getting settlers to Kansas, but would not agree with Forbes's suggestion to support the settlers until their crops could be cultivated and harvested. Forbes quipped that the gentlemen of property who could afford to go west might have to "cultivate with slaves before a sufficient number of poor, but really free emigrants could be sent there to vote the stain from that portion of the land." In preparation for sending local radicals west, the internationalist group appointed a committee to inspect Forbes's military work.[7]

Through the rest of 1854, the radicals at New York, hosted by La Montagne at 80 Leonard Street, not only tried to find their way into the Kansas struggle, but also to disabuse Europeans about the actual conditions here. Veteran land reformers—Ira B. Davis, William Arbuthnot and George H. Evans—participated on behalf of the Ouvrier Circle. In response to a letter from Victor Hugo, echoing the old timeworn republican appeals for aid for refugees in Europe, Benjamin F. Price declared "it is a great mistake to suppose that any but the rich have their rights in the United States."[8]

The nearly sixty delegates to that year's NIC gathered over June 7–9 at Trenton's Temperance Hall. They acknowledged support from prominent antislavery officeholders, though a single adamantly Democratic, Saxe Gotha Laws of Delaware wanted to mention only Andrew Johnson. When he proposed scheduling the next year's meeting "in a Southern State, so as to remove any imputation of being local," Nathaniel W. Brown of the Massachusetts NRA, backed by Donald C. Henderson, a *Tribune* reporter and Brother of the Union underscored the inconsistency of their purposes and a Southern meeting place.[9]

The NIC directly took up slavery as well as "the infamous Nebraska Bill." Henderson's proposed organizing "for the purpose of settling in Kansas and Nebraska, to prevent the extension of Slavery" and incorporating opposition to the law into the basic pledge required of candidates seeking land reform support. David Marsh urged the body to "give expression to its feelings against slavery," and Brown thought it gained nothing "by temporizing with an institution that was inimical to all rights of free labor." In the end, the NIC inscribed on its banner for the next national elections: "Free Homes, Land Limitation, Free Schools, Free Speech, a Free Soil for Free Men, an Elective Judiciary, Elective Functionaries, and Religious Liberty." Delegates expressed solidarity with "the fugitive freeman, whom we swear to protect by the rights of our States and the strength of our arms." By their adjournment, delegates discussed resistance to the Fugitive Slave Act. Laws walked out, snarling that land reform was "resolving itself into an Abolition Society, under a nice name."

The metamorphosis of the Ceresco phalanx reflected changes in the nature of communities generally. These came primarily out of practical experimentation in the Midwest. "Socialism is, in my opinion, the goal of humanity," wrote William Denton, "but we can not arrive there at a bound." In the interim, he—with many others—had simply aspired "to form neighborhoods of intelligent, reformatory persons" Others also became active in "casting about for a location for a Reform Neighborhood." They discussed locations as far as Florida and the Yucatan, and the French efforts in Texas, and personally scouted various sites in the west, noting several efforts out of Pittsburgh and St. Louis, establishing small settlements in western Virginia and northwestern Arkansas.[10]

Josiah Warren's innovative cooperative version of Owenism did not even require removal to a community. For a quarter of a century, he had developed his "Time Stores," where participants purchased goods with promissory "labor notes" redeemable for set amounts of time working at their own trade for the recipient. It offered a flexible process of transition from capitalism to a more equitable society.[11]

These western innovations informed the 1851 founding of Modern Times, one of the most influential and curious communitarian ventures of the day. Three of the most important critics of early American capitalism—Josiah Warren, Stephen Pearl Andrews, and Edward N.

Kellogg—shaped its course. A Yankee abolitionist driven out of Texas, Andrews anticipated a "Universology" of liberation that would draw together the various strands of radicalism. Kellogg, a businessman who went broke during the depression, made his idea of a national paper currency complimentary to Warren's Labor Notes.[12] The community paradoxically attracted eccentric individualists. Dr. Edward Newberry, a London native had turned to dentistry, and proposed a preventative NRA treatment for a decaying society. Another Londoner, Emma Floyd, had struggled for a career in show business— as a singer, actress, and pianist—before turning to occultism under her married name, Hardinge, under which she became one of the most prolific and serious spiritualist writers. She and her mother were most likely the pair of resident nudists in the community scandalizing early passengers on the Long Island Railroad.[13]

Modern Times already had a natural constituency in the city. Henry Clapp—the veteran abolitionist and Fourierist—had become enamored with life in the Parisian neighborhoods on the Left Bank of the Seine, and began drawing similarly alienated souls to a unique social life centered at Charles Pfaff's restaurant and saloon just up Broadway from Taylor's Hotel. Fourierist and former Fourierist visitors to Pfaff's included Brisbane, William H. Fry, and George Arnold, the son of a New Jersey phalanx leader; they mingled alongside future socialists like Albert L. Rawson. Practitioners of the arts, music and theatre, as well as writers, created this Bohemian subculture, which provided a vital introduction to the city for writers from the outside like William Dean Howells, or the yet unrecognized local genius of Walt Whitman.[14]

Roots of an International and a New Mass Insurgency 1854–5

Elsewhere, the bipartisanship efforts to secure slavery sparked a growing political response. Early in 1854, former NRA secretary, Alvan E. Bovay organized meetings at Warren Chase's former Wisconsin phalanx at Ceresco, recently renamed Ripon. Regardless of their previous party affiliations, participants called for a new party and Bovay suggested "a cherished name with our foreign population of every nationality. They call themselves *Republicans, Republicains, Republikaner, Republicanos*— or by some modification of it in all European countries, and this name meets them here like an old friend."[15] Horace Greeley publicized it nationally.

More importantly, the coalition around the radical émigrés essentially absorbed the city's Free Democratic League, planning ultimately "to enter into communication with all such as seek liberty and progress" beyond New York. D. L. Szpaczek of the Polish Democrats protested any attempt to take a position on Kansas as "interference with the domestic politics of the United States, which had received them with hospitality as exiles and wanderers." Forbes and others, though, insisted upon "opposition to despotic measures and men on this side of the Atlantic" to be "a service rendered to the cause of freedom universally."[16]

The group endorsed Forbes's *Manual for the Patriotic Volunteer* as "indispensable for the Revolutionists," and his political "Catechism," describing the Democrats and Whigs as existing "to procure public occupation in the diplomatic service, custom house, post office, treasury, patent office, land office, municipality, police, or any other where salary and profit can be enjoyed," and to maintain slavery. He did praise the Free Democrats (and later editions quoted him as saying the same for the Republicans) for opposing the two-party system, though fearful that the price of their governing would be placating the powers that be. The abolitionist *Independent* not only praised the *Manual* for its contribution to "the oppressed peoples of Europe," but quickly reported that "a few copies have gone to Kansas."[17]

Meanwhile, New York seriously lagged as Republican state parties formed in Wisconsin, Michigan and parts of the Midwest, though the pace towards independence lagged in the East. In New York, Calvin Pepper—an abolitionist, NRA veteran and Free Democrat—called to order the August 1854 statewide "Anti-Nebraska" conference, but could not dissuade it from simply fusing with the remnants of the Whigs. Old-line politicians dominated the September convention at Auburn, not only declined to endorse land reform but refused to affiliate with the emergent Republican Party nationally, leading to a walkout by Leonard Gibbs of the old NRA and other radicals.[18]

Radicals determined to sustain their organizational coherence. On October 11, William Arbuthnot, Ira B. Davis and Benjamin F. Price attended a convention hosted by the French Society of "The Mountain," with the ubiquitous Forbes as secretary. Other groups represented included the Arbeiterbund, the new socialist organization launched by the veteran Communist Leaguer Joseph Weydemeyer. Davis and others urged the émigré radicals to join their effort to establish a radical political presence locally.[19]

Davis, Arbuthnot, Price and a broad spectrum of veteran radicals launched their "Practical Democrats" at an October 1854 mass meeting. Even the hostile *Herald* acknowledged theirs to be "an organization of some importance." Along with Price, Donald C. Henderson, and William Rowe, they revived the application of NRA principles to municipal reforms. When the internationalist body met on October 17, Forbes suggested that any questions to candidates begin with slavery, because it would be "useless further to question any candidate for the Legislature" should they not be publicly antislavery. Prevaricating, Davis thought opposition to slavery meant nothing in the government of a state that did not have it. Nevertheless, "a protracted discussion" led the meeting "to give the priority to the question of Slavery" with only two votes opposed.[20]

Meanwhile, the Practical Democrats filled their ticket, usually endorsing Democratic or Whig candidates, but making some key independent nominations: Bailey made an independent bid for Congress from the Fifth C.D.; Davis, Arbuthnot, Alexander Ming, William V. Barr, Daniel Ullman, and J. W. Bryce ran for the state assembly; John H. Keyser for alderman; and Price for Surrogate Court Judge. The radical émigrés likely sustained the slate, because they put Davis in the chair for their November 15 meeting.[21] Political action remained high on the list.

Already, the crisis in the party system found elite opponents of the Democrats locally turning briefly to Nativist "American Party," which created a serious Irish and German backlash, that helped the Democrats. "Colonel" Ming (wedded to an Irish Catholic) became so disgusted with those who "disgrace the American flag" with their narrow-mindedness that he turned back to the Democrats, whose more reform-minded leaders sought to coax radicals into another unification meeting at Tammany.[22] This time, determined radicals struggled to maintain their independence.

In particular, radicals sought to channel the energies of the election into a movement to assist the unemployed. Through the bitter weeks of winter 1854–5, they acted, with the support of the trade unions, to mobilize the unemployed. The newly elected Democratic Mayor Fernando Wood—reportedly the richest man in the city—repeatedly brushed aside movement proposals, promising "a plan of my own for the relief of the unemployed workingmen."[23]

The movement determined to hold him to it. Land reformers and German émigrés dominated the mass meeting on January 8, 1855. The former Fourieriest and "bohemian" Edward F. Underhill helped shape the resolutions. Davis described their thrust, that "the unoccupied lands on this island should be thrown open to the occupancy of the people. [Loud cheers.] When it was known that men had a right to pitch a tent or build a hut on these waste lands, landlords would loose the grip with which they now hold their tenants." Introducing some of the Germans, Bailey noted that the movement "recognized every man as an American who had an American heart."[24] This common sense emergency measure reappeared in every subsequent depression, though any government move to shelter the poor or permit them to grow food on unoccupied ground would naturally reduce what landlords could charge as rent or grocers for food.

The ideas of Modern Times began percolating through the deliberations of these unemployed demonstrations. Davis presided over "a discussion arose on the propriety of embracing currency reform in the Homestead bill." Others suggested that "the land question and the currency question as one, and that they ought to be presented in the same memorial."[25] Nationalization of Labor Notes, coupled to Agrarian radicalism, foreshadowed the Greenbackism that would emerge in another twenty years.

At the same time, those internationalist bodies took up the cause of labor with plans for a petition to the Congress "to reform sundry evils which press hard on the working man." Forbes "thought it was their duty to notice the labor movement," and agreed to establish a "conference committee" with the movement in the streets. Davis and others of the "Ouvrier Circle (American workmen)" had taken pains to refute the misimpression that unemployment had been restricted to foreign-born newcomers to the city. The internationalists assigned Forbes "to make a report on the condition of the laboring classes, and the origins of the present distress."[26]

The *Times* reported a conference committee meeting of only six persons at which Forbes and Davis agreed that unemployment was not "a casual and transitory malady in the United States; for, in fact, the disease is *chronic*, and it has for a long time been increasing in intensity."

However, Forbes worried that land reform would ultimately be a "delusion," to which Arbuthnot replied that much of the country was fertile enough to where "a mechanic could dig a living out of the ground with nothing but a sharp stick."[27] The key to the radicalism of the NRA had always been its challenge to the idea of unlimited private ownership of land and capital, rather than some vision of a society of small farmers or a dubious grasp of agronomy.

Within days, on March 6, Forbes, Davis, Arbuthnot and William West hosted a mass meeting that endorsed a new report on the conditions of the laboring classes, and urged joint action with "the Workingmen's Association," likely the socialist Arbeiterbund. Their report on the condition of the American working class was sponsored by the new Universal Democratic Republicans. In short order, they affiliated with the new International Association that emerged with its headquarters in London. Proscribed French, German and Polish socialists joined English and Belgian democrats to establish an International Association that put Forbes on its Central Committee.[28]

The 1855 NIC demonstrated how all of these plans had become strongly anchored in the broader antislavery political movement. A broadly representative body of "persons favorable to the Land and other cognate reforms" assembled in Cleveland's Sons of Temperance Hall on Wednesday, June 6, 1855. An active milieu of literary reformers had made the city, George Lippard's favorite western community. For years, John Brainerd had issued the *Farmers' and Mechanics' Journal* with C. T. Blakeslee at nearby Chagrin Falls, passing it on into Cleveland where H. E. Calkins changed it into the *Spirit of Freedom*, soon transformed by a "Laboring Men's Association" into the *Laborer*. John Bell Bouton, a Dartmouth graduate and lawyer-turned-newspaperman became the editor of the *Plain Dealer* in 1851. With Brainerd, Bouton gained fame as one of the literary men of the new Midwest.[29] The NIC reaffirmed the old NRA measures.

The Cleveland NIC reflected the new importance of German émigrés. Most notably, Weitling's Arbeiterbund and a succession of similarly named associations led by Weydemeyer sustaining pro-NRA newspapers like *Der Kommunist* and *Waechter am Erie*. The Brotherhood of the Union, in turn, publicized the work of these German socialists among English-speaking radicals.[30] Increasingly, Germans would provide a ready-made national framework for labor radicalism.

The NIC also reflected the importance of the new Republican party. Ohioan John Hancock Klippart called the body to order, but Philadelphian John Sheddon was the key speaker at the first public meeting and served with Klippart as one of the three secretaries. The other two secretaries were George Gordon of Philadelphia and William H. Day of Cleveland. Both Klippart, Sheddon and the radical Germans had already become publicly identified with the new Republican Party. Day was not only one of the most prominent black leaders in Ohio but had himself more or less openly defied and violated the Federal Fugitive Slave Act. Indeed, Day periodically shifted his base of operations to Canada.

A bit later that June, another national gathering brought together those political abolitionists who repudiated the Republican acceptance of the constitutionality of slavery. In the months before, William Goodell, for fifteen years the editor of the *Friend of Man*, reorganized a New York Anti-Slavery Society around the arguments of Lysander Spooner and others that slavery simply violated the Constitutional guarantee of due process.[31]

Their racially mixed national convention at Syracuse resurrected the Liberty League as the Radical Abolitionist Party. Gerrit Smith called the body to order and Dr. James McCune Smith—the leader of the black allies of the Euro-American Internationals—presided over the three day convention of June 26–9. Other participants included Charles C. Foote of Michigan, Goodell, Gerrit Smith, Samuel J. May, Lewis Tappan, and J. W. Loguen. Letters of support arrived from John Pierpont and John McIntosh—possibly the future socialist editor—and twenty more in sympathy with the Convention. They rejected "as useless, all schemes for limiting, localizing, confining, or ameliorating slavery—all options for protecting the non-slaveholding States from the aggressions of slavery," demanding "the immediate and unconditional prohibition and suppression of slavery in all parts of the country." "There are spots where all men can breathe freely," declared Dr. Smith. "Syracuse is one of those places."[32]

In the course of the gathering, a gaunt figure attended with letters from his sons on the plight of Free State settlers in Kansas. An ardent abolitionist, John Brown had also gotten something of a taste for revolution when he had gone overseas in the aftermath of the 1848 risings, ostensibly in an effort to find a better market for his wool. He now appealed to the Radical Abolitionists "for men and means to defend freedom in Kansas.

His remarks deeply stirred the hearts of the audience." They decided not to endorse armed struggle as a party, but "a collection was taken up to aid the father in the objects, pistols and all."[33] Abolitionist involvement in active, often armed resistance to slavery became ever more widespread. Philadelphia on July 18, 1855, Passamore Williamson of the vigilance committee of the Pennsylvania Anti-Slavery Society simply approached and walked off with Jane Johnson and her two sons, slaves of U.S. Minister to Nicaragua, John H. Wheeler. Wheeler had already sold one of her sons and locked her and the others in a Philadelphia hotel room. The black porter contacted William Still of the vigilance committee who sent Williamson and two others to the docks when Wheeler tried to usher his property onto the ship. Williamson declared that Pennsylvania law did not recognize slavery and told her and her sons that they did not have to board with him. Black deckhands restrained Wheeler, who watched his human property disappear into the crowd with the abolitionists. When the authorities attempted to try the deckhands and the abolitionists for slave stealing, Johnson herself snuck back into the city to testify and was quickly smuggled out by the movement. In the end, the courts delivered convictions but only on very reduced charges.

Radical Abolitionist called a second national convention for October 23–5, 1855 at Boston, realizing that they would soon face a larger Republican Party with a very watered antislavery platform. The Tappans, Goodell, Dr. Smith and others turned up, launching the American Abolition Society. Starting with a few hundred, the convention nearly filled Melonian Hall by the second evening, forcing them to move to the Tremont Temple with at least 1500 people. They proposed that the AAS "form a National Abolition Party and find a remedy for Slavery in political agitation, claiming the Constitution is on their side."[34]

Across the country, the Free Democrats, also struggled to redefine themselves with relation to the broader current. Those at New York City proved as skeptical as the Radical Abolitionists about the state's anti-Nebraska coalition. The last Free Democratic state conventions placed alongside its universal hostility to slavery, "a natural right to a portion of the soil, and that as the use of the soil is as sacred as their right to life itself." By August 1855, the Free Democratic League called a state convention at Syracuse to meet on September 26, the same day and place as the Whig and Republican convention.[35]

The fall of 1855 in New York City created strong Democratic and American tickets, to which what had been the "Practical Democrats" reorganized as the "American Democrats." They offered a more thought-out municipal program, including the encouragement of cooperative protective unions, criminalizing attempts "to defraud working people out of their just wages for labor performed," and promoting the city construction of its own buildings to rent cheaply to the landless.

Meanwhile, the cultural radicals pulled the rug entirely out from under Mayor Wood's first administration. Clapp, Ingalls, Andrews and S. B. Brittan the spiritualist editor began discussing the extent to which people should exercise "great latitude to the 'freedom of the affections'." For two years, it held twice weekly lectures, followed by music and dancing upstairs at Taylor's Hotel at 555 Broadway. Then, Greeley's *New York Tribune* issued a sensationalist exposé, partly to disassociate Fourierism from it and to discredit Wood's administration for its failure to act against it. No sooner had Albert Brisbane and Clapp started the October 1855 meeting than the police descended on the hall. Angry "free lovers" broke the furniture into clubs and chased the municipal police out of the hall and down Broadway.[36]

Once the Wood administration sent the police to break up the meeting, the *Tribune* and other papers launched into a rigorous defense of free speech. It included detailed coverage of how the association had not actually been about destroying marriage. While often treated as an early kind of "culture war," the evidence points most clearly to the success of the "bohemian" newspaper writers in setting up the Wood administration for its downfall at the hands of what remained an evolving Republican coalition.

What moved politics everywhere was Kansas. In the fall of 1855, the New York anti-Nebraska forces finally held a "Republican State Convention." Within it, the well-established and tightly led former Whigs and Americans dominated the party. Nevertheless, land reformers and Fourierists, such as Jacob Seaman and William H. Fry participated in the founding Republican meetings on the Lower East Side. At the same time, John H. Tobitt, Freeman Hunt, and Watson G. Haynes helped launch the Republican Party in Brooklyn. With Tobitt's help, Thomas A. Devyr, James A. Pyne, and George Luther Stearns the abolitionists made a similar bid at Williamsburgh, through their Tax Payers Association.[37]

Even as the Republicans took form in New York, the Radical Abolitionists found it insufficient. Through 1856 and 1857, their small but vital national party reported organization in Ohio, Illinois, Pennsylvania and Vermont. By February 1857, black abolitionist Charles L. Remond presided over the state convention at Utica with about a hundred people present. Despite his long opposition to political action, William Lloyd Garrison spoke as did Dr. William P. Powell, and Parker Pillsbury. Several women rose to address the convention as well, including Miss Remond, Miss Sarah Clark, and one Susan B. Anthony.[38]

Kansas Bleeds

However, the regional shifts left some of the veteran eastern leaders of the land reform movement themselves pointed west to new epicenters of the antislavery agitation. In New Jersey, George Henry Evans— along with William Heighton—stumped for the Republicans, and an unexpected snowstorm left Evans soaked, after which he succumbed to "a nervous fever" on February 2, 1856. Evans had provided a voice for workers in the city over seven or eight years, developing a reputation for "perseverance and sagacity." His comrades praised him as "one of Nature's noblemen—a man of rare foresight and talent, though of unostentatious pretentions." Another recalled that he "never allowed himself to arise to a passion." He had been "so naturally imbued with the spirit of democracy that he brought it to bear on every question he discussed." A Boston radical thought him as "persevering and disinterested a Reformer as the laboring classes ever had."[39] Still, early labor historians favorable to business unionism mistrusted him for his political focus, and their Marxist successors described his politics as "utopian" and, through judicious cherry-picking of the evidence, quietly proslavery, ignoring the major achievements of his career as a political leader. John Windt convened the remnants of the movement in New York, which pledged to persist, which they did largely under the leadership of Ingalls and Commerford.[40]

In reality, though, many who had envisioned a radically transformed America looked to the west and Kansas. Barr, William Haddock, Alvan E. Bovay, and John Swinton, the Scottish-born bohemian from New York City had gone west, Barr and Swinton reaching Kansas. Edward Lynde with Augustus and John Otis Wattles from Ohio and William

Addison Phillips from Illinois plunged into the Kansas conflict, as did Richard J. Hinton. Erastus D. Ladd, of Wisconsin had witnessed the destruction of Lawrence. "For the last six or eight years," editorialized the *New York Tribune*, "a small band of earnest thinking men have been hard at work endeavoring to attract attention to the iniquities of our system of disposing of our Public Lands" by sale to "capitalists or speculators, native or alien." The *Tribune* predicted no change "unless the very magnitude and impudence of the evil should arouse the People to demand and secure a remedy."[41]

As radicals back east wrestled over electoral questions, John Brown joined his sons on October 7, 1855, at Osawatomie.[42] The Massachusetts Emigrant Aid Society of Thayer and Amos Lawrence and Thayer had gotten the first colonists to what became Lawrence. Nevertheless, the most unbending of the "Southern Rights" Democrats in Missouri sent large armed bodies of "Border Ruffians" into the territory to vote for slavery. Determined to prove the viability of popular sovereignty as a means to extend slavery, the Pierce administration sanctioned the vote and established the legitimacy of what most actual settlers called the "bogus" legislature.

This caused considerable difficulty for the administration, which had to replace its appointed territorial governors, regularly frustrated by their inability to control the situation. On the ground, the efforts of proslavery forces to drive out the Free States had sparked "the Wakarusa War." A heavily reinforced little army of armed Missourians actually marched on Lawrence at the start of December and were dissuaded from attacking it. The majority of the three-man Congressional committee inspecting the situation in April, 1856, issued a report indicating that popular sovereignty had failed, indicating the sectional collapse of the Democratic Party, and a serious challenge to the survival of the Union. On May 21, an estimated 700 armed "Border Ruffians" attacked Lawrence, destroying the Free-State Hotel, smashing the presses and scattering the type of the newspapers. The next day, South Carolina Congressman Preston Brooks assaulted Senator Charles Sumner with a cane, crippling him on the floor of the Senate.

Lawrence braced for another attack on May 24, when John Brown organized his local free state company to march there to defend the place. Apparently under advice of James H. Lane, Brown first made a pre-emptive attack on local proslavery settlers who had threatened to burn out the Free Staters. His men killed five of them in the Pottawat-omie Massacre, for which Brown assumed full responsibility, but never fully discussed them. Thereafter, though, his mistrust of political leaders deepened.

Advocates of communitarian experiments went west with other Free Staters hopeful of peopling Kansas. In May 1856, about a hundred settlers arrived on the site—roughly fifty miles beyond Fort Scott—inspired by the interest of the phrenologist and spiritualist Orson Squire Fowler in octagon buildings, one of which the denizens of Modern Times constructed for their community. The reality of mosquitoes, malnutrition, exposure, malaria, and alternating thunderstorms and drought brought a quick end to the experiment, leaving only four of the original group by 1857.[43]

Nevertheless, by the end of the year, more experienced advocates looked to Kansas. After scouting the area around St. Louis, Denton—the visiting spiritualist and socialist from Dayton—headed to Kansas and lectured in Lawrence and at Twin Mounds, a short distance west of Lawrence, where a handful of secularists led by Henry Hiatt had founded the hamlet of Bloomington. Early in 1858, one visitor wrote that he "never saw any country where so many persons were ready to defend progression in proportion to the population."[44]

Later, when the proslavery forces captured two of his sons, Brown gathered twenty-nine men and successfully attacked them on June 2, at Black Jack on the Santa Fe Trail. Afterwards, they returned to Lawrence, from which they raided Franklin in an effort to recover materials seized in the earlier attack. On August 16, a later Free State raid had better luck raising "Fort Titus," another fortified building near Lawrence.

John Brown's band represented a remarkably diverse group. Although widely reputed to have been an intolerant Christian fanatic, he inspired and held together fighters of various backgrounds. The Wattles brothers—Augustus and John Otis—were even spiritualists, as was Aaron D. Stevens. In one skirmish, Theodore Weiner and August Bondi called to each other in Yiddish. Freethinkers among them appreciatively circulated works by Tom Paine.[45] Certainly, Hinton and Phillips rode regularly with Brown.

As much as any of them, Brown saw what they fought for in Kansas as part of an international struggle. He had personally gone to Europe in the aftermath of the 1848–9 uprisings to discuss the problems of revolution with its contemporary proponents. He discussed with real appreciation the Haitian revolution, the attempts at slave rebellion on the American mainland, and the Servile War of Spartacus in antiquity. He saw chattel slavery as both one of "an infinite number of wrongs" and the "sum of all villainies" that pervaded American life. "If the American people did not take courage, and end it speedily," he warned William A. Phillips, "human freedom and republican liberty would soon be empty names in these United States." When back east, he associated William H. Day, Gerrit Smith and Thaddeus Hyatt, who had gone into partnership with Ingalls in the street lighting business.[46]

Too, Brown and most of his men saw what they fought for in Kansas as part of an international struggle. He had personally gone to Europe in the aftermath of the 1848–9 uprisings to discuss the problems of revolution with its contemporary proponents. Back in Kansas, veterans of those risings fought alongside him. Charles W. Lenhardt, a Polish printer who had fought in Germany and Hungary, rode with Brown's band, as did two Austrian Jews, Bondi and Weiner, the former a veteran of the Vienna rising of 1848. Among such figures, Brown not only criticized slavery but "our forms of social and political life," declaring that he "thought society ought to be organized on a less selfish basis; for, while material interests gained something by the deification of pure selfishness, men and women lost much by it."[47]

The most militant of the abolitionists found ready allies among the native peoples. The Seminole, Creek, Ottawa, Shawnee and others had a long history of aiding runaways, which had contributed to their removal to the West. "God make white man, God make red man, God make black man," declared one Kansas Indian, "but God never make slave." The Delaware provided guides and protection through their reserve lands for armed antislavery bands in conflict with government-backed proslavery forces. When the proslavery forces had converged on Lawrence, both they and the Shawnee "volunteered the services of the warriors of their respective tribes to aid in repelling the invaders." The respectable leadership of the Free Staters declined the offer, but John Brown and the radicals forged particularly close ties with Chief John Tecumseh Jones of the Ottawa and Baptiste Peoria.[48] The issue struck through the Kansas bleeding over slavery directly to the heart of western expansion.

Quindaro on the Missouri River embodied this association. Dr. Charles Robinson—a Yankee land reformer and veteran leader of the so-called Squatters' movement in California—had quickly become a leader among the Free Staters. Eager to find a way into the territory without passing through the populous proslavery towns like Westport, he joined some of the Wyandots and Delawares to establish a town under a high bluff over the river in September 1856. They named the settlement for the wife of one of the founders, whose Wyandot name was Seh Quindaro, roughly meaning a "Bundle of Sticks." Runaways found something of a natural refuge in the multi-racial community at Quindaro, where the militant feminist Mrs. Clara Nichols also published her journal, *The Cradle of Progress*.[49] All of this framed the activities of John Brown.

Throughout the conflict, Hinton shuttled back and forth from the territory through the conflict. Working as a freelance reporter most of this time, he had also fallen in with Clapp, Whitman, and the bohemian circles in New York City. He also noted that things had gotten "more exciting in Boston than elsewhere north of Mason and Dixon's line. For a few of us they were almost as much as Kansas was in Fifty-Six." Republicans on the rise were fearful of the plans to kidnap those implicated.[50]

The shadow of Kansas extended back east. Decades later, Ingalls recalled how the attack on Senator Charles Sumner galvanized public sentiment, along with "the Kansas Embroglio, fugitive slave law, and other matters of national concern." Generally pleased with the new party, but concerned that land reform be ignored, he, Windt, Price, Arbuthnot, Bailey and others planned a reorientation of the land reform movement at the upcoming 1856 NIC scheduled for New York City. However, on May 24, Radical Abolitionists such as William Goodell and Gerrit Smith joined their effort, persuading the NRA core to announce a "National Land Reform Convention" on the Fourth of July at Albany.[51]

* * *

Radical Abolitionism, revolutionary émigrés, bohemians, land reformers and others generally shared a range of concerns, if not yet a common priority in those concerns. Gerrit Smith wrote, "There are more than a hundred thousand of us. What an attractive nucleus we would have been had we all remained together!" The Germans "constitutionally and educationally abolitionists," he continued:

Emphatically true is this of such of them as breathed the revolution-ary spirit of 1848. The Land Reformers too, whose name is legion would have stood by us, had we stood by our principles. Every real land reformer is an abolitionist—for as every real land reformer holds that every man is the owner of his equal share of the soil, he must, of course, hold preliminarily, that every man is the owner of himself. But that every man owns himself, is the only distinctive doctrine of the abolitionists.[52]

Nevertheless, the transition from ideas to practice would have to be carried by the hands of individuals making a choice for themselves. Across the country, on August 30, 1856, John Brown quickly rallied a small band of men at Osawatomie, as several hundred armed proslavery men attacked the town, eventually driving off the Free Staters and looting the community. The next day, Brown and his men emerged from the woods into the charred ruins of town, and tallied their losses, which included his son Frederick. To another son, Jason, he said:

I have only a short time to live—only one death to die, and I will die fighting for this cause. There will be no more peace in this land until slavery is done for. I will give them something else to do than extend slave territory, I will carry this war into Africa.[53]

9

The Spark: Small Initiatives and Mass Upheavals, 1856–60

By 1858, adherents of the International Association in New York City, Chicago, Cincinnati and elsewhere sponsored a series of mass demonstrations. Conservative papers at New York acknowledged that the action by these *"Revolutionists of all the Nationalities"* proved to be "a much more imposing affair than was generally anticipated." An estimated fifteen to twenty thousand lined the route of the parade from Union Square to the City Hall under the protection of a rifle company of Turners including contingents from Williamsburg, Brooklyn and Manhattanville. Americans, Irish, French, Italians and Cubans joined the Germans in flaunting "the most exceptional features, of Red Republicanism." Conspicuous by his absence, the principled organizer of the coalition, Hugh Forbes was off in the West, hoping to assist John Brown in finding a way to make revolution in the New World practical.

As Free Staters and Border Ruffians waged low intensity warfare in Kansas, radicals elsewhere waged a persistent struggle for the soul of the new Republican Party. Although directly involved in all this, the revolutionary internationalists directly moved onto the stage in their own name, taking to the streets several times in 1858 under their own red flags for their own sweeping goals, which converged with Radical Abolitionism. Radicals of all sorts decided to nationalize the lessons of Kansas in one way or another. Determined to have an immediate impact on a debate that had already gone on for too long, a core of veterans under John Brown chose to take action that would, at long last, force a decision on the entire nation.

The Global Struggle for Freedom

The Radical Abolitionists called a convention for Syracuse in May 1856. Kansas overshadowed their deliberations. In preparation, supporters circulated a massive list of endorsers. They also discussed a "direct and emphatic encouragement to the immediate employment of physical force to rescue Kansas." Frederick Douglass declaring himself "ready to fight, when satisfied it would accomplish anything." However, the timing of the gathering indicated that it also subsumed a planned convention of National Reformers largely disorganized with the death of George Henry Evans. Participants with old land reform ties included James C. Jackson, the health reformer and Charles C. Foote, the vice presidential candidate of the old Liberty-National slate of eight years earlier. So did young Peter H. Clark, the black schoolteacher from Cincinnati, introduced by Douglass. Ernst Helde declared that his German constituency "are Revolutionists. They are all of them, or nearly so, enemies of slavery. ... The Turners, numbering many thousands, are with us."[1]

The Republican state convention took place "the same day, only a few rods distant." Some Radical Abolitionists crossed over to make another effort to span the divide. Helde and Gerrit Smith sat among the Republicans, though a severe cold plagued the latter.[2] This body selected delegates for the new party's first national convention, scheduled to make its first presidential nomination.

Back in the city, a few anti-electoral radicals—together with some who still clung to Democratic illusions—convened their own NIC at Convention Hall on Wooster Street during the time-honored first week of June. Robert McDonald, a Delaware Democrat presided and the Philadelphian J. Sidney Jones and his wife, Fanny Townsend—famed for their role in the Dorr War—turned up, she with "her usual quota of jewelry and curls." The group displayed "that exuberance of beard for which the pioneers and disciples of the beard and land reform school should be noted." They held a stormy first day, though only "eight persons assembled, including two ladies." By the next day, McDonald had faded away. Dr. William J. Young turned up from those involved in the internationalist coalition to make an apparently successful argument for its adjournment *sine die*, in the interests of the upcoming joint convention with the abolitionists.[3]

A few days later, on June 17, the Republican National Convention took place. It included some genuine radical delegates, as well as friendly politicians such as David Wilmot, Joshua R. Giddings, Cassius M. Clay, Charles Sumner and others. Some of the vice presidential ballots went to Abraham Lincoln, the former one-term Whig Congressman from

Illinois, but the ticked that emerged consisted of John C. Fremont for president and William L. Dayton for Vice President.[4] Yet, as the NIC of two years before had suggested, some of the state parties even took up the causes of "Free Homes, Land Limitation, Free Schools, Free Speech, a Free Soil for Free Men, an Elective Judiciary, Elective Functionaries, and Religious Liberty."

Meanwhile, the planned Fourth of July radical convention got rescheduled to Rochester, and then "indefinitely postponed." The unexpected rise of Republicanism and the desperation of the struggle in Kansas clearly took priority. August saw "the largest political meeting of our German fellow citizens which ever assembled in this country" at the Tabernacle. Dr. Froebel chaired, though the vice presidents included William Cullen Bryant, Charles A. Dana, with Friedrich Jacobi and Freidrich Kapp of the German communists, as well as Franz Siegel, Dr. Adolph Hexamer serving as secretaries. Up from Texas, Karl Adolphus Douai addressed "opposition to slavery among workingmen of the South." Senators John P. Hale and Governor Salmon P. Chase send letters.[5]

Through September and October, John Windt, William Rowe, Keyes Arthur Bailey, John H. Keyser, Charles A. Guinand, and others went to work in earnest for the new party. They sustained the "Mechanics and Workingmen's Central Republican Union" from a reading room at 163 Bowery. On the Lower East Side, Lewis Ryckman ran for the state assembly as a Republican. Senator Henry Wilson addressed "Free Labor" on their behalf at the Broadway Tabernacle on October 4, and, three weeks later, even the hidebound Henry Raymond of the *Times*, talked on "the great struggle for Free Labor and the Freedom of the Public Lands." When Fremont visited the city, he reassured them that he supported land and labor reform.[6]

Democrats had relatively little to offer, though old habits still tugged at the movement. A projected meeting at Tammany simply did not come off, though they sponsored a public rally in the City Hall Park. Commerford presided and the long list of participants included the long-time Democratic ally John Cochrane. Ira B. Davis allegedly told the gathering that he had an interview with James Buchanan "who assured him that he had always been and always would be, in favor of the dominant principles of the Homestead Bill.[7] Such hopes were in vain.

The Radical Abolitionists, meanwhile, remained aloof. They noted in the wake of the Republican convention that the new platform even prevaricated on "the determination cherished by the old 'Free Soil' party, to prevent the admission of any new slaves." Others, they noted, hoped Fremont's victory "will be the termination of the anti-slavery excitement in this country." Goodell expected the Republicans would not outlast the Kansas crisis. Gerrit Smith thought his comrades to be generally "looking after ballots when their eyes should be fixed on bayonets—they are counting votes when they should be mustering armed men—they are looking after civil rulers when they should be searching after military ones." In September, the Radical Abolitionists convened at Syracuse, nominating Goodell for Governor. Despite their national nomination of Smith for president, the candidate himself came to agree with the land reformers and those black abolitionists, such as Frederick Douglass in supporting Fremont, to whom Smith contributed $500.[8] In the end, Fremont got more than 1,300,000, a bit under a third of the total, outpolling former president Millard Fillmore, running for the American Party, a faint hope at breathing new life into the Whigs.

The Radical Abolitionists survived without supplanting the Republicans. It seemed to prove that the dominant classes in America were "a commercial, not an enthusiastic nor a metaphysical people." Radicals hoped "to make Kansas a free State, and, at the same time, preserve the country from civil war. But we have little expectation that this course will be pursued." At the same time, most of them had "no conscientious scruples against fighting for their rights." In the fall of 1857, the remnants of the Liberty Party of New York convened alongside the American Abolition Society, the organization of the Radical Abolitionists. Prominent black participants included Samuel J. May and William H. Day, former secretary of the 1855 NIC. In addition, a Vermont convention of the Radical Abolitionists brought together Benjamin W. Dyer, William Wells Brown, Charles L. Remond, and Parker Pillsbury. In May 1858, Lewis Tappan and Henry Highland Garnet attended the national convention of the American Abolition Society on Union Square.[9]

Land reformers maintained their New York's Mechanics and Workingmen's association, and even moved to statewide organization. They had sent Democratic President-elect James Buchanan an alternative proposal for building a Pacific Railroad, and Commerford read his rejection. William J. McCabe chaired a later meeting. Joshua K. Ingalls, Benjamin F. Price, Henry Beeny and others spoke on "the aims and objects of the Free-Soil Party," and Ingalls went to lobby for a Homestead Bill at Washington, though critics described his goal as "the rights of the Workingmen and Mechanics to an equal division of the uncultivated soil of the country." On June 30, a Mechanics' and Workingmen's State Committee met at Troy, later announcing forty-two functioning clubs with a total membership of 11,310, with requests from nine new clubs, and talk of a state newspaper. They noted that a committee of Democrats had come courting the previous day one of the Republicans would arrive.[10] More than ever, officeholders of both parties strained to shoehorn a radical vision of social transformation into a homestead bill.

The "Red Republican and Ultra-Liberal émigrés from the European Continent" also continued to maintain a public presence. Early in 1857, a hundred and fifty French, German, Italian, Hungarian and Poles (including half a dozen ladies) gathered in "a spacious bar-room in one of the back slums off Broadway" toasted the abolition of the death penalty and the memory of Brutus."Among the Germans, Friedrich Adolph Sorge, Friedrich Jacobi, Friedrich Kamm and Albert Komp were also organizing the Communist Club to regroup émigré veterans of the Communist League of Marx and Engels.[11]

While developments in Kansas loomed large over these developments, events abroad informed the efforts of radicals, particularly in New York. In London, Polish, French, German, Italian, and Hungarian émigré associations formed a short lived "International Committee" to celebrate the February revolution. The effort to extend this into a permanent organization included such figures as the French socialist Louis Blanc, the Russian revolutionary Alexander Herzen, the cooperationist George J. Holyoake, the Chartist land reformer Bronterre O'Brien, the English Garibaldian Forbes, and the German Communists with Karl Marx and Friederich Engels. In June 1857, they sent copies of their resolutions to their comrades at New York City.[12]

Frustration and desperation over Kansas moved those who had hoped in the power of moral suasion to take up arms in their own self-defense, even as the stunning news from Paris inspired hope in the efficacy of direct action. An old member of Giovane Italia, Felice Orsini had served in the Constituent Assembly of the Roman Republic, protected by the guns of Garibaldi, Forbes and their men. He escaped capture to work in the underground until his 1854 arrest on a mission to Hungary, recounted in his *Austrian Dungeons in Italy*, which appeared in 1857. Convinced that Napoleon III represented the chief architect of reaction throughout Europe—especially Italian unity and independence—he went to Paris. On January 4, 1858, Orsini and three accomplices lobbed bombs at the carriage of the emperor and empress on their way to Gioachino Rossini's *Guillaume Tell*, an opera on the legendary Swiss freedom fighter. The blast left eight killed, 142 wounded, and the royal couple unscathed. Orsini met his execution on March 13 bravely and calmly.

Within weeks, the émigrés in the U.S. prepared a public demonstration of their defense of tyrannicide. On April 13, 1858 "delegates from various nationalities" met at 291 Bowery under the chairmanship of Lyman Case—garbled by the press into "Lisen" or "Leon." A Connecticut lawyer associated with land reform, he had moved to New York, where he became intimately associated with the bohemian circle around Pfaff's. "Several Americans among the male portion of these congregations belong to the Red Republican associations which have sprung up in the City," grumbled the Republican *New York Times*, "and some of these figured conspicuously in the obsequies held in honor of ORSINI. The old Socialist champions are busy with the propagation of their disrupted theories."[13]

The Republican *Times* joined the Democratic *Herald* and the rest of the press in denouncing "the Moloch of Radicalism" among "cosmopolitan sympathizers, who would be utter savages were they not absolute simpletons," venting its journalistic spleen on the most loyally Republican of them, the "foolish Teutons." Above their headquarters at the Steuben House at 293 Broadway hung a banner showcasing "the Goddess of Reason—embracing a white man and a negro, under the auspices of the Universal Republic"

In fact, that April march of "Revolutionists of all the Nationalities" proved to be "a much more imposing affair than was generally anticipated." It started with at least "two thousand persons in line, with three hundred torches distributed among them." The parade included rifle company of Turners, different national contingents, Williamsburg, Brooklyn and Manhattanville Turners. Each marcher "wore a band of crape on the left arm and nearly all had a badge on the left breast." They hauled "a huge catafalque, erected on a large fourwheeled wagon" topped by "an Egyptian sarcophagus, covered with crape." A critic complained that the Irish and majority of Germans displayed "the worst qualities," and to exhibit the most exceptional features, of Red Republicanism." About 15,000 to 20,000 stood along the line of the march, which came down Broadway to Great Jones, then to Bowery and down to Canal to Broadway, round the park "to a platform erected in front of the City Hall steps.

The march ended at the Steuben House, Bowery. Around 10 p.m., the demonstration passed the reviewing stand and entered the park. John Allen—formerly associated with the *Voice of Industry* and later the leader of Fourierist efforts in the Midwest—"announced that 20,000 freemen had gathered together there for the purpose of doing homage to the memory of the sainted ORSINI and PIERRI, and to announce themselves as friends of the *Republique Univeselle*."[14] Around 11:30 pm "the managers and big men of the affair sat down to a supper which had been prepared, and enjoyed themselves for some time with speeches, toasts and songs, of the most ultra character. During the evening, a Committee of one hundred was chosen, as a Permanent Revolutionary Committee, for the spread of true liberty throughout the world."

Significantly, these actions demonstrated how others had moved to the fore to take up the slack in Forbes's absence, but these reflected internal changes among the various émigré organizations. The French groups had already shown a marked difference between the old republican orders and a broadly socialist perspective. At these demonstrations for Orsini, the tailor François Latour spoke for the latter, which also enjoyed the recent appearance of *Le Libertaire*. Its editor, Joseph Déjacque was a Paris-born wall paperer and a veteran of the revolutionary movement. He had gone into exile, passing briefly at New York before heading to New Orleans where he had publicly called for a slave insurrection. Upon returning, in early June 1858, he launched his new paper on a shoestring budget, urging revolutionary action upon largely anarchist principles.[15]

However, major shifts took place among these communities. Many of the French headed home in some safety after the abortive revolutions of 1848 had faded a decade into their past. Meanwhile, developments back in Italy offered new promise in the struggle for national unification and began drawing large numbers back. As a result, the Germans increasingly emerged as the mainstay of radicalism among the émigrés.

Among them, Friedrich A. Sorge began to emerge as a new leader. The "German Socialists" called a meeting at Harmony Hall, Essex Street on June 23. The large building seemed "pretty well filled by Germans, their wives and children, a considerable contingent of the French, a number of Poles, and a very small admixture of native Americans." At 8:30 p.m., he took his seat before "the *drapeau rouge*" with tricolors, and personally spoke in German, French and English. They had letters from Gustave Struve, and Friedrich Kamm "apostrophizing the Red flag" "going over a good deal of Red Republican thunder." Turners marched in with a band "and bearing the Republican flag and the stars and stripes."[16]

The Politics of Radicalism

At Boston, the same German Turners who defended abolitionist meetings sponsored the gathering of "friends of universal freedom" in Boston on Thursday April 29.[17] The abolitionist John W. Barnes presided over a "largely attended and quite enthusiastic" rally that heard speeches in French, Italian, German and English. Although William Lloyd Garrison had been expected, he sent a letter "ardently sympathizing with the purpose of the meeting." "How can America sympathize with any struggle for freedom in the Old World?" asked Garrison.

She holds every seventh person of her vast population in fetters of iron, as a brute beast, as an article of merchandise. With four millions of slaves in her ruthless grasp, she has not only lost all reverence for human rights, but she ridicules and rejects her own Declaration of independence; and hence, her instincts and feelings are with every tyrant in Europe, and against its down-trodden masses, and such will be her state and attitude until she breaks every fetter, and liberates every slave, on her own soil: then shall she lead the nations of the earth to universal freedom.

The International abroad continued to face the issue because the British authorities prolonged the issue by sending to trial the Foureiriest Dr. Simon François Bernard as a collaborator of Orsini. That spring, the International noted the responses in America as "extensive" and "truly wonderful" with new affiliates reaching beyond the east coast. On May 17, the Turners at Chicago led a torch-bearing "Red Republican demonstration" through the streets. The local press sought to denigrate a similar march at Cincinnati.[18]

In the U.S., however, radicals took heart at the Federal concession to the determination of the actual settlers in Kansas. The *Radical Abolitionist* hinted that the conflict would not end with the victory in Kansas:

> private information, from a high source, to the same effect, and still further. The movement will not stop in Missouri. The war, if it begins, will run through the slave States. It will be a war of revolution, and make other work for the administration, besides subduing Kansas. It will probably embroil the whole nation.[19]

Indeed, a small group of determined abolitionists combined their efforts to get armed parties where they might be needed. George Luther Stearns began moving them west from Worcester. Samuel Gridley Howe, Theodore Parker, Franklin Benjamin Sanborn and Gerrit Smith participated. Thomas Wentworth Higginson cast his lot with what came to be remembered as "the Secret Six." They began imagining the armed protection of the "slave stampede." Meanwhile, John Brown visited Boston and, on March 8, left the city.[20]

A Federal fugitive himself at this point, Brown had grown a long white beard to disguise his identity and looked like a Biblical prophet. Under the advice of "the Secret Six," he approached Forbes. In his paper for the émigrés, *The European*, Forbes had long defended the right of black resistance to slavery in the South, up to and including mass insurrection, and had little interest in the electoral effort to secure "Kansas for white people." The abolitionist *Independent* reported that "a few copies" of his *Manual for the Patriotic Volunteer* had gone to Kansas.[21] Brown now offered him an opportunity to do something to encourage such a rebellion.

For his part, Forbes went west expecting to find a small army to train in Iowa, but found around a dozen irregularly armed veterans of the Kansas conflict, hoping to involve "some twenty-five to fifty (colored and white mixed), well armed and bringing a quantity of spare arms, to beat up a slave quarter in Virginia." Forbes questioned sending such a hopeless force against a Federal arsenal in the hopes it would immediately detonate the necessary numbers, particularly with "no preparatory notice having been given to the slaves." Forbes also doubted Brown's optimistic faith that non-slaveholding Southern whites would tend not to assist in the repression of the rising and, indeed, join in the revolt at places. If Brown's gamble failed, warned Forbes, the raid would be suicidal. Moreover any slave rebellion would sweep "like a prairie fire from Mason and Dixon's line to the Gulf of Mexico," in such a localized fashion that would likely be "easily subdued" piecemeal.[22] As an alternative, Forbes suggested that posting small armed bands making regular emancipator raids into the slave states would destroy the value of slavery, and roll back the borders in which the institution could function.

After being overruled, Forbes found that the funding had trickled away, so he headed back east where he stalked antislavery leaders with entirely accurate forebodings of disaster. By May 1858, concerns about the security of the project turned on the fear that Forbes might go to John P. Hale, Henry Wilson or other antislavery political leaders he knew. Hinton—who knew everybody involved—assured them that Forbes would not "have been deliberately or intentionally treacherous," and Sanborn doubted that he would betray them. Still, Gerrit Smith favored abandoning the project and the other four of the other "Secret Six" became concerned enough that Higginson came in from Worcester for a three hour discussion with Brown in Boston. The entire experience left Brown as disillusioned with his backers as Forbes had become. Nevertheless, Brown's "Secretary of State" Richard Realf got $250 to seek help in England, a venture that produces nothing.[23] The project rested entirely on the "Secret Six."

News that Brown had something in the works began to leak out. While Forbes remained silent, James Redpath published a piece on black insurrection, and Lysander Spooner issued his own manifesto calling for an armed revolt by slaves, free blacks and their allies. Spooner Higginson hurriedly set up a meeting with him at Monk's Bookstore on Broomfield Court. Without any apparent connection to Forbes, a black student at Oberlin, William Ellaby Lincoln had similar responses to the Harpers Ferry project, and offered particularly sage advice that Brown learn from the maroons, anchor his force someplace like the Florida swamps, and engage in "an armed diversion a la Garibaldi."[24]

Brown took advantage of the delay to root the legitimacy of his project among African American supporters. On May 8, 1858, a small convention gathered at Chatham, Canada to authorize his initiative. By then, thousands of African Americans had taken up residence in that part of Ontario, supporting Henry Bibb's *Voice of the Fugitive* at Sandwich. George De Baptiste and William Lambert later said, "the expedition was armed here and started from here, and there are still living in Detroit several colored men who helped arrange the plan, and are familiar with it from its first inception."[25]

At Chatham, Brown surprised some of his African American comrades by his placement of the Stars and Stripes at the fore, but he had his reasons. Certainly, almost all of the proposed alternatives made more sense as a means of subverting and destroying slavery over time, but the defeat of slavery was not enough for John Brown. He hoped the American nation would defeat slavery, to invest itself into a future as more than a white republic.

In this, he reflected the sense of the Radical Abolitionists and Libertymen. They, with notable allies such as Lucius A. Hine followed Spooner's insistence that the Constitution had been, however inadvertently, an antislavery document. Goodell insisted that "the people of this country as constituting ONE NATION—a nation remarkably tenacious of its nationality." "What nation ever perished? What Government was ever overthrown? What people ever lost their liberties, but by neglecting to 'execute judgment for the oppressed'?" he asked. "Do your banks, your palaces, your quiet habitations need the defenses of protecting law? Then make those defenses offered for the protection of the lowly cabins of the outraged slaves. Understand, that if there is to be protection for *you*, there must be protection for *them*."[26] So, too, proclaimed Brown's insistence on the presence of the U.S. flag at Chatham.

Chatham enlisted a good contingent of Prince Hall Masons, including Martin R. Delany who presided, and Osborn P. Anderson who decided to join the planned raid. One of Brown's comrades from Kansas, Luke Parsons found out about the "African Mysteries" or "African-American Mysteries," and told the other white abolitionists with Brown that blacks had their own secret society to take direct action against slavery. Indeed, the convention included members of the order such as William Lambert and probably William C. Munroe.[27] In the end, the convention ratified a constitution for the self-government of slave rebels and authorized Brown to serve as the commander-in-chief of a paramilitary venture.

Back in the U.S., Internationalists, Radical Abolitionists, and working-class land reformers remained critical of the Republican alternative, even though some saw it as a usable vehicle for their views. On

October 4, with Commerford in the chair and Price as secretary, what was left of the local NRA endorsed the state Republican ticket. A week later, representatives of the 43 local groups held a state convention at 163 Bowery, with Theodore C. Wittemberg, an NRA veteran from upstate. It declared for land reform, prison labor, ten hours on public works. "The Republican candidates were all declared nominated, they having received the largest number of votes."[28]

Among the émigrés, the German radicals sponsored a rally on October 13 "principally composed of the ultras of the Socialist, Communist and Red Republican Parties, about eight hundred in number." They proposed "to take steps for the organization of a new and independent party" to which the *Times* snidely added, would be "composed exclusively of Germans." Struve's resolutions denounced Democrats over slavery and Americans and Republicans as "antagonists of the emigrant's rights." The "People's party" they advocated "must advocate the rights of the workingmen, and the equality of employers and employed—must seek the abolition of all monopolies—must reform the laws and the system of their administration—purify the Judiciary—oppose the election of Judges by the people—oppose the Sabbatarian spirit, which is seeking to deprive the workingman of his recreation, and finally stand erect for Universal Freedom, Civil and Religious."[29]

In mid-January, the Allegemeiner Arbeiterbund hosted another convention "composed of delegates from various socialistic organizations throughout the country." After meeting at Philadelphia the previous month, the group reassembled at the Steuben House, and then the Metropolitan Rooms in Hester Street. Joined by the French and Italian groups, they agreed to "labor to elect a President of the United States pledged to carry out its principles."[30]

Their American comrades had much more attainable goals. That summer, Commerford opened a land reform meeting to hear the report of Senator Benjamin F. Wade, who described the Slave Power as playing "the game of the monopolist." In August, the New York State Radical Abolitionist convention at Syracuse decided to run Gerrit Smith for governor. He proposed to use "the military power of the State" to protect fugitive slaves. He also spoke out bluntly against the "greedy and oppressive speculators" seeing to control the nation's land policy. Even those NRA veterans predisposed to the Republicans, such as Devyr, embraced the Radical Abolitionist ticket. The movement hosted his campaign meetings at Brooklyn and the Cooper institute in New York.[31]

Quickly forgetting their own experience as a third party, the Republicans disparaged the Smith campaign with a series of now-familiar tropes used against third party movements. They advocated "Voting for Morgan to keep Out Parker," and urged "Don't Throw Away Your Votes!" "It is quite clear," sniffed the *New York Times*, "that, in the approaching canvass, as always heretofore, Radical Abolitionism will be found fighting on the side of Slavery."[32]

In the middle of this campaign, the American Abolition Society held a multi-racial national convention on September 29–30. Charles C. Foote, Frederick Douglass, and James McCune Smith participated. For some years, the African Americans involved had been discussing colonization, and been organizing themselves to that purpose as early as the 1854 convention at Cleveland. In addition to Smith and Martin Delany, Lambert, William C. Munroe, and Richard De Baptist of the Detroit circle attended. This had a broad variety of meanings, from going as far as Africa or as nearby as Canada. Nor did it preclude armed resistance as the recollection of Haiti demonstrated.[33]

One of the great problems the Radical Abolitionists had with the Republican Party centered on the party's idealization of social conditions in the North. This concern brought about the actual convergence between the persistent agitation of white workers in the non-slaveholding states and the growing independent voice of African Americans such as Dr. Smith, who took up the pen to correct the assertions of the *Tribune* about the actual condition of "colored people" in the city.[34]

The emergence of a mass movement against slavery and, ultimately, the outbreak of war overshadowed the delusion of colonization, and a new generation of leadership began to emerge. Born a North Carolina slave, the recently ordained Baptist minister John Sella Martin became the first black pastor of Tremont Temple in Boston and threw his prestige behind the ACS. Although sold repeatedly when younger, he managed to become literate enough to forge papers that had allowed his escape north only two years earlier.[35] The postwar leader of the National Colored Labor Union pointed towards a juncture of race and class that understated neither.

Those familiar with the institution understood the burden it imposed on the South. "The poor laboring white man of the South is looked down upon with as withering a contempt as the slave," declared Frederick Douglass. Radical Abolitionists celebrated indigenous anti-slavery sentiments in the South among the "hundreds of thousands of oppressed whites and free people of color, and from millions of slaves." It publicized the case of the printer William S. Bailey of Newport, who used his *Kentucky News*—later the *Free South*—to develop a class under-standing of the need for interracial solidarity against slavery. They also promoted the hostility of James B. Gardenshire of Jefferson City Land Company against the return of fugitive slaves, the legality of the insti-tution, and the Dred Scott decision. Socialist circles—largely German émigrés—functioned in Baltimore, Washington, Louisville, St. Louis, New Orleans, San Antonio, and even Richmond, Virginia.[36] Withal, though, the Smith campaign expected 50,000 votes and Greeley even anticipated as many as 25,000, but, in the end, got 5,470.

In short, radicals remained skeptical of Republican shortcomings. Some Republican leaders began to urge the party to make common cause with Northern Democrats around popular sovereignty, inspiring Redpath to say, "I would give ten thousand to Mr. [Gerrit] Smith if I had them, no matter whom the Republicans nominated." In Abraham Lincoln's own state, Ira Porter's *North-West Excelsior*, a small spiritualist sheet from Waukegan complained of the Topeka constitution "proscrib-ing the colored race." Democrats "boldly demands equal rights for slavery with freedom," while Republican "denies the right of suffrage to the colored race." "In the present contest between Sham Republi-canism and Satanic Democracy, has the friend of freedom any cause to sympathize with either?"[37]

Nevertheless, the Republicans in Congress made good their promises for a Homestead Act. In the House of Representatives, Alexander Hamilton Stevens of Georgia and other Southern Democratic Con-gressmen demanded discussion, when Galusha Grow called up the measure for a vote in February 1858. Grow quipped that it had been "discussed for eight years or more," and, in a largely sectional vote, the House passed the bill 120 to 76. About two weeks later, Senators Wade, Andrew Johnson, Henry Wilson, James Shields, and William H. Seward got the measure through the Senate.[38] Then, President James Buchanan vetoed the Homestead Bill.

Thereafter, even those land reformers who called themselves Democrats and had a nostalgic affection for Andrew Jackson's antimonopoly rhetoric had repudiated the party. By the end of the year, Thomas A. Devyr had toured the old Antirent communities upstate for the Radical Abolitionists. Commerford wrote Andrew Johnson that, while he had resisted Fremont's appeal, "in the next Presidential Contest, I shall have to cast my ballot for the Republican Candidate."[39]

Too, the more skeptical of electoral politics, such as Garrison, remained as unmoved by the Radical Abolitionists as by the Republicans. 'The so-called government of this republic, I regard as a stupid, grim, malignant conspiracy," declared Beriah Green in declining a nomination. "I cannot recognize it as a government without assailing the prerogatives of God and the rights of men."[40]

This faith in the irreducible equality of the individual *human spirit* found a great cultural expression in a massive and pervasive new spiritualism. Supporters believed literally that trance mediums and seances permitted communication with the souls of the departed, who were nudging the nation and the world towards a new standard of human rights. Faith in practical spirit communication sweep precisely the same districts as created the Republican political insurgency. Higginson thought a Satan "decked as a gentleman, and acting through some fashionable system of wrong or institution of despotism, should be the object of actual terror—not the defunct, imaginary devil aforesaid."[41] Of the tens of thousands of active promoters of spiritualism, a core of several thousand regularly engaged in the cooperative, land reform and antislavery agitations.

So, too, spiritualist efforts at organization invariably drew out its most radical possibilities. A mass "Free Convention" at Rutland, Vermont in June 1858 drew several thousands to what became a discussion of capitalism, slavery, and, particularly, patriarchy. Mrs. Julia Branch shocked the press, if not the participants with her denunciations of the family and marriage, coupled to her demand that the state declare all children legitimate. Others followed at Utica and elsewhere.[42] The distant sound of the guns in Kansas proved not yet loud enough to focus their attention on slavery.

Spiritualism opened the platform to scores of talented and otherwise excluded female voice. A succession of prominent spiritualists tied their beliefs to women's rights. These included Ernestine Rose, Hannah F. M. Brown, and Mathilde Anneke. Conversely, leaders of the women's rights movement, such as Elizabeth Cady Stanton and Susan B. Anthony found spiritualism entirely compatible with their feminism. In the decade after the 1848 Seneca Falls gathering, state efforts to revise their constitutions had inspired a series of women's conventions, from which produced a network of women, largely participants in the antislavery cause, who also contended for their own rights.

Nationalizing Kansas

Victory in Kansas had required the opponents of slavery to thwart the plans of the Federal government for their territory. The U.S. Supreme Court then issued its Dred Scott decision to nail down the national commitment to slavery, but the people had defied them or, in most cases, declined to crush those who did. Even the U.S. Army had found Kansas to be ungovernable by the designated autocrats.

Brown, Forbes and others had no more patience with electoral games. They were not a small group choosing to take up arms, but part of a massive number who had essentially had arms put into their hands in self-defense. Nor did they propose to transform the world through their own small numbers. Their hope was to detonate a mass revolt, and—in the end—mass action to secure emancipation, particularly by those currently held in slavery. Brown's hope was that some decisive action could force the issue sooner than would otherwise be the case.

What Brown and his men did after the Chatham convention became well-documented. He sent John E. Cook to Harpers Ferry. He went to work on the Chesapeake and Ohio Canal on the Maryland Heights, just across the Potomac from town, and, eventually, got a job teaching school. He familiarized himself with the town, the armory, the arsenal, the surrounding countryside, as well as the state of the militia.[43]

Brown, meanwhile, headed back to Kansas where events quelled the last of his doubts about the project. A runaway Missouri slave found help at the homes of Augustus Wattles and James Montgomery just over the Kansas line, pleading for help to rescue his family due to be sold south. On December 20–21, Brown and Aaron D. Stevens led a small band on a night raid into Missouri, freeing the man's family with other slaves, and taking the wagons, horses, and mules necessary to speed their own rush back into Kansas.[44] In the aftermath, the Federal authorities offered a reward of $250 for Brown's capture.

Hinton, meanwhile, scouted what he hoped would be "the best place of attack in the South-Western States." The often mixed race peoples of the Indian Territory just south of Kansas had their own antislavery traditions that the national movement had never fully tapped. Noting the history of "the Maroons" among the Creeks, he found some white support for a revolt in adjacent Arkansas and Texas, particularly Douai's San Antonio Germans already discussing the idea of an independent non-slaveholding territory in northern Texas. Between them, free Kansas, the Indians, and a free territory in west Texas would effectively block the further expansion of slavery.[45] After returning from a scout through this area, Hinton heard about the Harpers Ferry plan from John Henry Kagi, who acknowledged that it would probably be suicidal.

That winter, Brown's comrades had to accommodate his plan. In February 1859, Mr. and Mrs. Samuel G. Howe and the veteran Fourierist George Ripley escorted Theodore Parker—eager to get his tuberculosis out of the New England winter—onto a ship bound for Cuba with his wife, a voyage from which he would not return. In mid-March, those slaves Brown had extracted from Missouri reached the radical circles in northern Illinois, where the ex-Chartist railroad detective Allan Pinkerton got them on their way into Canada.[46]

As the weather warmed, Brown arrived in the east. Using a pseudonym, he rented the Maryland farm of Dr. Booth Kennedy, only a few miles into Maryland from Harpers Ferry. In ones and twos, the volunteers began showing up. Some had already told friends that they expected not to survive through the raid, and all were ready for that end. Meanwhile, Kagi settled into a rented house at Chambersburg in August, and began receiving arms, which he forwarded to the farm. At one point, a disguised Brown met Frederick Douglass and Shields Green at a stone quarry near Chambersburg. Douglass told Brown that it was likely Virginia would "blow him and his hostages sky-high, rather than that he should hold Harpers Ferry an hour." However, Green, an escaped slave from South Carolina, saw the glimmer of a chance to liberate his family and joined the raid.

Brown and his men had long worked alongside African Americans and believed that slaves could ultimately gain freedom only by their own hand. Osborn P. Anderson and Dangerfield Newby added two more black faces to the group. On October 14–15, John A. Copeland, a black former student at Oberlin and his uncle Lewis Leary joined the growing band. They, with Green, made five of the nineteen raiders black.

Nevertheless, the operation reflected the weakness of Brown's politics. As James M. Smith later complained, they slated mostly whites to deliver the initial blow. Too, though they had struggled alongside Indians in the West, none rode with them. Nor could the old patriarch bring himself to lead a Garibaldian uprising involving armed women, so he sent his daughter-in-law and her own fifteen-year-old daughter who had been keeping house at the farm back to Brown's own wife back at North Elba.

On Sunday night, October 16, the group waited around 8 p.m. before mounting up and heading out into a nasty drizzle over the last few miles, after which Brown fully disclosed his plans. Sanborn later repeated the account he got from Charles Plummer Tidd. Looking down from the heights of the Maryland shore, Brown sketched the plans. With Harpers Ferry visible below them, the group generally saw themselves likely to wind up with their backs to the river near a railroad that could bring legions of armed men down upon them. At one point, all but Owen Brown "refused to take part in it," but Brown insisted that "he would make the attack with a single man, if only one man would obey him." In the end his sons would not desert him, and the others ultimately decided not to make the odds worse by their individual absence. Sanborn later wrote, "We have no reason to doubt that Tidd's statement was true in substance."[47]

The story of the raid has been oft told. They moved into action around 10:30 p.m., seizing the Potomac Bridge into Harpers Ferry, cutting the telegraph and stopping a Baltimore and Ohio train before letting it continue, possibly in hopes that news of the raid might spark a rebellion along the line. They descended on the armory and began taking hostages, dispatching some raiders to take the arsenal, near where the Shenandoah flowed into the Potomac, and Hall's Rifle Works on Lower Hall Island.

By morning on October 17, locals realized that they faced an armed, mixed-race force and began putting down sufficient fire to hold the raiders until a company of militia came up by train. It quickly captured the bridge, isolating Brown and his men, with nine captives barricaded into the smaller engine house. Episodic gunfire continued dropping casualties, including the mayor. Meanwhile, individual raiders scattered or usually fell. Brown sent out a small detail with a white flag to negotiate a surrender, but the militia and townsmen gunned them down.

On the morning of October 18, Colonel Robert E. Lee, on leave from his posting in Texas, steamed into town with a company of U.S. Marines. After deploying them for an assault on the engine house, Lee sent Lieutenant J. E. B. Stuart under a white flag of truce to the engine house to demand a surrender. After a short parlay, Stuart wheeled and gave a thumbs-down signal to the waiting Marines. Almost immediately, the troops had battered their way into the building, overwhelming the defenders. Broken and bloodied, the handful of surviving raiders emerged to see what Forbes, William Ellaby Lincoln, and Frederick Douglass had predicted.

Yet, what their captors saw was a badly injured old white man who had chosen to walk the same path as Gabriel Prosser, Nat Turner and unnumbered slave rebels, and a number of others, black and white, who had made the same choice. Mulling over what was incomprehensible to him, Lee reported it the next day as "the attempt of a fanatic or madman." He confirmed that the blacks captured with Brown "gave him no voluntary assistance," and none of the raiders would say otherwise. More silently, the slave population in the area began falling off in the aftermath of the raid.

Lee headed back Texas to resume his general command of the U.S. forces there, only to face revolt, if not revolution, in the Rio Grande Valley. Years before, the Anglos had driven out the family and countrymen of Juan N. Cortina. After the Anglos took the area, he had returned to the family's ranch at Santa Rita, only five miles from what had begun to be Brownsville. Thereafter, the Texas officials indicted him for rustling, though his popularity among the Chicano peoples kept him from arrest. On July 13, 1859, the city marshal assaulted and arrested one of Cortina's former employees, alleged to have been drunk and disorderly. In response, Cortina shot the marshal and released him.

After the continued harassment and brutalization of Mexicans in Texas, Cortina returned on the morning of September 28, with an armed band. After shooting five men, including the jailer for resisting them, they seized control of the town. Some of the townsmen appealed for help to the Mexican authorities in Matamoros, who sent José María Jesús Carbajal (also spelled Carvajal, Caravajal, Carabajal and Carbahal) to negotiate Cortina's evacuation of Brownsville. Once back on his ranch, though, Cortina issued a proclamation on September 30, warning Anglo Texans to respect the rights of the Chicano people.

Over the next few days, a posse from Brownsville, aided by a Mexican militia company from Matamoros recaptured Cortina's compañero, and attacked Cortina's ranch. The small group of defenders drove them off, and Cortina threatened to burn the town should the authorities not release Cabrera. In early November, Captain William G. Tobin arrived with a company of Texas Rangers, whose presence emboldened the locals to hang Cabrera and fight another skirmish with Cortina's men. On November 23, Cortina issued a second proclamation urging Governor Samuel Houston to protect his Spanish-speaking citizens.[48]

Backed by Lee and the power of the U.S. military, Captain John "RIP" Ford replied to Cortina's request with a second contingent of Rangers, and a regiment of the U.S. Army. Cortina retreated up the Rio Grande, but the Texas and Federal forces hit his band with overwhelming force on December 27, ending the so-called First Cortina War. It hardly resolved the problem of La Raza on the border.

Similar forces at work in California, since its U.S. acquisition, extended the policy of ethnic cleansing begun centuries before on the other end of the continent. In 1858–1859, whites had perpetrated the Round Valley Massacres and the army reported on May 1, that settlers had slaughtered six hundred Yuki Indians in the previous year. In September, they butchered another seventy Achomawi, sixty of them women and children, on the Pit River. The assault on a Maidu camp near Chico Creek killed another forty Indians. Bret Harte covered events near Hydesville, on February 26, 1860, where whites waged a series of nearly simultaneous attacks on Wiyot Indians in Humboldt County. Most of the two hundred to two hundred fifty killed at Indian Island, Eureka, and Rio Dell had been women, children and elders, with others following over the next few days. That same year, another sixty-five Yuki met their end at Bloody Rock in Mendocino County.

Back in Virginia, where these policies started, the authorities brought to trial a handful of men who offered a very different vision of the nation's future. On October 25, a grand jury at Charlestown formally indicted the lot of them, and the authorities began John Brown's trial the next day. Meanwhile, Hinton, Augustus Wattles, James Montgomery and others scurried about to raise money and volunteers for a rescue. In the end, though, the authorities concentrated a large militia force, and Brown personally discouraged any further violence on his behalf.

The old man waved aside a proposed insanity defense as a "miserable artifice and pretext." Although lawyers argued that Brown could not be tried for treason by Virginia because his crimes had been committed on property belonging to the Federal government, prosecutors successfully countered the argument on the basis of states' rights.

Brown's trial came very quickly and drew the eyes of the nation to it.[49] For the first time, a non-office-holding Northern white had a national platform from which to address the issue. The old man deigned to hide his purposes or do anything to sugar-coat its means. Addressing the court, he freely acknowledged the charges that he had interfered with the arrangement of the slaveholders in the interests of slaves, adding that had he done so in their interests, "every man in this court would have deemed it an act worthy of reward rather than punishment." The court sentenced him to be hanged on December 2.

Even those unsympathetic to abolitionism realized that nothing would be able to stay the same after the slaveholding interests used their power to hang John Brown. Rescue plans resumed as the courts turned to Brown's surviving comrades. Green, Copeland, Cook, and Barclay Coppoc faced trial on December 16. On March 16, 1860, Stevens and Albert Hazlett, who had been captured in Carlisle, followed.[50] The authorities consigned their bodies to unmarked graves away from the cemeteries.

* * *

The soul that Brown left behind went marching on to move the reputedly immoveable iron laws of history, as he himself saw it before his execution. Before leaving his cell, he wrote, "I John Brown am now quite certain that the crimes of this guilty land will never be purged away but with Blood. I had as I now think: vainly flattered myself that without very much bloodshed; it might be done." Radicals such as Lyman Case had already been arguing that, like it or not, the unwillingness of the power structure to acknowledge the necessity of history or the will of the people meant that freedom "could only be achieved through blood."[51] This would not be a matter of choice but the recognition of necessities imposed by an inflexible ruling class.

By the middle of the nineteenth century, radicals in the U.S. addressed the idea of a special divinely ordained American exceptionalism. Shortly after the Civil War, Cora L. V. Tappan declared bluntly that "a government that has for nearly a century enslaved one race (African), that proscribes another (Chinese), proposes to exterminate another (Indians), and persistently refuses to recognize the rights of one-half of its citizens (women), cannot justly be called perfect." Even where the property requirement for voting no longer existed, her colleague Benjamin N. Kinyon tallied up the racially excluded, the women, and minors under the age of twenty-one to conclude that six out of seven Americans "so far as the Government is concerned, are as powerless as the serfs of Russia." The structure of power left the preponderant majority of that remaining sixth fundamentally marginalized and powerless within the system.[52] Without equality, the only liberty permissible would be defined by the rich and powerful in their own interests, leaving the new American republic no more exceptional than anywhere else in the world.

As with Old John Brown, whatever these striking insights would mean in the long run of history would be in the hands of those who came after them.

EPILOGUE

Survival and Persistence: The Lineages and Legacies of the Early American Movement

The slaves who buried the last of John Brown's raiders shared the location with Gabriel Newby, the brother of Dangerfield. Decades later, these local African Americans told some sympathetic whites. In late July 1899, a group of them—free now but still moving in secret and at night—sunk their shovels into a washed-out slope overlooking the river. They struck the remains of a soaked mud-filled coffin after only three feet, and quickly gathered the remaining bones into a trunk. Professor Orin Grant Libby, the nephew of Charles Plummer Tidd, then smuggled them out of Virginia. Another group simultaneously retrieved the remains of those buried at Perth Amboy. They all converged on the old Brown farm near North Elba, where he had been buried. In a short ceremony on August 30, Dick Hinton personally reminisced about each of the ten men whose bones went into a single coffin placed alongside John Brown's.[1] Within months, the last of the century that had inspired their hopes faded into history, and Hinton himself left on a research trip to England from which he would not return in hopeful pursuit of Brown's connections to the revolutionary movement in Europe.

Already, liberal ideas of a gradual, inexorable "progress" had begun to come to the fore. Not the old spirit of change but the nosier, more tangible, and profitable wheels of industry would define what that could mean. Contrary to the hopes of the old radicals, no lesson would be learned so thoroughly as not to require a continued relearning. Already, a much more powerful Federal Union crushed the last of the free and independent native peoples, and established a system of racial apartheid, while showing no interest in preventing the systemic lynchings of African Americans largely enslaved by impoverishment. The women who had anticipated equal rights in the war's aftermath remained subordinate, and that the right of property trumped the human rights of those without property remained as persistent as ever.

Of course, so did the radical critique of these notions.

History and the Domestication of the Past

John Brown's soul may be marching on, as the old song ran, but the authorities began mapping its permissible course no sooner than they had hanged him. U.S. Senators James M. Mason and Jefferson Davis launched a formal committee to investigate Harpers Ferry. The official probe hinted at a dark, hidden conspiracy. They investigated the activities of Brown's followers in Kansas. Although Hugh Forbes had left for Italy to fight rejoin the campaigns of Giuseppe Garibaldi and his old comrades, the *New York Herald* bribed his landlord to seize his trunk before it could be sent on.[2]

Ultimately, officialdom thought it wiser to minimize the importance of the raid. In the end, they embraced the description of Brown as a lunatic, casting his allies and friends as deluded. This suited many in the North, including the more moderate critics of slavery. The basis for Brown's posthumous diagnosis was not taking up arms in a nation which had resorted to arms over such questions for years, but his uncompromising advocacy of the abolition of property rights in human beings.

Indeed, this reflects the broad predispositions of those with power and wealth to rationalize their standing and the status quo. "Utopian extremes cannot long live upon the soil of this Republic," the *New York Times* told itself. The "Red Republican Jacobinism" of Tom Paine, it noted with little regard for accuracy, had "died before he did." Such currents "have been succeeded by myriads of others, each of which has been equally short-lived." In other words, radicalism demonstrably had no place in the American experience because it died as soon as it appeared, the *Times* complaining that it cropped up repeatedly in "myriads." Behind the first official burial of Paine's legacy, for example, Gilbert Vale, Horace Seaver, Josiah Mendum and many others kept it quite alive, as did younger radicals, such as the union printer Joseph N. Moreau, whose projected biography of Paine would be cut short in 1863 by secessionist lead.[3]

In reality, Brown was the product of a long and self-conscious radical continuity. After the investigation struck on "the Secret Six," New England officials descended on the Concord home of Franklin Benjamin Sanborn, in hopes of getting him to Boston, and thence to Washington. Almost immediately, his neighbors surrounded and seized the deputies until lawyers could file papers to save Sanborn, after which they also began planning "to appear in force at the state supreme-court room." In the wake of Brown's hanging, Hinton, who had stopped by the home of Wendell Phillips to escort him to a meeting, saw the mild-mannered Boston gentleman slip a Colt revolver from his desk drawer to his inside pocket. At that meeting, Phillips found the stage protected by "over 400 gallant young fellows in the hall ready to offer their lives in his defense." Such figures organized in hopes of making a mass armed raid into Virginia to free the prisoners.[4] All this implied organization.

The platforms of the meetings commemorating John Brown and the raid not only included names prominent in abolitionism—black and white—but former Owenites and Fourierists, as well as participants in the annual conventions around freethought, women's rights, and land reform. Over a generation, these distinctions had come to mean less and less, a process hastened by the influx of the refugees of the European revolutionary movements.

The rescue network evolved into the variously named League of Freedom or John Brown League, which served as an abolitionist "Minute Man" organization. They functioned as a paramilitary secret society, with secret signs, grips, passwords and obligations such as the Carbonari or the Blanquists on the continent. Members took "a binding oath ... to engage in no occupation that could prevent our marching at an hour's notice, and to obey an order to march without question." One member later estimated that it "numbered 25,000 members, scattered through Kansas, Iowa, Northern Ohio, New York and Canada."[5] Although surely exaggerated in numbers, what they represented was essentially the professionalization of revolutionary politics in America.

Participants included the usual suspects. Black and white veterans of the Underground Railroad formed something of a core, but if that "league" assumed anything like the numbers attributed to it, it would have absorbed what remained of that loose internationalist network of radicals that Forbes had constructed. Certainly, Karl Heinzen immediately began "to organize a force of Turners." Joseph Déjacque praised Brown in *Le Libertaire*, and the Polish speaker at a meeting of his countrymen "made some very lengthy remarks about John Brown and Harpers Ferry, eulogizing Brown as a hero of the first order, whom he regarded as a victim of the slave power. Slavery he denounced as a crime equal to assassination." Later, Giuseppe Garibaldi himself offered to return to the U.S. and fight for the Union on the condition that it take up the cause of the Harpers Ferry raiders. The German Jewish secularist Max Langenschwartz described history as "but the record of a perpetual struggle for social equality," adding that "talking is of no use. His remedy for social wrongs is *revolution*. ... His model Reformer is John Brown. He would make every despot a head shorter."[6]

To them—and to growing numbers in the North—the conduct of the Virginia authorities and their apologists reflected the aggressive desperation of a threatened elite. The fact that the slaveholders had law and the institutions of power on their side had come to matter less and less to the people of the non-slaveholding states. "I think that for once the Sharp's rifles and the revolvers were employed in a righteous cause," declared the long-standing pacifist Henry David Thoreau. "The tools were in the hands of one who could use them," he declared in "A Plea for Captain John Brown," who "has a spark of divinity in him." The antislavery religious weekly the *Independent* agreed that the raid may have been "insane," but "the controlling motive of his demonstration was sublime."

The intransigence of the old order seemed so inoffensive that it stirred a respectable health reformer such as Dr. James C. Jackson to look up from his fresh water and vegetables. The emerging conflict had clarified "the true position of the people of the North, and the people of this country; and it seems to me that this position is one of *revolution*! We are, whether we will it or not, in the midst of a revolution!" In this, he declared, "our sympathies are with the mass of the people."[7]

The Radical Abolitionists persisted in keeping the broader antislavery movement from getting too comfortable. In May, they hosted a broader gathering at Boston that drew nationally prominent spiritualists such as Bela Marsh and John Pierpont, as well as Hinton and James Redpath. Their stated goal was no less than to consider forming a new party, as the German socialists had recently advocated.[8]

The Radical Abolitionists held their national convention at Syracuse towards the end of August. Frederick Douglass, Elizabeth Cady Stanton, and Charles C. Foote heard an opening appeal from William S. Bailey, the Southern editor of the *Free South*. They formulated a militant platform: "we demand at the hands of our National Government, a Homestead Bill, which shall not only leave every landless settler the opportunity to acquire a home without money and without cost (save the cost of transfer.) but we also demand of it a statute against land monopoly." Embracing the legacy of John Brown, they nominated Gerrit Smith for president. "The ballot-box, if used to that end would speedily bring slavery to a peaceful death," he replied. "But the ballot-box must be left to serve slavery, and slavery must be left to go out in blood."[9] Yet, hoping against hope, Smith and other radicals generally wound up supporting the insurgent campaign of Abraham Lincoln.

The Republican victory in the November elections heralded that anticipated "Second American Revolution," though not in a straightforward way. With the election of Abraham Lincoln, the governments of the Southern states voted to secede from the United States, and, in April 1861, opened fire on Fort Sumter, forcing the hand of the new government. As the war loomed longer and larger, it forced more innovative and far-reaching measures on the Federal authorities. The Lincoln administration promulgated a radical wartime monetary policy centered on printing paper currency and a progressive income tax. 1862 finally brought a Federal Homestead Act—land reform seriously shorn of its most radical features—and the fall brought a proclamation emancipating those slaves held in Confederate territory. In the end, the very power structure that had found it convenient to treat Harpers Ferry as the work of lunatics embraced that very "lunacy" as a national policy.

Radicals themselves had anticipated something like this. Lucius A. Hine had long expected that events would "bring more skillful anti-slavery players to the board." They would sway "public sentiment that they [slaveholders] will soon be unable to make anything out of it." In hindsight, Hinton thought that Kansas had brought in "growing northern and western business interests" to bear. "The danger of the possible nationalization of slavery or the threatened dissolution of the union," he continued, "was so imminent that business and ethics fused into statesmanship."[10]

Radical participation in the war pushed this process along. The handful of Brown's raiders that had survived Harpers Ferry entered the service of the Union. Officers and participants in the ranks of abolitionist, land reform and socialist currents donned the uniform and took up arms. While conditions back in Europe drew many of the Italian and French radicals back to their homelands, the largest remaining bloc, the Germans threw themselves heavily into the war effort.

Beyond the war, a looming reconstruction increasingly posed the question of what kind of Union they hoped to restore, a matter for which the radicals already had an agenda of sorts. Too, by the time of the war, radical currents of all sorts discussed "slavery" as more than the "chattel slavery" ended by wartime emancipation. In that sense, they expected Republicanism, Unionism, and Reconstruction to go far beyond. Harriet Tubman and African American participants in the underground—with legions of others fleeing slavery—would carry such aspirations into the war and beyond.

None of this could happen without addressing those systemic exclusions—and we mean by this the exclusion of entire peoples and not the cosmetic acceptance of symbolic tokens—would leave a reconstructed republic little more than a mere aggregate of exploitable human beings rather than a community of citizens. Alvan E. Bovay described a prerequisite for radical reform in reconciling the aspirations and concerns of the "Spanish, Indian, Negro, and Anglo-Saxon races" in the New World. Peter H. Clark spoke to a gathering that included many who had shared this view. "The doctrine of the universal brotherhood of man is the foundation of all good government in the world," he argued. "If you wish to abolish Slavery, you must combat it wherever it is found, wither in political parties, in churches, or in your own homes."[11]

For a brief period, Unionist radicalism threatened to integrate the maroon traditions into American experience. Even as Brown and his people created alliances with Ottawa Jones and Baptiste Peoria, John Beeson, a white farmer in Oregon, overtly advocated the resistance of various tribal groups in what became the "Rouge River War." Beeson took representatives of the Indians touring the country under the sponsorship of antislavery whites and blacks, culminating in a mass wartime meeting for native rights under the dome of the U.S. capitol. The Lincoln administration appointed an ad hoc commission, consisting of three critics of Indian policy, including Augustus Wattles, who had already advocated dual citizenship for native peoples and civic equality within the United States. One of his cousins from Nebraska joined W. A. Phillips, Hinton and others and raised a tri-racial Federal Union army on the western border. The last of the great Seminole war chiefs, Su-nuk-mik-ko (also known as Halpatter Micco or, among the whites, "Billy Bowlegs")—a man who had fought the U.S. to a standstill over many years back in Florida—took an officer's commission in its ranks and died in the service of the Union.

The antebellum settlement of Quindaro, Kansas on the Missouri River embodied this convergence. The population included Indians, who had originally owned the land and were not dispossessed. It became a conduit for escaped slaves heading north and white Free Staters coming into the territory, some of whom remained. One of its most prominent residents, Clarina I. H. Nichols, had joined the Wattles and other of John Brown's allies to found the territory's first woman's rights organization.

Too, leaders that had emerged from the women's conventions of the decade, such as Susan B. Anthony, Elizabeth C. Stanton, and Ernestine Rose had also participated in broader radical deliberations. In the wake of the war, Stone and Anthony forged a remarkably efficient organizing team. The postwar spread of the agitation for women's rights had deep abolitionist roots, particularly in that part of the movement concerned with politics and advocating a broad social program that included radical land reform and economic egalitarianism.

While many factors disinclined the Second American Revolution from meeting the radical aspirations it inspired, it marked a qualitative shift in American radical history. In organizational terms, the veteran American land reformers and the German émigrés formerly associated with Hugh Forbes re-established their alliance a decade later in the International Workingmen's Association. John Commerford first wrote Karl Marx on their behalf, and their ranks included most of those with whom he had worked for decades still in the land of the living. The Brotherhood of the Union directly contributed to the wartime emergence of the Union Leagues, which went south and became overtly radical largely in the African American political current, and provided some of the founders of the Knights of Labor.

Antebellum politics and political issues continued to inspire radical activism through the century. The "land question" became essential to the programs of groups as diverse as the Knight, the IWA, and the succession of independent political parties ranging from the early Republicans through the Greenbackers to the Populists. That rather mild latter-day land reformer Henry George wrote, "that absolute political equality does not in itself prevent the tendency to inequality involved in the private ownership of land." Wealth remained no less polarized in the U.S. because "simple citizens" rather than nobles controlled the "thousands of miles of railroad, millions of acres of land, the means of livelihood of great numbers of men; who name the governors of sovereign states as they name their clerks, choose senators as they choose attorneys, and whose will is as supreme with legislatures as that of a French king sitting in a bed of justice."[12] By then, the last of the old land reformers were holding the last of their gatherings as the "National Land Reform Association."

A number of them were in or around the emergence of distinct socialist parties in the 1870s. The list included prominent Fourierists such as John Orvis, Alcander Longley, and J. Homer Doucet, as well as veterans of abolitionism and land reform, such as Peter H. Clark and William West. Indeed, the story unfolded most clearly in their local communities.

For the first century of national existence, what proved to be the most effective radicalism fostered the movement of the most people on a principled basis, independent from the conservatizing entanglements with the institutional power structure. Indeed, the builders of a genuinely distinct and independent American Left paradoxically learned that radicalism, to be effective, could not be distinct and independent of the people it sought to serve.

Decades of experience had taught them that talk was ultimately cheap. The owners and rulers of the society prattle endlessly about democratic values, egalitarianism, and community, and a self-gratifying radicalism that ultimately did no more than talk would not suffice. Radicals not only act to promote such goals but cannot actually foster them without, in some small part, leading in demonstrating that such goals are practical and must be, in some important respect, implemented.

Serious radicalism does not even try to pull a movement out of thin air or build it to a blueprint. The women's movement posed an unarguably correct critique of the new United States and its civilization, but its founders had to take their concerns into movements around other issues, particularly the antislavery movement. Freethought and land reform offered a thoroughly principled—even revolutionary—perspective on the American experience, but their concerns mattered only in that adherents were willing to carry them into a broader movement hostile to—and resisting of—the constitutional and legal ownership of human beings.

Within the spectrum of legitimate, principled concerns, serious radicals learned the power of the people moving independently of the dead-end institutional channels of designated authority. The logic of mass self-organization naturally generated new layers of leadership, and expanded the power of the movement. In Kansas, that power had defeated Congress, the presidency, the Supreme Court, and the military.

Growing power carried extensive responsibilities, primarily to cultivate and sustain the process. That is, participants needed to keep the movement as massive and principled as possible, which meant avoiding the perennial systemic efforts to undercut its independence with electoral politics. Had the early movement sought to subvert human slavery by voting for the lesser evil proslavery candidates of the proslavery parties, they would have contributed to their own marginalization, and salved nothing but their own bruised sensibilities.

The weight of institutional power systemically offers a comfortingly symbolic assuagement without any substantive change. For this reason, if no other, radicalism offers no lessons that can be simply won and built upon. All need continual relearning, and a democracy systemically refreshed. There are no lessons of the past that are not lessons of the present. So, long after their death, John Brown and his men could inspire that second raid on Harpers Ferry.

No university rewarded Professor Libby any grants or chairs for his role in commemorating Harpers Ferry. Neither of the Tidds had survived the war. Libby had managed to survive the new history graduate program at the University of Wisconsin, where he impressed Frederick Jackson Turner enough to be kept on at Wisconsin. However, his peers saw his serious interest in science as a lack of focus on history, and his research focus on such subjects as the Greenback and Populist movements irritated them. Later, after exposing the plagiarism of two other historians, Libby would find himself driven out of his job at Wisconsin and forced to take a teaching post in North Dakota, where his compilation of Arikara versions of the Custer massacre pioneered the documentation of western history from an Indian perspective.[13] In so institutionally conservative a profession as history, Libby's being on the real cutting edge, by definition, left him on the margins of the field.

*   *   *

Like that handful of black and white admirers of the antebellum radicals working to disinter the bones of John Brown's men, radicals labor with no media fanfare, no fair recourse to the courts, and no grants. Metaphorically, they, too, may have to wait until nightfall and slip beyond the streetlights of Harpers Ferry, stumbling their own way through the darkness of the woods beyond sight of the town. When they relocated the spot they wanted, they put shovels into the muddy earth until they uncovered the crumbling bones of the executed raiders.

Notwithstanding a culture of intellectual arrogance and institutional neglect, the graveyards of the past remain as embattled and muddied as the present. It is, after all, part of the same living struggle that has continued.

Notes

Introduction

1. Judith Mulcahy, "James McCune Smith: The Communipaw Connection," *Nineteenth-Century Prose*, 31 (Fall 2007), pp. 349–58; Graham Russell Hodges, "Free People and Slaves, 1613–1664," in his *Roots and Branch: African Americans in New York and East Jersey* (Chapel Hill, NC: University of North Carolina Press, 1999), pp. 6–33.
2. *Maroon Societies*, ed. R. Price (3rd edition; Baltimore, MD: Johns Hopkins University Press, 1997). For a broader, Transatlantic context, see Peter Linebaugh and Marcus Rediker, *The Many-Headed Hydra: Sailors, Slaves, Commoners, and the Hidden History of the Revolutionary Atlantic* (Boston, MA: Beacon Press, 2000).
3. George Henry Evans in "Agrarian League," *Working Man's Advocate*, June 1, 1844, p. 1.

Chapter 1   Liberty: Eighteenth-Century Transatlantic Legacies and Challenges

1. *Familiar Letters of John Adams and His Wife Abigail Adams During the American Revolution*, ed. Charles Francis Adams (New York: Hurd & Houghton, 1876), pp. 262, 263 and 265; *Letters of Mrs. Adams, the Wife of John Adams* (3rd edition; Boston, MA: Charles C. Little & James Brown, 1841), vol. 1, pp. 109–10, reprinted in *The Spirit of Seventy-Six*, ed. Henry Steele Commager and Richard B. Morris (New York: Harper & Row, 1967), p. 787. See also Richard B. Morris, *Government and Labor in Early America* (2nd edition; New York: Columbia University Press, 1946), pp. 124–5; and, Mary Beth Norton's *Liberty's Daughters: the Revolutionary Experience of American Women, 1750–1800* (Boston, MA: Little, Brown and Company, 1980).
2. Edward Countryman, *A People in Revolution: The American Revolution and Political Society in New York, 1760–1790* (Baltimore, MD: Johns Hopkins University Press, 1981); Patricia U. Bonomi, *A Factious People: Politics and Society in Colonial New York* (New York: Columbia University Press, 1971); Paul A. Gilje, *The Road to Mobocracy: Popular Disorder in New York City, 1763–1834* (Chapel Hill, NC: Omohundro Institute of Early American History and Culture and the University of North Carolina Press, 1987).
3. Quoted in Edmund S. Morgan and Helen M. Morgan, *The Stamp Act Crisis: Prologue to Revolution* (rev. edition; New York: Norton, 1973), p. 237. On the Revolution, see Francis D. Cogliano, *Revolutionary America, 1763–1815: A*

Political History (3rd edition; New York: Routledge, 2017); Gordon S. Wood, *The Radicalism of the American Revolution* (New York: Vintage Books, 1992); and Staughton Lynd, *The Intellectual Origins of American Radicalism* (New York: Pantheon Books, 1968). On the artisans, see Howard B. Rock, *Artisans of the New Republic: the Tradesmen of New York City in the Age of Jefferson* (New York: New York University Press, 1979); Charles S. Olton, *Artisans for Independence: Philadelphia Mechanics and the American Revolution* (Syracuse, NY: Syracuse University Press, 1975); Richard W. Walsh, *Charleston's Sons of Liberty: A Study of the Artisans, 1763–1787* (Columbia, SC: University of South Carolina Press, 1959); Charles G. Steffen, *The Mechanics of Baltimore, MD: Workers and Politics in the Age of Revolution* (Urbana, IL: University of Illinois Press, 1984); and Jesse Lemisch, *Jack Tar vs. John Bull: The Role of New York's Seamen in Precipitating the Revolution* (New York: Garland Publishers, 1997).

4. On the rioting, see Pauline Maier, *From Resistance to Revolution: Colonial Radicals and the Development of American Opposition to Britain, 1765–1776* (New York: Alfred A. Knopf, 1972), pp. 51–60, 61–76; Pauline Maier, *The Old Revolutionaries: Political Lives in the Age of Samuel Adams* (2nd edition; New York: Vintage Books, 1982); and George P. Anderson, "Ebenezer Mackintosh: Stamp Act Rioter and Patriot" and "A Note on Ebenezer Mackintosh," *Colonial Social of Massachusetts, Publications*, 26 (1926–27), pp. 15–64, 348–61.

5. Gov. Francis Bernard, quoted in Morgan and Morgan, *The Stamp Act Crisis*, 171; Jonathan Boucher, *View of the Causes and Consequences of the American Revolution* (London: printed for G. G. and J. Robinson, Paternoster-Row, 1797), p. 309.

6. Mitch Kachun, *First Martyr of Liberty: Crispus Attucks in American Memory* (New York: Oxford University Press, 2017). See also W. Jeffrey Bolster, *Black Jacks: African American Seamen in the Age of Sail* (Cambridge, MA: Harvard University Press, 1997).

7. Staughton Lynd, "The Mechanics in New York Politics," *Labor History*, 5 (Winter 1964), p. 226. On specifics in the cities, see Gary B. Nash, *The Urban Crucible: Social Change, Political Consciousness, and the Origins of the American Revolution* (Cambridge, MA: Harvard University Press, 1979); and Gary B. Nash, *The Unknown American Revolution: The Unruly Birth of Democracy and the Struggle to Create America* (New York: Penguin, 2006). For comparative views of the Pennsylvania achievement, see Elisha P. Douglas, *Rebels and Democrats: the Struggle for Equal Political Rights and Majority Rule during the American Revolution* (Chapel Hill, NC: University of North Carolina Press, 1955).

8. David Freeman Hawke, "Dr. Thomas Young—Eternal Fisher in Troubled Waters: Notes for a Biography," *New York Historical Society Quarterly*, 64 (January 1970), pp. 9, 10, 11 and n, 13–14, 15, 16–18, 18–22; Maier, *The Old Revolutionaries*, pp. 116–18. On Allen, see Charles Jellison, *Ethan Allen: Frontier Rebel* (Taftsville, VT: Countryman Press, 1969); G. Adolf Koch, *Republican Religion: The American Revolution and the Cult of Reason* (2nd

edition; Gloucester, MA: Peter Smith, 1964), pp. 528–50.

For rural discontent, see Sung Bok Kim, *Landlord and Tenant in Colonial New York: Manorial Society, 1664–1775* (Chapel Hill, NC: University of North Carolina Press, 1978); and Staughton Lynd, *Class Conflict, Slavery, and the United States Constitution: Ten Essays* (Indianapolis, IN: Bobbs-Merrill, 1968).

9. Richard A. Ryerson, *The Revolution is Now Begun: the Radical Committees of Philadelphia, 1765–1776* (Philadelphia, PA: University of Pennsylvania Press, 1978); Steve Rosswurm, *Arms, Country, and Class: the Philadelphia Militia and "Lower Sort" During the American Revolution, 1775–1783* (New Brunswick, NJ: Rutgers University Press, 1990); David Freeman Hawke, *In the Midst of a Revolution* (Philadelphia, PA: University of Pennsylvania Press, 1961).

10. Paine has inspired a growing list of biographers, the most extensive and classic "movement" study being Moncure D. Conway's classic *The Life of Thomas Paine*, ed. Hypatia Bradlaugh Bonner (London: Watts, 1909), a one-volume edition that expanded parts of the original two-volume set (New York: G. P. Putnam's sons 1892). See also Eric Foner, *Tom Paine and Revolutionary America* (New York: Oxford University Press, 1976); and Eric Foner, *Thomas Paine and the Promise of America* (New York: Hill & Wang, 2005).

11. See Hawke, *In the Midst of a Revolution*, pp. 101, 102–4, 105, 106–7, 112–13.

12. On Young and the Congressional delegates, Hawke, "Dr. Thomas Young," pp. 22–4, 27–8, 29.

13. For this narrative of the Revolution in Pennsylvania, see the sources cited in notes 8 and 10 above.

14. Quoted Hawke, *In the Midst of a Revolution*, pp. 176–7.

15. Anonymous, *The People the Best Governors: Or a Plan of Government Founded on the Just Principles of Natural Freedom* [1776], reprinted in Frederick Chase, *A History of Dartmouth College and the Town of Hanover New Hampshire*, ed. John K. Lord (2 vols.; Cambridge: John Wilson & Son, 1891), vol. 1, p. 654.

16. Matt Bushnell Jones, *Vermont in the Making* (Cambridge, MA: Harvard University Press, 1939), pp. 341, 342, 346–51, 356; see also ibid., pp. 356–9, 360, 361, 362, 373, 375–81, 383n.; Hawke, "Dr. Thomas Young," p. 28n. For its subsequent course, see Randolph A. Roth, *The Democratic Dilemma: Religion, Reform, and the Social Order in the Connecticut River Valley of Vermont, 1790–1850* (New York: Cambridge University Press, 1987).

17. For an overview of the historians' debate over this, see Alfred F. Young and Gregory Nobles, *Whose American Revolution was It? Historians Interpret the Founding* (New York: New York University Press, 2011).

18. "An Address to the UNITED STATES in General, the LEGISLATURE of VIRGINIA in particular," *Virginia Gazette*, November 13, 1779; *The Journals of Each Provincial Congress of Massachusetts in 1774 and 1775 and of the Committee of Safety* (Boston, MA: Dutton & Wentworth for the state, 1838), 319. See also Bernard Mason, *The Road to Independence: The Revolutionary Movement in New York, 1773–1777* (Lexington, KY: University of Kentucky Press, 1966), pp. 244–49.

19. *Journals and Essays of John Woolman*, ed. Amelia M. Gummere (New York: The Macmillan Company, 1922), p. 403; "Queries and Remarks Respecting Alterations in the Constitution of Pennsylvania," and Franklin to Robert Morris, December 25, 1783, in *The Writings of Benjamin Franklin*, ed. Albert H. Smyth (10 vols; London: Macmillan & Co., 1905–7), vol. 10, pp. 158–9, and vol. 9, p. 138.

20. Rosswurm, *Arms, Country, and Class*, pp. 104, 195–6; Warren to Edmund Dana, March 19, 1766, in Richard Frothingham, *Life and Times of Joseph Warren* (Boston, MA: Little, Brown, 1865), pp. 20–21. For John Locke's primitive labor theory of value, see "ninety-nine hundredths are wholly to be put on the account of labour," *Two Treatises of Government*, ed. Thomas I. Cook (New York: Hafner Press, 1947), pp. 134, 141.

21. "An Address to the UNITED STATES in general, the LEGISLATURE of VIRGINIA in particular," *Virginia Gazette*, November 13, 1779, p. 1.

22. *Familiar Letters of John Adams and His Wife Abigail Adams During the American Revolution*, ed. Charles Francis Adams (New York: Hurd & Houghton, 1876), pp. 262, 263, 265; *Letters of Mrs. Adams, the Wife of John Adams* (3rd edition; Boston, MA: Charles C. Little & James Brown, 1841), vol. 1, pp. 109–10, reprinted in *The Spirit of Seventy-Six*, ed. Henry Steele Commager and Richard B. Morris (New York: Harper & Row, 1967), p. 787. See also Richard B. Morris, *Government and Labor in Early America* (2nd edition; New York: Columbia University Press, 1946), pp. 124–5; and Mary Beth Norton's *Liberty's Daughters: the Revolutionary Experience of American Women, 1750–1800* (Boston, MA: Little, Brown & Company, 1980).

23. Anonymous, *The People the Best Governors* [1776], 4, in Chase, *A History of Dartmouth College and the Town of Hanover*, 654; Richard B. Morris, "Labor and Mercantilism in the Revolutionary Era," in *The Era of the American Revolution*, ed. Richard B. Morris (New York: Harper & Row, 1939), pp. 105–10; "An Address to the UNITED STATES in general, the LEGISLATURE of VIRGINIA in particular," *Virginia Gazette*, November 13, 1779; and for a discussion of the proposal, see the issues of *Virginia Gazette* for December 11, 1779 and February 5, 1780.

24. Robert L. Brunhouse, *The Counter-Revolution in Pennsylvania* (New York: Octagon Books, 1971), p. 68; Thomas Paine, "To the People of America," in *The Complete Writings of Thomas Paine*, ed. Philip S. Foner (2 vols., New York: Citadel Press, 1945), vol. 2, p. 141, though see too pp. 171–6 on Wilson.

25. Supreme Executive Council Minutes, *Pennsylvania Colonial Records* (13 vols.; Harrisburg: Printed by T. Fenn & Co., 1831–53), vol. 11, pp. 664, 665.

26. Brunhouse, *The Counter-Revolution in Pennsylvania*, pp. 69–71; Morris, "Labor and Mercantilism," p. 114; Elias P. Oberholtzer, *Robert Morris* (New York: Macmillan & Co., 1903), pp. 51–6.

27. Paine, *Complete Writings*, vol. 2, pp. 1176–8 expresses his utter frustration with the Congress in May and June 1779. For this and the next two paragraphs, see Morris, "Labor and Mercantilism," 122, 135–6. See also Brunhouse, *The Counter-Revolution in Pennsylvania*, pp. 72–6.

28. Arthur Zilversmit, *The First Emancipation: the Abolition of Slavery in the North* (Chicago, IL: University of Chicago Press, 1967), pp. 122–35; Charles Royster, *A Revolutionary People at War: the Continental Army and American Character, 1775–1783* (Chapel Hill, NC: University of North Carolina Press, 1979).

29. Carl Van Doren, *Mutiny in January: The Story of a Crisis in the Continental Army* (New York: Viking Press, 1943). For a more general treatment of such behaviors on a much smaller scale, see John A. Nagy, *Rebellion in the Ranks: Mutinies of the American Revolution* (Yardley, PA: Westholme Publishing, 2008).

30. Van Doren, *Mutiny in January*, pp. 97, 45–6, 57–8. The chairman of the Board was English-born Sergeant John Williams; another Englishman, John "Macaroni Jack" Maloney of the artillery, whose wife and family were among the women and children travelling with the army; Daniel Connell of the Eleventh, William Bowzar, a quartermaster; and George Gonzall of the Second.

31. Van Doren, *Mutiny in January*, pp. 189–91, 64–7, 205–6, 208–9, 210, 211–12, 217–24. Leaders of the New Jersey Line had been: George Grant of the Third; Jonathan Nichols, John Minthorn and John Tuttle of the First; and David Gilmore (or Gilmour) of the Second.

32. For enlisted men later killed, with and without trials, see Van Doren, *Mutiny in January*, pp. 234–7, 250–57.

33. Woody Holton, *Abigail Adams: A Life* (New York: Free Press, 2009).

34. William Cooper Nell, *The Colored Patriots of the American Revolution: With Sketches of Several Distinguished Colored Persons: to which is Added a Brief Survey of the Condition and Prospects of Colored Americans* (Boston, MA: Robert F. Wallcut, 1855).

35. William L. Stone, *Border Wars of the American Revolution* (New York: A. L. Fowle, 1900); Alan Taylor, *The Divided Ground: Indians, Settlers, and the Northern Borderland of the American Revolution* (New York: Alfred A. Knopf, 2006); Rev. Eleazer Williams, "The Life of Colonel Louis Cook" [1851], Papers of Franklin B. Hough, Darren Bonaparte (trans.), New York State Archives, retrieved from www.wampumchronicles.com/colonellouis.html.

36. Allan D. Gaff, *Bayonets in the Wilderness: Anthony Wayne's Legion in the Old Northwest* (Norman, OK: University of Oklahoma Press, 2004); John Sudgen, *Blue Jacket: Warrior of the Shawnees* (Lincoln, NE: University of Nebraska Press, 2000); John F. Winkler, *Fallen Timbers, 1794: The U.S. Army's First Victory* (London: Osprey, 2013).

37. To Joseph Reed, December 16, 1780, quoted in Van Doren, *Mutiny in January*, p. 33.

38. Anonymous, *The People the Best Governors* [1776], reprinted in Chase, *A History of Dartmouth College and the Town of Hanover*, p. 659.

39. Raymond Walters, *Albert Gallatin: Jeffersonian Financier and Diplomat* (Pittsburgh, PA: University of Pittsburgh Press, 1969).

40. Thomas Paine, "Public Good: Being an Examination into the Claims of Virginia to the Vacant Western Territory and of the Right of the United States to the Same," in *Complete Writings*, vol. 2, 305, 329, 332.

Chapter 2   Equality: The Mandates of Community
and the Necessity of Expropriation

1. James Cheetham, *Life of Thomas Paine* (New York: Southwick & Pelsue for the Author, 1809), pp. 276–78.

2. George R. Minot, *The History of the Insurrection in Massachusetts, in the Year Seventeen Hundred and Eighty-Six, and Rebellion Consequent Thereon* (Freeport, NY: Knopf, 1970; reprinting the 2nd edition of 1810).

3. Staughton Lynd, "Abraham Yates's History of the Movement for the United States Constitution," in his *Class Conflict, Slavery, and the United States Constitution: Ten Essays* (Indianapolis, IN: Bobbs-Merrill, 1967), pp. 218–20, 227.

4. See Marion L. Starkey, *A Little Rebellion* (New York: Knopf, 1955), pp. 77, 153, 213–14; David P. Szatmary, *Shay's Rebellion: the Making of an Agrarian Insurrection* (Amherst, MA: University of Massachusetts Press, 1980); Leonard L. Richards, *Shays's Rebellion: The American Revolution's Final Battle* (Philadelphia, PA: University of Pennsylvania Press, 2002); Sean Condon, *Shays's Rebellion: Authority and Distress in Post-Revolutionary America* (Baltimore, MD: Johns Hopkins University Press, 2015).

5. See Thomas P. Slaughter, *The Whiskey Rebellion: Frontier Epilogue to the American Revolution* (New York: Oxford University Press, 1986); William Hogeland, *The Whiskey Rebellion: George Washington, Alexander Hamilton, and the Frontier Rebels Who Challenged America's Newfound Sovereignty* (New York: Scribner, 2006). For the ideological underpinnings of this dissonance, see Ann Fairfax Withington, *Towards a More Perfect Union: Virtue and the Formation of the American Republic* (Oxford: Oxford University Press, 1991); and Gordon S. Wood's overview of *The Radicalism of the American Revolution* (New York: Alfred A. Knopf, 1992).

6. On Brown, see *The Faith of Our Fathers: An Anthology Expressing the Aspirations of the American Common Man, 1790–1860*, ed. Irving Mark and Eugene L. Schwaab (New York: Alfred A. Knopf, 1952), pp. 42, 44–7; and James M. Smith, *Freedom's Fetters: the Alien and Sedition Laws and American Civil Liberties* (2nd edition; Ithaca, NY: Cornell University Press, 1966), pp. 257–70. On William Manning, see his *The Key of Libberty, Shewing the Causes why a Free Government has always Failed and a Remidy Against It* (Billerica, MA: Manning Association, 1922), pp. v, xii, vi, 3, 53, 51, 67–9, 65.

7. For a comparative approach, see Hugh McLeon, *Secularisation in Western Europe, 1848–1914* (New York: St. Martin's Press, 2000); and Moncure D. Conway, *The Life of Thomas Paine*, ed. Hypatia Bradlaugh Bonner (London: Watts, 1909), pp. 292, 296, 299, 301, 315, 325.

8. *Massachusetts Soldiers and Sailors of the Revolutionary War: A Compilation from the Archives* (17 vols.; Boston, MA: Wright and Potter Print. Co., 1896–1908), vol. 5, p. 595; Albert Post, *Popular Freethought in America, 1825–1850* (New York: Columbia University Press, 1943), p. 149; Conway, *The Life of Thomas Paine*, pp. 292, 296, 299, 301, 315, 325; Rocellus S. Guernsey, *New York City and*

Vicinity during the War of 1812 (2 vols.; New York, 1889–95), vol. 1, p. 443;
G. Adolf Koch, *Republican Religion: The American Revolution and the Cult of Reason* (2nd edition; Gloucester, MA: Peter Smith, 1964), p. 147.

9. *The Radical*, I (April 1841), p. 63. On Christian: Charles Christian, *A Brief Treatise on the Police of the City of New-York: By a Citizen* (New York, 1812), his *Notes on the Police of the City of New-York* (New York, 1813), and the *Military Minutes of the Council of Appointment of the State of New York, 1783–1821*, ed. Hugh Hastings (4 vols.; Albany, NY: New York State Historian, 1901–2), vol. 1, pp. 666, 923, vol. 2, 1158, 1298, 1643, 2203. Alexander Ming, much more modestly, gained enough status to hold the rank of captain; *Military Minutes*, vol. I, pp. 694, 817, vol. II, p. 1132.

10. Jeffrey S. Kahana, "*Imperium in Imperio* and the Political Origins of the American Labor Conspiracy Doctrine," *Law and Policy*, 30 (July 2008), pp. 364–84.

11. *Equality; or, A History of Lithconia* (2nd edition; Philadelphia, PA: Liberal Union, 1837), pp. 96, 97, 101, 102, 104. The reprinting of this 1802 work by the "Liberal Union" involved the circle involved in fostering the workers' movement in the city as well. Earlier attributed to Dr. James Reynolds. Michael Durey, "John Lithgow's Lithconia: The Making and Meaning of America's First 'Utopian Socialist' Tract," *The William and Mary Quarterly*, 49 (October 1992), pp. 675–94.

12. Amos Gilbert, "A Sketch of the Life of Thomas Skidmore," *Free Enquirer*, March 30, 1834. See also my compilation of his three articles of March 30, April 6 and 13 in Mark Lause, *The Life of Thomas Skidmore* (Chicago, IL: Charles H. Kerr, 1984), pp. 24–5; David Lee Clark, *Charles Brockden Brown, Pioneer Voice of America* (Durham, NC: Duke University Press, 1952); and Charles Brockden Brown, *Arthur Mervyn; or Memoirs of the Year 1793* (2 vols; 2nd edition; Philadelphia, PA: McKay, 1887), vol. 1, pp. 12–13, 22.

13. Maria Aletta Hulshoff, *Peace Republican's Manual or the French Constitution of 1793 and the Declaration of the Rights of Man and of Citizen … Extracts from Pieces Seized in Baboeuf's Rooms …* (New York: J. Tiebout & Sons, 1817), cited in R. B. Rose, *Gracchus Babeuf: the First Revolutionary Communist* (Stanford, CA: Stanford University Press, 1978), pp. 329, 403n.1. David Thompson, *The Babeuf Plot: the Making of a Republican Legend* (London: Kegan Paul, Trench, Trubner, 1947), p. 59 states that young Babeuf moved to the U.S., but see also Victor Adville *Histoire Gracchus Babeuf et du Babouvisme* (2 vols.; Paris: by the Author, 1884), vol. 1, pp. 342, 345–7.

14. James H. Billington, *Fire in the Minds of Men: Origins of the Revolutionary Faith* (New York: Basic Books, 1980), pp. 138–9, cites Follen's association with Buonarroti, and for his later abolitionist preoccupations see Charles Follen, *The Works of Charles Follen* (5 vols.; Boston, MA: Hilliard, Gray, and Company, 1841–2). On Gall, see Carl Stegmann and C. Hugo, *Handbuch des Socialismus* (Zurich: Verlag-Magazin, 1894), pp. 272–89. See also Adam Zamoyski, *Holy Madness: Romantics, Patriots, and Revolutionaries, 1776–1871* (Harmondsworth: Penguin Books, 2001).

15. David Ricardo, *On the Principles of Political Economy* (Harmondsworth: Penguin Books, 1971), pp. 55–6 (1st American edition: Georgetown, 1819). See also Patrick Collquhoun's *Treatise of the Wealth, Power, and Resources of the British Empire* (London: Joseph Mawman, 1814), and Jamie L. Bronstein, *Land Reform and Working-Class Experience in Britain and the United States, 1800–1862* (Stanford, CA: Stanford University Press, 1999).

16. Stewart, *The Moral State of Nations, or Travels Over the Most Interesting Parts of the Globe and The Apocalypse of Nature* (Middletown, OH: George H. Evans, 1837), originally 1790. See also William Thomas Brande, *The Life and Adventures of the Celebrated Walking Stewart: Including His Travels in the East Indies, Turkey, Germany, & America* (London: E. Wheatley, 1822); Gregory Claeys, "'The Only Man of Nature That Ever Appeared in the World': 'Walking' John Stewart and the Trajectories of Social Radicalism, 1790–1822," *Journal of British Studies*, 53 (2014), pp. 1–24; and Bertrand Harris Bronson, "Walking Stewart," *Essays and Studies*, xiv (Berkeley, CA: University of California Press, 1943), pp. 123–55.

17. Thomas Spence, *The Real Rights of Man: A Lecture Read at the Philosophical Society in Newcastle on November 8th, 1775*, reprinted in *The Pioneers of Land Reform: Thomas Spence, William Ogilvie, Thomas Paine*, with an introduction by Max Beer (London: Bell, 1920; New York: Alfred A. Knopf, 1920), which also reprints William Ogilvie, *An Essay on the Right of Property in Land* (London: J. Walter, [1782?]). Helene Zahler, *Eastern Workingmen and National Land Policy, 1829–1862* (New York: Columbia University Press, 1941), p. 22f, citing Olive Rudkin, *Thomas Spence and His Connections* (London: n.p., 1927), p. 184. Erma S. Griffith sought to find a connection between the Evans family and Spence, "Requests Early Family Data," April 2, 1945, *Binghamton Press*, April 5, 1945, p. 6. On the other hand, Malcolm Chase, *"The Peoples' Farm: English Radical Agrarianism* (Oxford: Clarendon Press, 1988) mentions McDiarmid and Warden.

18. See *Daily National Intelligencer*, December 1, 1824, quoted in Arthur E. Bestor, *Backwoods Utopias: The Sectarian and Owenite Phases of Communitarian Socialism in America: 1663–1829* (Philadelphia, PA: University of Pennsylvania Press, 1950), p. 96; this work included a pioneering exploration of the movement before Owen's arrival. See also A. L. Morton, *The Life and Ideas of Robert Owen* (New York: International Publishers, 1969), p. 75.

19. *National Intelligencer*, May 29, 1819. Joseph Gales, Jr. regularly published such issues, including the *Life of Theobald Wolfe Tone, Founder of the United Irish Society, and Adjutant General and Chef de Brigade in the Service of the French and Batavian Republics* (2 vols.; Washington, DC: Gales & Seaton, 1826).

20. Since the pioneering work of Edward Deming Andrews, the Shakers have inspired a small library of work, perhaps most interestingly around the peculiar importance of women in the shaping and leading of the group.

21. On Dorsey, see *History and Biographical Cyclopaedia of Butler County, Ohio* (Cincinnati, OH: Western Biographical Publishing Co., 1882), pp. 60–61; Miami University, *General Catalogue of the Graduates ... 1809–1909* (Oxford,

OH: Miami University, 1910), p. xvii; Harry W. Newman, *Anne Arundel Gentry* (Baltimore, MD: Lord Baltimore Press, 1933), p. 19. Also William Ludlow, *Belief of the Rational Brethren of the West* (Cincinnati, OH: for the Society, 1819), and Bestor, *Backwoods Utopias*, pp. 207–8. See also John F. C. Harrison, *Robert Owen and the Owenite Movement in Britain and America: The Quest for the New Moral World* (London: Routledge & Kegan Paul, 1969), pp. 107, 168.

22. Captain Adam Seaborn's *Symzonia* (New York: J. Seymour, 1820), reprinted with J. O. Bailey's introduction in a new edition (Gainesville, FL: Scholars' Facsimiles & Reprints, 1965). Scholars have challenged the old attribution to Symmes himself: "The Authorship of Symzonia," *Science-Fiction Studies*, 3 (March 1976), pp. 98–9; Hans-Joachim Lang and Benjamin Lease, "The Authorship of Symzonia: The Case for Nathaniel Ames," *New England Quarterly*, 48 (June 1975), pp. 241–52; and Francis B. Heitman, *Historical Register and Dictionary of the United States Army* (Washington, DC: Govt. Print Office, 1903).

23. Bestor, *Backwoods Utopias*, pp. 97–100, 104. On Raymond, see David Harris, *Socialist Origins in the United States: American Forerunners of Marx, 1817–1832* (Assen: Van Gorcum & Comp., 1966), pp. 20–33.

24. *Altruism and Idealism: Notes and Queries: A Monthly of History, Folk-Lore, Mathematics, Literature, Art, Arcane Studies, etc.* (Manchester, NH: S. C. and L. M. Gould, 1900), vol. 18, p. 159, which also described him as "a Protestant Irishman of culture." War Office, September 18, 1802, *Cobbett's Weekly Political Register* [London], 2 (September 25, 1802), p. 382; Martin R. Andrews, *History of Marietta and Washington County, Ohio* (Chicago, IL: Biographical Pub. Co., 1902), p. 177. Edward Postlethwayt Page to Thomas Jefferson, January 10, 1809, Thomas Jefferson Papers Series 1, General Correspondence, 1651–1827, Library of Congress. Page's publications are too copious to cite, but can be found readily enough today on World Cat. Andrews, *History of Marietta*, p. 176.

25. R. Birkbeck, *The Birkbecks of Westmorland and Their Descendants* (London, privately printed, 1900); G. Flower, *History of the English Settlement in Edwards Co., Ill* (Chicago, IL: Fergus Printing Co.1882); T. C. Pease, *The Frontier State 1818–48* (Chicago, IL: McClurg, 1922).

26. Cornelius C. Blatchley, *Some Causes of Popular Poverty, Derived from the Enriching Nature of Interests, Rents, Duties, Inheritances, and Church Establishments, Investigated in their Principles and Consequences, and Agreement with Scripture*, in Thomas Branagan, *The Pleasures of Contemplation, being an Investigation of the Harmonies, Beauties, and Benefits of Nature ...* (2nd edition; Philadelphia, PA: for S. Eastwick, 1818), pp. 176, 205, 201; and Harris, *Socialist Origins in the United States*, 20–33. For background, the latter work also discusses Raymond, Byllesby, Maclure, and Skidmore.

27. Murray N. Rothbard, *The Panic of 1819: Reactions and Policies* (New York: Columbia University Press, 1962), p. 142.

28. Paul Brown, the author of *Disquisition on Faith* (Washington, DC: for the Author, 1822) and *An Inquiry concerning the Nature, End, and Practicabil-*

ity of a Course of Philosophical Education (Washington, DC: for the Author, 1822), encountered Blatchley's association as early as 1819, according to his own report on *Twelve Months in New Harmony: Presenting a Faithful Account of the Principal Occurrences which Have Taken Place there within that Period …* (Cincinnati, OH: William H. Woodward, 1827), p. 4. On Huestis, see Mark Lause, *Some Degree of Power: From Hired Hand to Union Craftsman in the Preindustrial American Printing Trades, 1778–1815* (Fayetteville, AR: University of Arkansas Press, 1991), pp. 97, 137, 138, 142, 143, 163, 210n.14, 222n.11.

29. *The Correspondent*, 1 (April 14, 1827), pp. 1, 3 (January 26, 1828), pp. 5–9, and (February 2, 1824), p. 24. For meetings of printers and carpenters at "Harmony Hall," see New York Typographical Society, Ms Minutes, 1809–1816 in Special Collections, Milton S. Eisenhower Library, Johns Hopkins University, and the *American Citizen*, May 23, June 23, 1810. The explosion of freethought in the 1820s was not without some precedents in the intervening years. Shortly after Paine's death, his New York City followers had launched the *Theophilanthropist*, a monthly journal, but by late 1811 it was gone.

30. J. Percy Moore, "William Maclure—Scientist and Humanist," *Proceedings of the American Philosophical Society*, 91 (August 1947), p. 247; Gerald Lee Gutek, *Joseph Neef: The Americanization of Pestalozzianism* (Tuscaloosa, AL: University of Alabama Press, 1978); Charles W. Hackensmith, *Biography of Joseph Neef, Educator in the Ohio Valley, 1809–1854* (New York: Carlton Press, 1973); Patricia Tyson Stroud, *Thomas Say: New World Naturalist* (Philadelphia, PA: University of Pennsylvania Press, 1992); Josephine Mirabella Elliott, *Charles-Alexandre Lesueur: Premier Naturalist and Artist* (New Harmony, IN: the Author, 1999).

31. Gutek, *Joseph Neef*; Charles W. Hackensmith, *Biography of Joseph Neef, Educator in the Ohio Valley, 1809–1854* (New York: Carlton Press, 1973); Patricia Tyson Stroud, *Thomas Say: New World Naturalist* (Philadelphia, PA: University of Pennsylvania Press, 1992); Josephine M. Elliott and Jane T. Johansen, *Charles-Alexandre Lesueur: Premier Naturalist and Artist* (New Harmony, IN: the authors, 1999); Marie D. Fretageot to William Maclure, Philadelphia, March 25, 1824, cited in Bestor, *Backwoods Utopias*, p. 100.

32. Shortly after Gates's paper, the *Liberal*, another short-lived Deist paper operated. J. Thomas Scharf and Thompson Westcott, *History of Philadelphia, 1609–1884* (Philadelphia, PA: L. H. Everts & Co., 1884), pp. 1990, 1991.

33. Don Blair, *The New Harmony Story* (New Harmony, IN: New Harmony Publication Committee, 1967). See also G. B. Lockwood, *The New Harmony Communities* (Marion, IN: Chronicle Co., 1902).

34. Robert Dale Owen spoke at Stillwell's farm during his first term in the Indiana legislature. George B. Lockwood, *The New Harmony Movement* (New York: D. Appleton & Co., 1907), p. 342; John C. Fory, *Correspondent*, I (July 7, 1827), p. 399; *Daily Sentinel*, July 9, 23, 1830; Vital Statistics of the Workingmen's Institute, New Harmony, cited in James J. Martin, *Men Against the State: the Expositors of Individual Anarchism in America, 1827–1908* (3rd edition; Colorado Springs, CO: Ralph Myles Publisher, 1970), p. 39f.

35. Robert Dale Owen, *Threading My Way: An Autobiography* (New York: G. W. Carleton & Co.; London: Trübner & Co., 1874), pp. 265–6, 267; E. P. Page to Jefferson, May 10, June 3, 1820, February 18, 1821, in Thomas Jefferson Papers, Library of Congress; *The Correspondent*, 3 (April 5, 1828), pp. 173–4; Bestor, *Backwoods Utopias*, pp. 101, 104; Andrews, *History of Marietta*, p. 176; quoted from the Ohio *American Friend*, March 12, 1828 in the New York *Correspondent*, 3 (April 5, 1828) 173.

36. Harrison, *Robert Owen and the Owenite Movement*, and his *Robert Owen and the Owenites in Britain and America* (New York: Taylor & Francis, 2009). Bestor, *Backwoods Utopias*, pp. 94, 99 pointed out that the American tracts "reached a humbler audience" than that of Owen, who "sought to reach the influential few rather than the many."

37. Wright quoted in A. J. G. Perkins and Teresa Wolfson, *Frances Wright, Free Enquirer: the Study of A Temperament* (New York: Harper & Bros., 1939), p. 201; Richard William Leopold, *Robert Dale Owen: A Biography* (Cambridge, MA: Harvard University Press, 1940; reprinted New York: Octagon Books, 1969).

38. The *Disseminator* and its successor, the *Disseminator of Useful Knowledge*, published much of Maclure, collecting scores of these essays in two volumes of his *Opinions on Various Subjects, Dedicated to the Industrious Producers* (2 vols.; New Harmony, IN: for the Author, 1831), which also included some essays censored by the authorities while he had lived in Paris and later published in the *New Harmony Gazette*. See also Jeffrey Douglas, "William Maclure and the New Harmony Working Men's Institute," *Libraries and Culture*, 26 (1991), pp. 402–14.

39. Elfrieda Lang, "The Inhabitants of New Harmony According to the Federal Census of 1850," *Indiana Magazine of History*, 42 (December, 1946), pp. 355–94. For a survey of the Owenite and earlier communities, religious and secular, see Robert S. Fogarty, *Dictionary of American Communal and Utopian History* (Westport, CT: Greenwood Press, 1980).

40. Richard Drinnon, *White Savage: The Case of John Dunn Hunter* (New York: Schocken, 1972); Dianna Everett, *The Texas Cherokees: A People between Two Fires, 1819–1840* (Norman, OK: University of Oklahoma Press, 1990).

41. Brown's *Twelve Months in New Harmony* came after his *Disquisition on Faith* and *An Enquiring concerning the Nature, End, and Practicability of a Course of Philosophical Education* (Washington, DC: J. Gideon, 1822).

42. William Bailie, *Josiah Warren: The First American Anarchist* (Boston, MA: Small, Maynard & Co., 1906); Martin, *Men Against the State*, pp. 8–106.

43. John Gray, *A Lecture on Human Happiness* (London: Sherwood, Jones, & Co, 1825; Philadelphia, PA: J. Coates, Jr., 1826), pp. 13, 34, 15, 69, 22. See also *Preamble and Constitution of the Friendly Association for Mutual Interests* (Philadelphia, PA: The Assoc., 1826); and Louis Arky, "The Mechanics Union of Trade Associations and the Formation of the Philadelphia Workingmen's Movement," *Pennsylvania Magazine of History and Biography*, 76 (April 1952), pp. 145–7. Owen introduced the ideas of William Thompson and Thomas

Hodskin. See Anthony F. C. Wallace, *Rockdale: The Growth of an American Village in the Early Industrial Revolution* (New York: Alfred A. Knopf, 1978), p. 287.

44. Wallace, *Rockdale*, p. 287. On Peter Kaufmann, see Loyd D. Easton, *Hegel's First American Followers: The Ohio Hegelians—John B. Stallo, Peter Kaufmann, Moncure Conway, and Aug. Willich, with Key Writings* (Athens, OH: Ohio University Press; Toronto: Copp Clark. 1967), pp. 95–122. The Valley Forge group seems to have moved to Ohio, as did Kaufmann; see the photocopy of the minutes of the Friendly Association for Mutual Interests Records at Kendal, Ohio, 1826–1829, Ohio Historical Society, Columbus, OH.

45. Andrews, *History of Marietta*, p. 176; *Altruism and Idealism*, vol. 18, p. 159; Page to James Gordon Bennett, February 19, 1846 (contents posted when sold on eBay by jkpaper27305, Bay Harbor Islands, FL).

46. Samuel Rezneck, "The Depression of 1819–1822: A Social History," *American Historical Review*, 39 (October 1933), p. 31. See also Rothbard, *The Panic of 1819*, pp. 179–80.

47. For Houston and Jennings, see Perkins and Wolfson, *Frances Wright, Free Enquirer*, pp. 154, 200, 201–3, 259; Harrison, *Robert Owen and the Owenite Movement*, p. 167.

48. For my assessment of Evans and the citing of earlier work on his background, see Mark Lause, *Young America: Land, Labor, and the Republican Community* (Urbana, IL: University of Illinois Press, 2005).

49. On Mack and Searing, see Lause, *Some Degree of Power*, pp. 164–8, 187–8; "Dialogue" and "Journeymen Tailors," *Museum and Independent Corrector*, May 14, July 16, 1824.

50. *The Correspondent*, 2 (January 19, 1828), pp. 401–2. For Evans on his housekeeping, see "Erratum," *Young America*, September 20, 1845.

Chapter 3   Solidarity: Coalescing a Mass Resistance

1. *The Confessions of Nat Turner ... Acknowledged by Him to be such ... Nov. 5, 1831* (Baltimore, MD: Thomas R. Gray, 1831), pp. 10, 11. See also David F. Allmendinger Jr., *Nat Turner and the Rising in Southampton County* (Baltimore, MD: Johns Hopkins University Press, 2014), pp. 21–2. For Evans's editorial in his *Daily Sentinel*, September 17, 1831, see *Nat Turner*, ed. Eric Foner (Englewood Cliffs, NJ: Prentice-Hall, 1971), pp. 76–7.

2. See *American Citizen*, April 10, 1809, cited in Mark Lause, *Some Degree of Power: From Hired Hand to Union Craftsman in the Preindustrial American Printing Trades, 1778–1815* (Fayetteville, AR: University of Arkansas Press, 1991), pp. 121, 213n.28. Bruce Laurie offers an excellent overview of the transformation in *Artisans into Workers: Labor in Nineteenth Century America* (New York: Hill & Wang, 1989).

3. For this account of the Philadelphia movement, see Louis Arky, "The Mechanics Union of Trade Associations and the Formation of the Philadelphia Working-

men's Movement," *Pennsylvania Magazine of History and Biography*, 76 (April 1952), p. 144; Bruce Laurie, *Working People of Philadelphia, 1800–1850* (Philadelphia, PA: Temple University Press, 1980); Edward Pessen, *Most Uncommon Jacksonians: The Radical Leaders of the Early Labor Movement* (Albany, NY: State University of New York Press, 1967), pp. 14–15, 35–6, 75–8, 80–85, 91–3, William A. Sullivan, *The Industrial Worker in Pennsylvania, 1800–1840* (Harrisburg, PA: Pennsylvania Historical & Museum Commission, 1955); Philip S. Foner, *History of the Labor Movement in the United States, Volume 1: From Colonial Times to the Founding of the American Federation of Labor* (New York: International Publishers, 1947), pp. 103–4, 127–9, 165; Helen L. Sumner in *History of Labour in the United States*, ed. John R. Commons, David J. Saposs, Helen L. Sumner, E. B. Mittelman, Henry Elmer Hoagland, John B. Andrews, Selig Perlman, Don D. Lescohier, Elizabeth Brandeis, and Philip Taft (2nd edition; 4 vols.; New York: Macmillan, 1947), vol. 1, pp. 167–332; and *A Documentary History of American Industrial Society*, ed. John R. Commons, Ulrich B. Phillips, Eugene A. Gilmore, Helen L. Sumner, and John B. Andrews, with preface by Richard T. Ely and introduction by John B. Clark (10 vols., reprinted; New York: Russell & Russell, 1958), vol. 5, pp. 80–84.

4. Philip S. Foner, *William Heighton: Pioneer Labor Leader of Jacksonian Philadelphia* (New York: International Publishers, 1991). On Dubois, see Lause, *Some Degree of Power*, pp. 143, 221–2n.10.

5. *An Address, Delivered before the Mechanics and Working Classes Generally, of the City and County of Philadelphia, At the Universalist Church, in Callowhill Street, on Wednesday Evening, Nov. 21, 1827, By the Unlettered Mechanic* (Philadelphia, PA: Printed at the Office of the Mechanics' Gazette, 1827). See also Owen's *Address Delivered by Robert Owen … at the Franklin Institute in Philadelphia … June 25th, 1827* (Philadelphia, PA: M. T. C. Gould, 1827).

6. Quoted in *History of Labour in the United States*, ed. John R. Commons, David J. Saposs, Helen L. Sumner, E. B. Mittelman, Henry Elmer Hoagland, John B. Andrews, Selig Perlman, Don D. Lescohier, Elizabeth Brandeis, and Philip Taft (2nd edition; 4 vols.; New York: Macmillan, 1947), vol. 1, pp. 188–9; *An Address, Delivered Before the Mechanics and Working Classes Generally*, p. 12. *An Address … before the Mechanics and Working Classes* had been printed at the office of the *Mechanics' Gazette*, which had evolved from the *Journeyman Mechanic's Advocate*. Preamble to the MUTA constitution reprinted in Commons et al., *Documentary History of American Industrial Society*, vol. 5, pp. 84–90. See also Nathan Fine, *Labor and Farm Parties in the United States, 1828–1928* (New York, 1928).

7. Commons et al., *Documentary History of American Industrial Society*, vol. 5, pp. 91–2.

8. By June, several hundred carpenters had won the ten-hour day and issued an Address encouraging others to maintain their cause. By November 1829, the number of dues-paying trade unions affiliated to the Mechanics' Union had dropped from fifteen to four and it adjourned *sine die*.

9. The Union Benevolent Society of Journeymen Brushmakers pledged its 113 members to the party and formed its own campaign committee.

10. On Baltimore, see Arky, "The Mechanics Union of Trade Associations," p. 154n. Milton J. Nodworny, "New Jersey Working Men and the Jacksonians," *Proceedings of the New Jersey Historical Society*, 67 (1949), pp. 185–98.

11. James J. Martin, *Men Against the State: The Expositors of Individualist Anarchism in America, 1827–1908* (DeKalb, IL: Adrian Allen Associates, 1953), pp. 4–8, with the exposition of his ideas and career on pp. 8–106.

12. John F. C. Harrison, *Robert Owen and the Owenite Movement in Britain and America: The Quest for the New Moral World* (London: Routledge & Kegan Paul, 1969), p. 48. See also Langdon Byllesby, *Observations on the Sources and Effects of Unequal Wealth; with Propositions toward Remedying the Disparity of Profit in Pursuing the Arts of Life, and Establishing Security in Individual Prospects and Resources* (New York: Lewis J. Nichols, 1826; reprinted New York: Russell & Russell, 1961).

13. *Correspondent*, 4 (December 20, 1828), pp. 369–70. Fay also served as the New York agent of the *Mechanics' Free Press*, starting with the issue of July 19, 1828. On Conrade, see Charles Sotheran, *Horace Greeley and Other Pioneers of American Socialism* (2nd edition; New York: Haskell House Publishers, 1915), pp. 102–3.

14. See also Horace Secrist, the Anti-Auction Movement and the New York City Workingmen's Party, *Transactions of the Wisconsin Academy of Sciences, Arts, and Letters*, 17: Part 1 (1911), pp. 149–66; New York *American*, September 18, October 15, 1828. See also the chapters on the Workingmen's party in Walter Hugins, *Jacksonian Democracy and the Working Class: A Study of the New York Workingmen's Movement, 1829–1837* (Stanford, CA: Stanford University Press, 1960), pp. 11–23; Pessen, *Most Uncommon Jacksonians*, pp. 9–33, and Sean Wilentz, *Chants Democratic: New York City and the Rise of the American Working Class, 1788–1850* (Oxford: Oxford University Press, 1984), pp. 173–217.

15. Robert Dale Owen to the [Washington, DC] *Madisonian*, February 13, 1838, p. 3; Evans, "History of the Origin and Progress of the Working Men's Party in New York," *The Radical*, 2 (January 1842), p. 1.

16. Amos Gilbert, "A Sketch of the Life of Thomas Skidmore," *Free Enquirer*, April 13, 1834. Gilbert's series of three articles in the issues of March 30, April 6 and 13, reissued these with my introduction and annotation as Gilbert's *The Life of Thomas Skidmore* (Chicago, IL: Charles H. Kerr, 1984), pp. 24–7, 74. See also *Muster Rolls of the Soldiers of the War of 1812: Detached from the Militia of North Carolina in 1812 and 1814* (Raleigh, NC: C. C. Raboteau, 1851). On the dry goods association, see *Nile's Weekly Register*, 21 (October 13, 1821), p. 103, and Rothbard, *The Panic of 1819*, pp. 179–80.

17. For his telescope letters, see Skidmore to Clinton, August 22, 1822 in Letterbook X, No. 53, DeWitt Clinton Papers, Manuscript Collections, Columbia University Library; Skidmore to Jefferson, August 18, 1822, and Jefferson to Skidmore, August 29, 1822, Thomas Jefferson Papers, Library of Congress.

18. Thomas Skidmore, *The Rights of Man to Property! Being a Proposition to Make it Equal Among the Adults of the Present Generation: And to Provide for its Equal Transmission to Every Individual of Each Succeeding Generation, on Arriving at the Age of Maturity; Addressed to the Citizens of New-York, Particularly, and to the People of other States and Nations, Generally* (New York: Alexander Ming, 1829). Perhaps, too, the presence among Owenite sympathizers of the Wilmington industrialist Thomas Gilpin may have inspired little confidence in the capacity of Owen's followers for ushering in the new moral world. Anthony F. C. Wallace, *Rockdale: The Growth of an American Village in the Early Industrial Revolution* (New York: Alfred A. Knopf, 1978), pp. 284–5.

19. John Bach McMaster, *A History of the People of the United States, from the Revolution to the Civil War* (2nd edition; 8 vols.; New York, 1913), vol. 5, pp. 101–2. Freethinkers and Owenites associated with the movement include Henry A. Fay, George Anderson, John M. Bruce, John C. Fory, William F. Kells, Frances Pares, Solomon Hewes Sanborn, Thomas George Spear, and Thomas Hertell, as well as John Ditchett, Benjamin Offen, and James B. Sheys.

20. Hanes Walton, Jr. *The Negro in Third Party Politics* (Philadelphia, PA: Dorrance, 1969), p. 7, citing Dixon Fox's "The Negro Vote in Old New York," *Political Science Quarterly*, 32 (January, 1917), p. 264.

21. On Townsend, see Lause, *Some Degree of Power*, pp. 143, 144, 204n.38, 222–3n.11.

22. Both the *Working Man's Advocate* and the *Evening Journal* covered Skidmore's activities, but no copy of his *Friends of Equal Rights* has been located.

23. Jabez D. Hammond described the *Journal* faction's allies as many of them zealous Clay men. *History of Political Parties in the State of New-York, from the Ratification of the Federal Constitution, to Dec., 1840*, ed. Jabez D. Hammond (4th edition; 2 vols.; Syracuse, NY: Hall, Mills, 1852), vol. 2, pp. 330–33.

24. George Henry Evans, "Man's Inalienable Right to Land," *The Radical*, 1 (April 1841), p. 52.

25. Stephen B. Oates, *The Fires of Jubilee: Nat Turner's Fierce Rebellion* (New York: Harper Perennial, 1990); *Nat Turner: A Slave Rebellion in History and Memory*, ed. Kenneth S. Greenberg (Oxford: Oxford University Press, 2003); David F. Allmendinger, *Nat Turner and the Rising in Southampton County* (Baltimore, MD: Johns Hopkins University Press, 2014); Patrick H. Breen, *The Land Shall Be Deluged in Blood: A New History of the Nat Turner Revolt* (Oxford: Oxford University Press, 2015); and Thomas R. Gray, *The Confessions of Nat Turner, the Leader of the Late Insurrections in Southampton, Va.* (Baltimore, MD: Lucas & Deaver, 1831), fictionalized by William Stryon, *The Confessions of Nat Turner* (New York: Random House, 1993).

26. J. L. Landers, "Traditions of African American freedom and community in Spanish Colonial Florida," in *The African American Heritage of Florida*, ed. D. R. Colburn and J. L. Landers (Gainesville, FL: University Press of Florida, 1995), pp. 17–41; Kenneth W. Porter, *The Black Seminoles: History of a Freedom-seeking People*, revised and ed. by A. M. Amos and T. P. Senter (Gainesville, FL: University Press of Florida, 1996); K. Mulroy, *Freedom on*

the Border. The Seminole Maroons in Florida, the Indian Territory, Coahuila, and Texas (Lubbock, TX: Texas Tech University Press, 1993).

27. Robert L. Hall's "Eleazer Williams, 'Mohawk Between Two Worlds'," *Voyageur: Northeast Wisconsin's Historical Review*, 19 (Summer/Fall 2002), retrieved from www.uwgb.edu/wisfrench/library/articles/eleazer.htm.

28. Byrdsall became an early historian of the movement with his *The History of the Loco-Foco or Equal Rights Party* (New York: Clement & Packard, 1842).

29. On slavery, see Skidmore, *The Rights of Man to Property!* 27, 54–5, 159, 270; Evans's editorial in his *Daily Sentinel*, September 17, 1831, reprinted in *Nat Turner*, ed. Eric Foner (Englewood Cliffs, NJ: Prentice-Hall, 1971), pp. 76–7.

30. Luther, *An Address on the Origins and Progress of Avarice* (Boston, MA: the Author, 1834), pp. 38–40; Lewis Masquerier's lectures in the John A. Lant Papers, his "Politicology" essay appended to his *Sociology* (New York: the Author, 1877); and "A Stray Leaf from a Modern Dictionary," Ann Arbor *The Signal of Liberty*, November 11, 1844, p. 112.

31. Gary Kulik, "Pawtucket Village and the Strike of 1824: The Origins of Class Conflict in Rhode Island," *Radical History Review*, 17 (Spring 1978), pp. 5–38.

32. Frances Wright, "The People at War," *Free Enquirer*, November 27, 1830, p. 38, in Commons et al., *Documentary History of American Industrial Society*, vol. 5, p. 178.

33. Ibid.

Chapter 4   The Movement Party: Beyond the Failures of Civic Ritual

1. Walter Hugins, *Jacksonian Democracy and the Working Class: A Study of the New York Workingmen's Movement, 1829–1837* (Stanford, CA: Stanford University Press, 1960), pp. 29–30; Edward Pessen, *Most Uncommon Jacksonians: The Radical Leaders of the Early Labor Movement* (Albany, NY: State University of New York Press, 1967), pp. 95–7, 98; Sean Wilentz, *Chants Democratic: New York City and the Rise of the American Working Class, 1788–1850* (Oxford: Oxford University Press, 1984), pp. 292–4; Philip S. Foner, *History of the Labor Movement in the United States, Volume 1: From Colonial Times to the Founding of the American Federation of Labor* (New York: International Publishers, 1947), pp. 143–66. The elected officers of the mass meeting included former Workies Edward J. Webb and John Windt, the latter also being a prominent freethinker and president of the New York Typographical Association.

2. "The Times," "The Times and Mr. Carr," and "Ninth Ward," *The Man*, May 21 (p. 2), 22 (pp. 1–2), December 22 (p. 1), 1834.

3. For a concise overview of "The Trades' Union Movement," see Edward B. Mittelman in *History of Labour in the United States*, ed. John R. Commons, David J. Saposs, Helen L. Sumner, E. B. Mittelman, Henry Elmer Hoagland, John B. Andrews, Selig Perlman, Don D. Lescohier, Elizabeth Brandeis, and Philip Taft (2nd edition; 4 vols.; New York: Macmillan, 1947), vol. 1, pp. 335–73, 373–471; Foner, *History of the Labor Movement in the United States*, vol. 1, pp. 97–120; *A*

Documentary History of American Industrial Society, ed. John R. Commons et al. (10 vols., reprinted; New York: Russell & Russell, 1958), vol. 5, pp. 203–322, 325–92.

4. In addition to previously cited material, see Arthur M. Schlesinger, Jr., *The Age of Jackson* (Boston, MA: Little, Brown & Co., 1945), pp. 258, 261, 261n., 407; Helene Zahler, *Eastern Workingmen and National Land Policy* (New York: Columbia University Press, 1941), pp. 103–4, 172f; Foner, *History of the Labor Movement in the United States*, vol. 1, pp. 130, 151; Lewis Masquerier, *Sociology* (New York: the Author, 1877), pp. 102, 125. This was several years before the 1842 ruling that trade unionism in itself, did not constitute a criminal conspiracy. Alfred S. Konesfky, "As Best to Subserve Their Own Interests: Lemuel Shaw, Labor Conspiracy, and Fellow Servants," *Law and History Review*, 7 (1989), pp. 219–40.

5. Carl Gersung, "Seth Luther—the Road from Chepachet," *Rhode Island History*, 30 (1974), pp. 47–55; Arthur B. Darling, "The Working Men's Party in Massachusetts, 1833–1834," *American Historical Review*, 29 (1923), pp. 81–7. See also Tom Juravich, William F. Hartford and James R. Green, *Commonwealth of Toil: Chapters in the History of Massachusetts Workers and Their Unions* (Amherst, MA: University of Massachusetts Press, 1996).

6. Fitzwilliam Byrdsall, *The History of the Loco-Foco or Equal Rights Party* (New York: Clement & Packard, 1842), pp. 99–113. Van Buren himself came to the city to seal the reassimilation of the Locofocos, attending the Bowery Theater in the summer of 1839 with Alexander Ming and his wife. Arthur M. Schlesinger, Jr., *The Age of Jackson* (Boston, MA: Little, Brown & Co., 1945), *The Age of Jackson*, p. 259.

7. Byrdsall, *The History of the Loco-Foco or Equal Rights Party*, 188.

8. On Windt: Masquerier, *Sociology*, pp. 106, 107; Thomas A. Devyr, *The Odd Book of the Nineteenth Century, Or, "Chivalry" in Modern Days* [American section] (New York: the Author, 1882), p. 39; Foner, *History of the Labor Movement in the United States*, vol. 1, p. 567; Commons et al., *Documentary History of American Industrial Society*, vol. 8, pp. 305, 326; George A. Stevens, *New York Typographical Union No. 6: Study of a Modern Trade Union and Its Predecessors* (Albany, NY: J. B. Lyon Company, State Printers, 1913), p. 106.

9. Masquerier, *Sociology*, pp. 155–8. See also Mark Lause, "'The Unwashed Infidelity': Thomas Paine and Early New York City Labor History," *Labor History*, 27 (Summer 1986), pp. 385–409; Jamie L. Bronstein, *Land Reform and Working-Class Experience in Britain and the United States, 1800–1862* (Stanford, CA: Stanford University Press, 1999), pp. 24–5; Kenneth W. Burchell, "New York Beacon: Hidden Influence in the Life and Works of Thomas Paine," MA thesis, University of Idaho, May 2005; and "We Are Reforming Democrats: Gilbert Vale, Thomas Paine, and Nineteenth-Century Transatlantic Reform," PhD dissertation, University of Idaho, 2005; *The Radical*, I (April 1841), p. 63; Post, *Popular Freethought in America*, pp. 157, 159.

10. Carol A. Kolmerten, *The American Life of Ernestine L. Rose* (Syracuse, NY: Syracuse University Press, 1999).

11. Hugins, *Jacksonian Democracy*, pp. 95–96, and *Appleton's Encyclopedia of American Biography*, 6: p. 225; Albert Post, *Popular Freethought in America, 1825–1850* (New York: Columbia University Press, 1943), pp. 157, 159; *The Radical*, 1 (February 1841), p. 32.

12. Charles W. McCurdy, *The Anti-Rent Era in New York Law and Politics, 1839–1865* (Durham, NC: University of North Carolina Pres, 2001); Reeve Huston, *Land and Freedom: Rural Society, Popular Protest, and Party Politics in Antebellum New York* (Oxford: Oxford University Press, 2000); and Reeve Huston, "Popular Movements and Party Rule: The New York Anti-Rent Wars and the Jacksonian Political Order," in *Beyond the Founders: New Approaches to the Political History of the Early American Republic*, ed. Jeffrey L. Pasley, Andrew W. Robertson, and David Waldstreicher (Chapel Hill, NC: University of North Carolina Press, 2004).

13. For a general look at abolitionism: Aileen S. Kraiditor, *Means and Ends in American Abolitionism: Garrison and His Critics on Strategy and Tactics, 1834–1850* (2nd edition; New York: Vintage Books, 1969); Lewis Perry, *Radical Abolitionism: Anarchy and the Government of God in Antislavery Thought* (Ithaca, NY: Cornell University Press, 1973); James Brewer Stewart, *Holy Warriors: the Abolitionists and American Slavery* (New York: Hill & Wang, 1976).

14. A solid literature has begun to emerge on the complexities of abolitionism and its interconnection with social radicalism in general. For overviews, see John Stauffer, *The Black Hearts of Men: Radical Abolitionists and the Transformation of Race* (Cambridge, MA: Harvard University Press, 2002); Bruce Laurie, *Beyond Garrison: Antislavery and Social Reform* (Cambridge: Cambridge University Press 2005); and Thomas Mitchell, *Antislavery Politics in Antebellum and Civil War America* (New York: Praeger, 2007). For the abolitionist roots of later working class radicalism, see Alex Gourevitch, *From Slavery to the Cooperative Commonwealth: Labor and Republican Liberty in the Nineteenth Century* (Cambridge: Cambridge University Press, 2014).

15. Richard H. Sewell, *Ballots for Freedom: Antislavery Politics in the United States, 1837–1860* (New York: Oxford University Press, 1976); Reinhard O. Johnson, *The Liberty Party, 1840–1848: Antislavery Third-Party Politics in the United States* (Baton Rouge, LA: Louisiana State University Press, 2009).

16. See also *The Address of the Southern and Western Liberty Convention, to the People of the United States; the Proceedings and Resolutions of the Convention; the Letters of Elihu Burritt, Wm. H. Seward, William Jay, Cassius M. Clay, William Goodell, Thomas Earle and Others* (Cincinnati, OH: Printed at the Gazette Office, 1845).

17. Larry Gara, *The Liberty Line: the Legend of the Underground Railroad* (2nd edition; Lexington, KY: University Press of Kentucky, 1996), pp. 30, 37–8. Literature on the subject is voluminous, if usually repetitive, but, for recent titles, see "Freedom's Railway," *Detroit Tribune*, January 17, 1887, p. 2.

18. See Carl J. Guarneri, *The Utopian Alternative: Fourierism in Nineteenth-Century America* (Ithaca, NY: Cornell University press, 1991), pp. 25–32; Albert Fein,

"Fourierism in Nineteenth Century America: A Social and Environmental Perspective," in *France and North America: Utopias and Utopians*, ed. Mathe Allain (Lafayette, LA: USL Press, 1978), pp. 133–48; Jonathan Beecher, *Victor Considerant and the Rise and Fall of French Romantic Socialism* (Berkeley, CA: University of California Press, 2001); and Vincent Prieur, "Unsyncretisme utopique: Le cas du Fourierisme Americain (1840–50)," in *1848: Les Utopismes Sociaux*, ed. J. Bartier et al. (Paris: SEDES, 1981), pp. 261–72.

19. For Brook Farm, see Richard Francis, "The Ideology of Brook Farm," in *Studies in the American Renaissance, 1979*, ed. Joel Myerson (Boston, MA: Twayne Publishers, 1978), pp. 1–48; Robert S. Fogarty, *Dictionary of American Communal and Utopian History* (Westport, CT: Greenwood Press, 1980), p. 183. This last source also compiled overviews of the many Fourierist and contemporary communities.

20. Guarneri, *The Utopian Alternative*, pp. 32–56; David Montgomery, *Beyond Equality: Labor and the Radical Republicans, 1862–1872* (2nd edition; Urbana, IL: University of Illinois Press, 1981), p. 414; Francis Wayland Orvis, *A History of the Orvis Family in America* (Hackensack, NJ: The Orvis Company, 1922), pp. 62, 64, 99. See also Lawrence B. Goodheart's *Abolitionist, Actuary, Atheist: Elizur Wright & the Reform Impulse* (Kent, OH: Kent State University Press, 1990).

21. L. M. Crist, *History of Boone County, Indiana: With Biographical Sketches of Representative Citizens and Genealogical Records of Old Families* (2 vols.; Indianapolis, IN: A. W. Bowen & Co., 1914), vol. 1, pp. 396–7, vol. 2, pp. 994–8; and *A History and Biographical Cyclopaedia of Butler County Ohio, With Illustrations and Sketches of its Representative Men and Pioneers* (Cincinnati, OH: Western Biographical Publishing Company, 1882), pp. 520–24.

22. Commentary on Longley's interpretation of Fourierism. To "begin at the first step of the ladder," see William McDiarmid, "Social Movements," *The Vanguard*, 1 (July 11, 1857), p. 147, which also published his "Practical Suggestions for Social Reformers," (October 31, 1857), pp. 257–8.

23. Martin R. Andrews, *History of Marietta and Washington County, Ohio* (Chicago, IL: Biographical Pub. Co., 1902), p. 176.

24. Guarneri, *The Utopian Alternative*, p. 57.

25. Alan M. Kraut, "The Forgotten Reformers: A Profile of Third Party Abolitionists in Antebellum New York," in *Antislavery Reconsidered: New Perspectives on the Abolitionists*, ed. Lewis Perry and Michael Fellman (Baton Rouge, LA: Louisiana State University Press, 1979), pp. 119–45; and Edward Magdol, *The Antislavery Rank and File: A Social Profile of the Abolitionists' Constituency* (Westport, CT: Greenwood Press, 1986), pp. 37, 110, 96–7, 137. See also Edward Magdol, "A Window on the Abolitionist Constituency: Antislavery Petitions, 1836–1839," in *Crusaders and Compromisers: Essays on the Relationship of the Antislavery Struggle to the Antebellum Party System*, ed. Alan M. Kraut (Westport, CT: Greenwood Press, 1983), pp. 45–70, esp. 54–5.

26. "Portraits of Reformers" [from *National Era*], *Wisconsin Freeman*, July 14, 1847.

27. "To My Old Friends," *The Radical*, 1 (January 1841), p. 15; Byrdsall, *The History of the Loco-Foco or Equal Rights Party*, pp. 14–15; "Dr. Jaques on Land Monopoly in 1835," *Working Man's Advocate*, July 20, 1844, p. 1. As a trustee of the seventeenth school district of Middleton, he participated in its purchase of land for an overdue schoolhouse. April 17, 1840 in Deed Book Z3, Office of Surrogate, Hall of Records, Monmouth County, Freehold, NJ, pp. 340–41.

28. Masquerier, *Sociology*, pp. 21, 62; "Man's Inalienable Right to Land," *The Radical*, I (April 1841), pp. 50–52. W. Whipple's *National Reformer* of Philadelphia was the organ of the American Moral Reform Society; it started in September 1838.

29. "To the Democratic Committee," *Young America*, June 14, 1845, p. 1; Jeriel Root, *Analysis of Theology, Law, Religion and the Rights of Man* (Peoria, IL: Benjamin Foster, 1855), p. 33; "Dr. Jaques on Land Monopoly in 1835," *Working Man's Advocate*, July 20, 1844, p. 1. See, for example, appeals to Jefferson in the *National Reform Almanac for 1848* according to *National Reform Almanac for 1849* (New York: Office of Young America, 1849), p. 47.

30. Jefferson's letter to Cornelius C. Blatchley, October 21, 1822, Jefferson to William Ludlow, September 6, 1824, Page to Jefferson, May 10, June 3, 1820, February 18, and December 16, 1821, Frances Wright to Jefferson, July 26, 1825, Jefferson to Wright, August 7, 1825, and Skidmore to Jefferson, August 18, 1822, Thomas Jefferson Papers, Library of Congress; Richard K. Matthew, *The Radical Politics of Thomas Jefferson: A Revisionist View* (Lawrence, KS: University Press of Kansas, 1984) offers a latter-day appreciation of this dimension to the views of a figure made so complex by his ambiguous slaveholding.

31. Regular advertisement for Evan's 2-volume edition of *The Political Writings of Thomas Paine*, and notice of "Vale's Life of Paine," *The Radical*, 1 (February, April 1841), pp. 32, 63; and Masquerier, *Sociology*, pp. 155–8. See also Lause, "'The Unwashed Infidelity,'" pp. 385–409. John Allen of Brook Farm and William West, "Reform Celebrations of the Fourth at Troy, N.Y.," *Albany Patriot*, July 7, 1847.

32. "Spirit of 'Seventy-Six," "Liberation of Gov. Dorr," and "Mammoth Mass Meeting of Fifty Thousand Democratic Men and Women," *Working Man's Advocate*, May 25 (p. 4), August 17 (p. 1), September 7 (p. 3), 1844; Devyr, *Odd Book*, pp. 44, 45; and Veterans' Memorial, February 6, 1851 in SEN31A-J1–4(tb), Tray 106, folder 3/13/50–2/28/51 in U.S. Senate, Ms Records, Legislative Records, National Archives.

33. "Remarks of Mr. Commerford," *Working Man's Advocate*, March 30, 1844, p. 4; "The World's Convention," *New York Daily Tribune*, October 6, 1845, p. 2; and "The Movement Party," *Young America*, March 29, 1845, p. 2.

34. Commerford in "Seventh Out-Door Meeting," *Working Man's Advocate*, July 20, 1844, p. 1; Price in "Free Homes To All!" *New York Daily Tribune*, May 28, 1852, p. 5; Van Amringe, "National Reform: No. 2," *Wisconsin Freeman*, January 26, 1848, p. 1.

35. Devyr, *Odd Book*, pp. 39, 41; Gary M. Fink, *Biographical Directory of American Labor Leaders* (Westport, CT: Greenwood Press, 1974), pp. 78–9; and Ray Boston, *British Chartists in America, 1834–1900* (Manchester: Manchester University Press, 1971), pp. 49–56.
36. Albert Schrauwers, *Union is Strength: W. L. Mackenzie, the Children of Peace, and the Emergence of Joint Stock Democracy in Upper Canada* (Toronto: University of Toronto Press, 2009), pp. 35–64.
37. Masquerier, *Sociology*, pp. 21, 62. Nick Salvatore makes this point in a later context in his *Eugene V. Debs: Citizen and Socialist* (Urbana, IL: University of Illinois Press, 1982), p. 19. See also Melvin Yazawa, *From Colonies to Commonwealth: Familial Ideology and the Beginnings of the American Republic* (Baltimore, MD: Johns Hopkins University Press, 1985).
38. New Harmony Free Land Association, Ms Minutes, in Workingmen's Institute, Archives, New Harmony Series III.v.44, New Harmony, Indiana.
39. "The Industrial Brotherhood," *Young America*, March 7, 1846, p. 3.
40. John H. Klippart, *Brotherhood of the Union: Address Delivered at Freedom, Portage County, Ohio; At a Festival of the B.U. (H.F.) C.A. of Circle No. 10.–98.* (Cleveland, OH: Sanford & Hayward, 1852), p. 14; Heighton's "True and Sham Reformers," and his "Slavery of Wages," *Young America*, November 8, 1845, February 7, 1846, both p. 1; as well as his *Principles of Aristocratic Legislation* (Philadelphia, PA: J. Coates, Jr. Printer, 1828), p. 5. See also "White Slavery" [from *New York Tribune*], *Young America*, February 7, 1846, p. 3; *The Jubilee* (New York, 1845), p. 2; Root, *Analysis of Theology, Law, Religion and the Rights of Man*, pp. 33–34, 40; Joshua King Ingalls, *Reminiscences of an Octogenarian* (New York: M. L. Holbrook and Company; London: L. N. Fowler, 1897), p. 51.
41. "Man's Inalienable Right to Land," *The Radical*, I (April 1841), pp. 50–52; Masquerier, *Sociology*, p. 12; Thomas Wentworth Higginson, *Cheerful Yesterdays* (Boston, MA: Houghton, Mifflin, 1898), p. 119. See also Elizur Wright's use of the phrase in "The Sisterhood of Reforms" [from the *Chronotype*], *The Signal of Liberty*, November 28, 1846, p. 2.
42. Elizur Wright on "Land Monopoly" [from Boston *Investigator*], *Voice of Industry*, November 13, 1846, p. 4; *Proceedings of the Seventh Industrial Congress ...* (Washington, DC: n.p., 1852), p. 7.
43. John C. Wheatcroft to Evans in New Harmony Free Land Association, Ms Mins., January 20, 1847, Workingmen's Institute, New Harmony, IN; "Address of Mr. Wait of Ill.," *Young America*, October 25, 1845, p. 1; Van Amringe, *Wisconsin Freeman*, March 8, February 16, 1848.
44. Masquerier, *Sociology*, pp. 13–19, 57, 67, 74, 76, 77, 98; *Working Man's Advocate*, June 18, 1844; Van Amringe in Adjournment of the Fifth National Industrial Congress," *New York Daily Tribune*, June 17, 1850, p. 3.
45. Skidmore, *Rights of Man to Property!*, pp. 5, 8, 10, 13–14, 209, 285, 299, 310, 333.
46. L. A. Hine, *A Lecture on Garrisonian Politics, before the Western Philosophical Institute; Delivered in Cincinnati, Sunday, April 24th, 1853* (Cincinnati, OH:

Longley, 1853), p. 18; Elizur Wright, "Philosophy of Labor No. IV" [from *Chronotype*], *American Freeman*, August 18, 1846, p. 1; and Van Amringe, "National Reform.—No. 1," *American Freeman*, January 19, 1848.

47. "The New Party," *Voice of Industry*, November 19, 1847, p. 2, which followed its call for the nominations of presidential and vice presidential candidates. "Industrial Congress," *Voice of Industry*, July 2, 1847, pp. 1–2. See too the "New England Labor Reform League," *Voice of Industry*, April 23, 1847, p. 2. The *Voice* proposed supplementing the three original NRA demands with: the ten-hour day; cooperative Protective unions; "a general Lien law for the protection of laborers"; and, "methods for the organization of Industry among small capitalists."

Chapter 5   Confronting Race and Empire: Slavery and Mexico

1. "Free Soil," *Western Quarterly Review*, 1 (January 1849), p. 10; "National Reform Banquet" [from the *Cincinnati Daily Herald*], *Harbinger*, 7 (June 10, 1848), pp. 45–6.

2. "Obituary of Alexander Bearse, John Lockley, Eunice Ames and John T. Hilton," *Liberator*, March 25, 1864, p. 51, also in William Cooper Nell, *Selected Writings 1832–1874*, ed. Dorothy Porter Wesley and Constance Porter Uzelac (Baltimore, MD: Black Classic Press, 2002), pp. 627–8, 644; "Presentation of a Portrait to a Masonic Grand Lodge," *Liberator*, October 10, 1862, p. 4.

3. Edward N. Palmer, "Negro Secret Societies," *Social Forces*, 23 (December 1944), pp. 208–9; David G. Hackett, "The Prince Hall Masons and the African American Church: The Labors of Grand Master and Bishop James Walker Hood, 1831–1918," in *Religion and American Culture: A Reader*, ed. David G. Hackett (New York: Routledge, 2003), pp. 289–314, originally in *Church History*, 69 (December 2000), pp. 770–802.

4. James Oliver Horton, *Free People of Color: Inside the African American Community* (Washington, DC: Smithsonian Institution Press, 1993), pp. 35, 42–3, 45, 49, 101–10, 111, 153; Maurice Wallace, "'Are We Men?': Prince Hall, Martin Delany, and the Masculine Ideal in Black Freemasonry, 1775–1865," *American Literary History*, 9 (Autumn 1997), p. 296; Caryn Cossé Bell, *Revolution, Romanticism, and the Afro-Creole Protest Tradition in Louisiana, 1718–1868* (Baton Rouge, LA: Louisiana State University Press, 1997), pp. 82, 83; James McCune Smith, "The Odd Fellows' Celebration," in *The Works of James McCune Smith: Black Intellectual and Abolitionist*, ed. John Stauffer (Oxford: Oxford University Press, 2006), pp. 159–61.

5. "Obituary of Alexander Bearse, John Lockley, Eunice Ames and John T. Hilton," *North Star*, July 6, 1849, p. 3, also in Nell, *Selected Writings*, p. 229; *Proceedings of the Black State Conventions, 1840–1865*, ed. Philip S. Foner and George E. Walker (2 vols.; Philadelphia, PA: Temple University Press, 1979–80), vol. 1, p. 36n.3; R. R. Wright, "The Negro in Unskilled Labor,"

Annals of the American Academy of Political and Social Science, 49 (September 1913), pp. 19, 24.

6. James McCune Smith, *The Works of James McCune Smith: Black Intellectual and Abolitionist*, ed. John Stauffer, foreword by Henry Louise Gates Jr. (Oxford: Oxford University Press, 2006).

7. "Death of George DeBaptiste," *Detroit Daily Post*, February 23, 1875; and "George DeBaptiste: His Death Yesterday," *Detroit Advertiser and Tribune*, February 23, 1875, Clarke Historical Library, Central Michigan University, retrieved from http://clarke.cmich.edu/undergroundrailroad/georgedebaptiste.htm; Patrick Rael, *Black Identity and Black Protest in the Antebellum North* (Chapel Hill, NC: University of North Carolina Press, 2002). See also Charles Testut, *Fleurs d'eté; poésies* (New Orleans, LA: n.p., 1851), and also his *Le vieux Salomon ou Une famille d'esclave au XIXe siècle* (Shreveport, LA: Cahiers du tintamarre, impr. 2003).

8. William J. Simmons, *Men of Mark: Eminent, Progressive and Rising* (Cleveland, OH: G. M. Rewell, 1887), pp. 546–8; Edward N. Palmer, "Negro Secret Societies," *Social Forces*, 23 (Dececember 1944), p. 209. Description of Lambert from "Freedom's Railway," *Detroit Tribune*, January 17, 1887, p. 2.

9. Simmons, *Men of Mark*, p. 547; W. H. Gibson, "Historical Sketch of the Progress of the Colored Race, in Louisville, Ky," pp. 42–3, separately paged in W. H. Gibson, *History of the United Brothers of Friendship and Sisters of the Mysterious Ten, in Two Parts: A Negro Order, Organized August 1, 1861, in the City of Louisville, Ky*. (Louisville, KY: for the author by Bradley & Gilbert Company, 1897).

10. "Order of the United Brothers of Friendship," pp. 7–9, independently paged in Gibson, *History ... of the Mysterious Ten*.

11. Manual *of the International Order of Twelve of the Knights and Daughters of Tabor, Containing General Laws, Regulations, ceremonies, Drill, and a Taborian Lexicon* (St. Louis, KY: A. R. Fleming & Co., 1891), pp. 7–9. For the importance of barbers such as Dickson and DeBaptiste, see Douglas W. Bristol's *Knights of the Razor: Black Barbers in Slavery and Freedom* (Baltimore, MD: John Hopkins University Press, 2009).

12. F. H. P. "Freedom's Railway," *Detroit Tribune*, January 17, 1887, p. 2, with "Death of George DeBaptiste," *Detroit Daily Post*, February 23, 1875, and "George DeBaptiste," *Detroit Advertiser and Tribune*, February 23, 1875; Katharine DuPre Lumpkin, "'The General Plan Was Freedom': A Negro Secret Order on the Underground Railroad" in *John Brown Mysteries: Allies for Freedom*, ed. Jean Libby (Missoula, MT: Pictorial Histories Publishing Company, 1999), p. 89. See also Foner and Walker, *Proceedings of the Black State Conventions, 1840–1865*, vol. 1, pp. 181–7, 190, 196.

13. Henry O. Wagoner, Chicago, to Frederick Douglass, August 17, 1849. "Union of the Oppressed for the Sake of Freedom," "The Union of the Opressed," and "Union of the Oppressed," *Frederick Douglass' Paper*, August 10, 17, 24, 1849, all p. 2.

14. Kenneth R. H. Mackenzie, *Royal Masonic Cyclopedia* (Wellingborough: Aquarian Press, 1987), pp. 328, 453, 457, 504; Simmons, *Men of Mark*, pp. 729–31; and Rev. Patrick Henry Alexander Braxton also became a member, 105. See also Betty M. Kuyk, *African Voices in the African American Heritage* (Bloomington, IN: Indiana University Press, 2003), pp. 53–9, 63, 66–7.

15. Albert L. Rawson. *Pronouncing Bible Dictionary*, quoted in Rev. J. J. Pipkin, *The Negro in Revelation, in History, and in Citizenship ... with Introduction by Gen. John B. Gordon* (St. Louis, MO: N. D. Thompson Publishing Company, 1902), pp. 35–6; Martin Delany, *The Origin and Objects of Ancient Freemasonry: Its Introduction into the United States and Legitimacy Among Colored Men ...* (Pittsburgh, PA: Haven: for the Author, 1853). On Rawson, see Mark Lause, *The Antebellum Crisis and America's First Bohemians* (Kent, OH: Kent State University Press, 2009), pp. 61–2.

16. E. J. Marconis, *The Sanctuary of Memphis or Hermes* (n.p., n.d. [1910]), pp. 3–4; Calvin C. Burt, *Egyptian Masonic History of the Original and Unabridged Ancient and Ninety-Six Degree Rite of Memphis* ([Utica, NY: White & Floyd], 1879), pp. 203–7, 314–17. See also Betty Fladeland, *Men and Brothers: Anglo-American Antislavery Cooperation* (Urbana, IL: University of Illinois Press, 1972); and Betty Fladeland, *Abolitionist and Working-Class Problems in the Age of Industrialization* (Baton Rouge, LA: Louisiana State University Press, 1984).

17. "Freedom's Railway," *Detroit Tribune*, January 17, 1887, p. 2; "George DeBaptiste," *Detroit Advertiser and Tribune*, February 23, 1875, both posted Clarke Historical Library, Central Michigan University, retrieved from http://clarke.cmich.edu/undergroundrailroad/georgedebaptiste.htm. Lambert identified John Brown's associate, Richard Realf as an unusual white member of the order.

18. "Freedom's Railway," *Detroit Tribune*, January 17, 1887, p. 2.

19. Bell, *Revolution, Romanticism, and the Afro-Creole Protest Tradition*, pp. 83, 84.

20. Foner and Walker, *Proceedings of the Black State Conventions, 1840–1865*, vol. 1, pp. 43–52; and Nell, *Selected Writings*, pp. 18n., 23n., 99–100, 278–9, 281, 432, 590.

21. Mary Kay Ricks, *Escape on the Pearl: the Heroic Bid for Freedom on the Underground Railroad* (New York: Harper Perennial, 2008), pp. 77–78.

22. Stanley J. Robboy and Anita W. Robboy, "Lewis Hayden: from Fugitive Slave to Statesmen," *The New England Quarterly*, 46 (December 1973), pp. 591–613, particularly 591, 593, *passim* 595–8, 607–11; and Nell, *Selected Writings*, pp. 194–5, 622, 632. On Cluer, see also Ray Boston, *British Chartists in America, 1834–1900* (Manchester: Manchester University Press, 1971), pp. 47–8.

23. William Monroe Cockrum, *History of the Underground Railroad as it was Conducted by the Anti-slavery League: Including Many Thrilling Encounters Between Those Aiding the Slaves to Escape and Those Trying to Recapture Them* (Oakland City, IN: J. W. Cockrum Printing Company, 1915), pp. 13–14.

24. "Freedom's Railway," *Detroit Tribune*, January 17, 1887, p. 2; Allan Pinkerton, *The Spy of the Rebellion* (New York: G. W. Dillingham Col., Publishers, 1883), pp. 354–7; and *Manual of the International Order of Twelve*, 9–10.

25. "Freedom's Railway," *Detroit Tribune*, January 17, 1887, p. 2.

26. "Mr. Birney's Letter" and Evans's "Reply to Mr. Birney," in *Working Man's Advocate*, July 27, 1844, pp. 1, 2; Brisbane in "National Reform Association," *Young America*, April 26 (p. 2), December 20 (p. 3), 1845; John H. Keyser's *The Next Step of Progress* (3rd edition; New York: for the Author, [1884?]), p. 42; and his letter, "Mr. Keyser in Self-Defense," *John Swinton's Paper*, September 20, 1885.

27. Nathaniel B. Sylvester, *History of Saratoga County, New York* (Philadelphia, PA: Everts & Ensign, 1878), biographical sketch inserted opp. p. 444; H. Royce Bass, *The History of Braintree, Vermont* (Rutland VT: Tutle & Co., state printers, 1883), pp. 131–2; B. W. Dyer and National Reform, "Industrial Congress," *Niles Weekly Register*, sixth series, 22 (July 10, 1847), p. 297.

28. See "The American Movement" [from the Chartists' *Northern State*] and Evans's reply, *Working Man's Advocate*, August 17, 1844, p. 4; "Mr. Brisbane's Address" and "National Reform Association," *Working Man's Advocate*, February 22, 1845, p. 3; and "Slaves in the British Islands" [from the *Guiana Times*], *Young America*, May 24, 1845, p. 2. See also Jonathan A. Glickstein, "'Poverty Is Not Slavery': American Abolitionists and the Competitive Labor Market," in *Antislavery Reconsidered: New Perspectives on the Abolitionists*, ed. Lewis Perry and Michael Fellman (Baton Rouge, LA: Louisiana State University press, 1979), pp. 195–218. William West saw slavery "peaceably abolished only by the political action of the legally qualified voters of the states in which it exists and to secure this action, the cause of the chattel slave should be united with that of the wage slave." West at "Reform Celebration of the Fourth in Troy, N.Y.," *Albany Patriot*, July 7, 1847.

29. On the role of immigrant workers are Clifton K. Yearley, Jr., *Britons in American Labor: a History of the Influence of United Kingdom Immigrants on American Labor, 1820–1914* (Baltimore, MD: Johns Hopkins University Studies in Historical and Political Science, 1957), and Bruce Levine, *The Spirit of 1848: German Immigrants, Labor Conflicts, and the Coming of the Civil War* (Urbana, IL: University of Illinois Press, 1992); and Hartmut Keil, "German-American Radicals, Antebellum Politics, and the Civil War," *Studia Migracyjne—Przeglad Polonijny*, 40 (2014), pp. 57–70.

30. "Slavery and Freedom," *New York Weekly Tribune*, June 29, 1850, p. 3, quoted in Arthur A. Ekrich, Jr., *The Idea of Progress in America, 1815–1860* (New York: Peter Smith, 1951), p. 246; and the unpacking of this discussion in my *Young America: Land, Labor, and the Republican Community* (Urbana, IL: University of Illinois Press, 2005), pp. 72–6.

31. *American Freeman*, November 17, 1847; "The American Oligarchy—Wherein Lies Its Strength! Number Fifteen," *The Principia*, 1 (July 21, 1860), p. 282.

32. "Wages and Chattel Slavery," "Black and White Slavery' [from the *Northampton Democrat*], *Voice of Industry*, May 7, August 14, 1847, both p. 2; "The Land Question," *Western Quarterly Review*, 1 (January 1849), p. 29; Jeriel Root, *Analysis of Theology, Law, Religion and the Rights of Man* (Peoria, IL: Benjamin Foster, 1855), p. 71. See also Bruce Laurie, *Rebels in Paradise: Sketches of*

Northampton Abolitionists (Boston, MA: University of Massachusetts Press, 2015).

33. For the first notation of black involvement, see "Milford" under "Working Men's Movements," *Working Man's Advocate*, September 21, 1844, p. 1; and Joshua King Ingalls, *Reminiscences of an Octogenarian* (New York: M. L. Holbrook and Company; London: L. N. Fowler, 1897), p. 35.

34. M. P. Hale on "Progress in Maine," *Young America*, February 21, 1846, p. 3; Salmon P. Chase to O. Johnson, J. H. Atkinson, G. McGregor, J. M. Cutter, and J. H. Rose, published as "Correspondence on the Subject of National Reform," [from *Cincinnati Herald*] in *Albany Patriot*, November 4, 1846.

35. The abolitionist *Albany Patriot* covered the campaign through October; Helene Zahler, *Eastern Workingmen and National Land Policy* (New York: Columbia University Press, 1941), p. 96 and n. See also "The 'Free Soil' Principle," *New York Daily Tribune*, October 13, 1846, p. 2.

36. "The Elections" [from *Young America*], and "Mike Walsh in Office," *Voice of Industry*, November 13, 1846, pp. 2, 3; *The Whig Almanac and United States Register for 1847* (New York: New York Tribune, 1847), p. 45 and *The Whig Almanac ... for 1848* (New York: New York Tribune, 1848), p. 40, both included in *The Tribune Almanac for the Years 1838 to 1868. Inclusive: Comprehending the Political Register with the Whig Almanac ...* (2 vols.; New York: New York Tribune, 1868). See also "The New Constitution," the critique of the New York convention and a call for "a *new era* on democratic progress." In *The Jubilee* (New York: [NRA], 1845), pp. 1, 2.

37. "Letter of Gerrit Smith" [from *Young America*], *Voice of Industry*, November 20, 1846, p. 3; and article on Smith's "Poor Man's Party," *Wisconsin Freeman*, November 24, 1846; Smith quoted in Thomas A. Devyr, *The Odd Book of the Nineteenth Century, Or, "Chivalry" in Modern Days* [American section] (New York: the Author, 1882), pp. 113, 112; Ingalls, *Reminiscences*, p. 26, which also offers a paraphrase of Smith's argument on the antislavery implications of land reform, p. 30. Significantly, the "Poor Man's Party" was the name of the first distinctly "Agrarian" organization in American history, founded in 1829–30 by Thomas Skidmore and others leaving the local Workingmen's Party.

38. U.S. Senate Ms, Committee on Public Lands, cited in Zahler, *Eastern Workingmen*, pp. 134, 135n.; "Letter of Hon. Moses G. Leonard, Tammany Candidate for Alms-House Commissioner to the National Reformers" [from *Young America*], "Mayor Brady and Land Reform," *New York Daily Tribune*, April 13, 15, 1847, both p. 2, the former referring to the National Reformers as "the Nationals," perhaps the first use of the term in American politics, and predating the pro-Greenback "Nationals" by almost thirty years. Dennis Lyons appeared in the accounts of local NRA meetings reported in *Young America*, October 4, 11, 1845, both p. 3.

39. "New York for National Reform," *Voice of Industry*, April 23, 1847, p. 2.

40. From the *Voice of Industry*, see "Industrial Reform Lyceum," March 13, 1846, p. 2; and "Anti-Slavery Convention," May 8, 1846, p. 2; "4th of July! Industrial Reform Celebration in Lowell!" July 3, 1846, p. 3 "Freedom of the

Public Lands" [from *Northampton Democrat*], February 19, 1847, p. 4; "Wages and Chattel Slavery," May 7, 1847, p. 2; "The Industrial Congress," June 11, 1847, p. 2; "Address of the Massachusetts National Reform convention, held at Boston, October 30, 1847," November 5, 1847, p. 3. See also Ryckman's "Union of All Reformers, For One Great Reform," *Harbinger*, 1 (August 23, September 27, 1845), pp. 169–70, 245–7; Elihu Burrit's "Universal Brotherhood," see *Albany Patriot*, September 30, 1846; Masquerier to Smith, October 5, 1847, John A. Lant Papers, Missouri Historical Society, St. Louis; and Zahler, *Eastern Workingmen*, pp. 86–7 and n.

41. "Industrial Congress," in *Voice of Industry*, June 18 (p. 2), 25 (pp. 1–2), July 2 (pp. 1–2), 1847. For the Louisville unions, see Ethelbert Stewart's "A Documentary History of Early Organizations of Printers," published as U.S. Department of Commerce and Labor, *Bulletin of the Bureau of Labor*, 11 (November 1905), pp. 908, 921, 933, 937, 944.

42. "Industrial Congress: Second Session—June, 1847" and "Industrial Congress on War: Address of the Industrial Congress to the Citizens of the United States," *Voice of Industry*, June 25, 1847, pp. 1–2, 4, and "Industrial Congress," July 2, pp. 1–2; Wright's "Victory" [from the *Chronotype*], *Harbinger*, 4 (April 24, 1847), p. 326; "The Mexican War" and "A Mexican Eden," in the *National Reform Almanac for 1849*, pp. 43, 44. An internal debate resolved opposition to annexation, according to accounts in the regular meetings reported in the *Working Man's Advocate* for January 18 through February 8, 1845. See also "Land Reform," *Wisconsin Freeman*, May 24, 1848, p. 1.

43. "Power of a Third Party" [from *Young America*], *Voice of Industry*, June 19, 1846, p. 4. See also "The 'Free Soil' Principle," *New York Daily Tribune*, October 13, 1846, p. 2. The "Free Soil building" appears in such publications as the National Reform Almanacs.

44. "Letter of Geritt Smith" [from *Young America*], *Voice of Industry*, November 20, 1846, p. 3; "A Call for a National Nominating Convention" [from *Albany Patriot*], "Proceedings of the Nominating Convention at Macedon Lock, N.Y.," and "Gerrit Smith—The Presidency" [from *Albany Patriot*] with "Resolutions Passed by the Macedon Lock Convention" in the *Voice of Industry*, May 21, July 2, 9, 1847, all p. 4. "Industrial Congress" and "Laws of the Industrial Congress," *Voice of Industry*, June 25, 1847, pp. 1–2.

45. West in *National Antislavery Standard*, March 22, 1849, p. 171; "Industrial Congress," *Voice of Industry*, June 18, 25, July 2, 1847, covered pp. 1–2; and, "Miscellany," October 8, 1847, p. 1; West in *Young America*, December 13, 1845.

46. "National Reform State Convention" and Fay's untitled letter to "Friend Jaques" *Voice of Industry*, September 24 (p. 3), October 1 (p. 2), 1847; "National Reform Meeting," *Voice of Industry*, October 29, 1847, p. 3. See also "Nomination of 'the Liberty Party' or 'Liberty league'—and of 'the National reform Association'," *Niles Weekly Register* (July 10, 1847), pp. 296–7. On Cluer, Mary H. Blewett, *Constant Turmoil: The Politics of Industrial Life in Nineteenth-century New England* (Amherst, MA: University of Massachusetts

Press, 2000), pp. 76, 84; W. Caleb McDaniel, *The Problem of Democracy in the Age of Slavery: Garrisonian Abolitionists & Transatlantic Reform* (Baton Rouge, LA: Louisiana State University Press, 2013), p. 157.

47. For this and the following paragraph, see "National Reform Convention," *Voice of Industry*, November 5, 1847, pp. 2–3, including resolutions and "Address of the Massachusetts National Reform convention, Held at Boston, October 30, 1847."

48. "Liberty Ticket," and "The New Party," *Voice of Industry*, November 5 (p. 2), 19 (p. 3), 1847, p. 2.

49. "The Elections" and "Returns," *Voice of Industry*, November 13, 20, 1846, both p. 2.

50. Grandin, "Land Reform," *Liberator*, April 28, 1848, p. 67. For his support for the labor movement, see also his "Working Men's Protective Unions," in the issue of April 23, 1847, pp. 68, 67.

51. "National Reform Vote in New York," *Voice of Industry*, December 24, 1847, p. 3. Oswego county gave 58 votes to Treadwell, as well as twenty-three for Washburn. See also, the *Whig Almanac … for 1848*, pp. 41, 42. On the Liberty ticket, see Bertram Wyatt-Brown's *Lewis Tappan and the Evangelical War Against Slavery* (Cleveland, OH: Press of Case Western Reserve University, 1969), pp. 47, and 57 n24. The *Albany Patriot*, December 15, 1847 also has returns.

52. "Letter of Alvan E. Bovay to the Auburn Convention," *Albany Patriot*, January 26, 1848.

53. Masquerier, "To Reformers, Tenants, Anti-Renters, Squatters, and Slaves," *Young America*, July 12, 1845, p. 1; and Van Amringe, "National Reform.—No. 2," *Wisconsin Freeman*, January 26, 1848, p. 1.

Chapter 6   Free Soil: The Electoral Distillation of Radicalism, 1847–8

1. On the Rosendale NRA, see letter in Waukesha, WI, *American Freeman*, March 1, 1848, p. 2.

2. "Democratic Mass State Convention of Barnburners, at Herkimer, N.Y." [from Charter Oak], *American Freeman*, November 24, 1847, p. 2, "Free Soil, Free Labor and Free Trade: A Barnburner's Response," January 5, 1848, p. 2. Active in this effort were C. C. Camberling and John Van Buren.

3. Untitled item from *Young American* in *American Freeman*, October 27, 1847, p. 2; "Gov. Young's Message," *New York Daily Tribune*, January 5, 1848, p. 2; Helene Zahler, *Eastern Workingmen and National Land Policy* (New York: Columbia University Press, 1941), pp. 51 and n., 96, 96n.–97n. See also "Land Reform," *Albany Patriot*, February 2, 1848; "The Auburn Convention" [from *Albany Patriot*], *American Freeman*, February 16, 1848; "Letter of Alvan E. Bovay to the Auburn Convention," *Albany Patriot*, January 26, 1848, p. 1.

4. For the radicals' critique of the Barnburners, see "A Call for a National Nominating Convention" [from *Albany Patriot*], "Proceedings of the

Nominating Convention at Macedon Lock, N.Y.," and "Gerrit Smith—The Presidency" [from *Albany Patriot*] with "Resolutions Passed by the Macedon Lock Convention" in the *Voice of Industry*, May 21, June 2, July 9, 1847, all p. 4. See also report from *Young America* in *Wisconsin Freeman*, October 27, 1847 and in all of the papers associated with the "broad platform" Libertymen.

5. On Ashton, see *Daily Sentinel*, July 6, 12, 1830; *A Documentary History of American Industrial Society*, ed. John R. Commons et al. (10 vols., reprinted; New York: Russell & Russell, 1958), vol. 8, p. 28. On Speakman: Arthur E. Bestor, *Backwoods Utopias: The Sectarian and Owenite Phases of Communitarian Socialism in America: 1663–1829* (Philadelphia, PA: University of Pennsylvania Press, 1950), pp. 100, 108, 109, 110, 112n, 154, 202, 213; Commons et al., *Documentary History of American Industrial Society*, vol. 8, pp. 26, 28; and *Young America*, May 10, 1845. On Fisk: *The Universalist Companion* for 1848, 58; Joshua King Ingalls, *Reminiscences of an Octogenarian* (New York: M. L. Holbrook and Company; London: L. N. Fowler, 1897), pp. 25–6; Philip S. Foner, *History of the Labor Movement in the United States, Volume 1: From Colonial Times to the Founding of the American Federation of Labor* (New York: International Publishers, 1947), p. 562; and Edward Pessen, *Most Uncommon Jacksonians: The Radical Leaders of the Early Labor Movement* (Albany, NY: State University of New York Press, 1967), pp. 92–3, although the implication that Fisk left the social reform movement is clearly wrong.

6. On Jones, Townsend and Dorrites, see *The Monthly Jubilee*, 4 (March 1854), p. 108, and his trip to Wilmington, p. 138. On Sheddon: "Membership Rolls" in Philadelphia Section, International Workingmen's Association, October 9, 1871 to August 18, 1873, Box 2, folder C, IWA Papers, and Sovereigns of Industry, Pioneer Council, No. 1, "List of Members, 1874–1877." The source also mentions John Mills and Thomas Phillips. See also Bruce Laurie, *Working People of Philadelphia, 1800–1850* (Philadelphia, PA: Temple University Press, 1980), pp. 165, 168, 196.

7. On Lippard, see David Reynolds's *George Lippard* (Boston, MA: Twayne Publishers, 1982) and his anthology, *George Lippard, Prophet of Protest: Writings of an American Radical, 1822–1854* (New York: P. Lang, 1986). The original biographies include that by his friend and cothinker John Bell Bouton, *Life and Choice Writings of George Lippard* (New York: H. H. Randall, 1855), particularly pp. 19, 20, and a series of reminiscences by J. M. W. Geist, O. W. C. Whinna and others in *Official Souvenir, Brotherhood of the Union* (Philadelphia, PA: [Brotherhood of the Union], 1900). For other examples, see advertisement for *Washington and His Generals; or, Legends of the Revolution* in Chester *Reveille*, February 10, 1849.

8. "Industrial Congress," *Philadelphia Daily Public Ledger*, June 12, 1848. Probably Thomas Speakman, the Fourierist. Most likely, he was the son or some relation to John Speakman, the local Owenite figure of twenty years before.

9. Ingalls, *Reminiscences*, 26. See also "Liberty Party Convention" [from *Rochester Advertiser*], *New York Daily Tribune*, June 20, 1848, p. 1; *Proceedings of the*

National Liberty Convention, Held at Buffalo, New York, June 14th & 15th, 1848 (Utica, 1848), especially pp. 9, 25 on land reform; Richard H. Sewell, *A House Divided: Sectionalism and the Civil War, 1848–1865* (Baltimore, MD: Johns Hopkins University Press, 1988), pp. 119–20, 121, 136.

10. On Foote, see William H. and Jane Pease, *Black Utopia: Negro Communical Experiments in America* (Madison, WI: State Historical Society of Wisconsin, 1963), pp. 115–17, 119; Abram William Foote, *Foote Family* (Rutland VT: Marble City Press, The Tuttle Co., 1907), p. 339, but also pp. 106, 107, 257.

11. Ingalls, *Reminiscences*, p. 25; Laurie, *Working People*, pp. 12, 165, 168, 192; and, Reynolds, *George Lippard, Prophet of Protest*, p. 7.

12. Notice of the meeting at an open lot on Second and Lombard in Schuylkill appeared in the *Daily Public Ledger*, June 14, 1848, p. 2, correcting the ascribing of the resolutions to the "Industrial Congress" in the issue of June 9.

13. "Liberty Party Convention" [from *Rochester Advertiser*], *New York Daily Tribune*, June 20, 1848, p. 1; *Proceedings of the National Liberty Convention ... 1848*, pp. 9, 25. See also "C. M. Clay and Gerrit Smith," *Working Man's Advocate*, October 5, 1844, p. 2; "The Liberty Party" and "Cassius M. Clay," *Young America*, November 1, 1845, p. 3, and January 17, 1846, p. 3; and Bertram Wyatt-Brown, *Lewis Tappan and the Evangelical War Against Slavery* (Cleveland, OH: Press of Case Western Reserve University, 1969), pp. 24, 47 and n., 57. On Wait, see Arthur M. Schlesinger, Jr., *The Age of Jackson* (Boston, MA: Little, Brown & Co., 1945), pp. 149, 312; "Constitution of the Industrial Congress," *Young America*, October 25, 1845, p. 3; Commons et al., *Documentary History of American Industrial Society*, vol. 8, pp. 21, 26, 27; and *History of Bond and Montgomery Counties, Illinois*, ed. William Henry Perrin (Chicago, IL: Baskin & Co., 1882), pp. 55, 57, 68. See also "Beginning at the Wrong End" and "Freedom of the Public Lands" for the NRA resolutions from Brooklyn, *Young America*, September 27 (p. 3), November 8 (p. 4), 1845.

14. Bovay (with Keyser listed as secretary) to Van Buren, June 24 and Van Buren to Bovay, July 20, 1848, in the Martin Van Buren Papers, along with a clipping from the *New York Evening Post*; "Free Soil Demonstrations," *New York Daily Tribune*, August 3, 1848, p. 1; and the Utica *Republic* and other newspapers with Van Buren's reply; Evans's comments on D. S. Curtiss's letter in "Real and Sham Free Soil," *Young America*, September 23, 1848, p. 2; Rochester National Reformers to Van Buren, July 28, 1848, and Van Buren to National Reformers, August 22 and 24, 1848, in Van Buren Papers.

15. "State Convention: To the Liberty Party of the State of New York," *Young America*, September 23, 1848, p. 2. On Buffum: *Young America*, May 10, 1845; and Commons et al., *Documentary History of American Industrial Society*, vol. 8, pp. 26, 27. On Andrews: "Letter from S. P. Andrews" [from Baltimore's *Saturday Visitor*], *National Anti-Slavery Standard*, October 10, 1844, p. 73; and Madeline B. Stern, *The Pantarch: A Biography of Stephen Pearl Andrews* (Austin and London, 1968), pp. 17–19, 28, 32–3, 35–9, 39–46, 48–55. Ingalls, *Reminiscences*, pp. 28, 35; and George W. Julian *Political Recollections, 1850–1872* (Chicago, IL: Jansen, McClurg & Company, 1884), pp. 231–2. John Carbutt,

Biographical Sketches of the Leading Men of Chicago (Chicago, IL: Wilson & St. Clair, 1868); and Tom Campbell, *Fighting Slavery in Chicago* (Chicago, IL: Ampersand Inc., 2009).

16. "Auxiliary Movements," *Young America*, March 21, 1846 and editorial April 29, 1848; "Land Reform," *Albany Patriot*, January 26, February 2, 1848, and also "The Auburn Convention" [from *Albany Patriot*], *Wisconsin Freeman*, February 16, 1848; Salem, Ohio *Anti-Slavery Bugle*, July 6, 1849. For Chapin, see Henry Christman, *Tin Horns and Calico* (New York: Collier Books, 1961), pp. 282–3; and Sewell, *A House Divided*, pp. 51–4, 56, 66–7, 117. "Anti-Slavery Convention," *Voice of Industry*, May 8, 1846. On Rogers, "An Idea" [from *Herald of Freedom*], *Working Man's Advocate*, June 29, 1844, p. 2. Concord in Merrimack county was the residence of Nathaniel Peabody Rogers and his *Herald of Freedom*, cited favorably by the NRA.

17. *Whig Almanac for 1849*, p. 49, and *Whig Almanac for 1851*, p. 42, both published by Greeley's *Tribune*, and "Popular Vote for President" in *National Reform Almanac for 1849*, p. 47.

18. Ingalls, *Reminiscences*, pp. 26, 37; *National Reform Almanac for 1849*, p. 47; "Reform" [from Peoria *Register*], *Young America*, April 29, 1848, p. 3; and Thomas A. Devyr, *The Odd Book of the Nineteenth Century, Or, "Chivalry" in Modern Days* [American section] (New York: the Author, 1882), p. 312. See also Richard H. Sewall's *Ballots for Freedom: Antislavery Politics in the United States, 1837–1860* (Oxford: Oxford University Press, 1976).

19. "Letter from Mr. Van Buren," *New Era of Industry*, July 27, 1848, p. 2, with earlier discussions in the issues of June 15, 19, July 6, 1848; *Albany Patriot*, May 3, 1848. On Pennsylvania, "Free Soil Movements," *American Freeman*, September 20, 1848; on Baltimore, see Snodgrass letter and Van Amringe's response under "Buffalo Convention," *Young America*, September 23, 1848, p. 4; and, Zahler, *Eastern Workingmen*, p. 97n.

20. James B. Doyle, *The Twentieth Century History of Steubenville and Jefferson County, Ohio and Reprentative Citizens* (Chicago, IL: Richmond-Arnold Publishing, 1910), pp. 314, 315; "Hon. Robert Smith" [from *Randolph County Record*], *Young America*, May 24 (p. 2), November 1 (p. 1), 1845. On Smith, see *Combined History of Randolph, Monroe and Perry Counties, Illinois* (Philadelphia, PA: J. L. McDonough & Co., 1883), pp. 195–6. See also *National Reform Almanac, for 1849* (New York: the NRA, 1849), p. 46, and also Ms Rolls of the Brotherhood of the Union in Brotherhood of America Papers, Pennsylvania Historical Society, Philadelphia.

21. James B. Stewart, *Joshua R. Giddings and the Tactics of Radical Politics* (Cleveland, OH: Press of Case Western Reserve University, 1970); Lewis Masquerier, *Sociology* (New York: the Author, 1877), p. 103; Joseph L. Norris, "The Land Reform Movement," the second essay in "Phases of Chicago History," published in the *Papers in Illinois History and Transactions for 1937* (Springfield, IL: Illinois State Historical Society, 1937), pp. 73–82; George W. Julian, *Political Recollections, 1840 to 1870* (Chicago, IL: Jansen, McClurg and Co., 1884), p. 103. See also Stephen E. Maizlish, *The Triumph of Sectionalism: the*

Transformation of Ohio Politics, 1844–1856 (Kent, OH: Kent State University Press, 1983); Frederick J. Blue, *The Free Soilers: Third Party Politics, 1848–54* (Urbana, IL: University of Illinois Press, 1973); John Mayfield, *Rehearsal for Republicanism: Free Soil and the Politics of Antislavery* (Washington, NY: Kennikat Press, 1980); Jonathan Earle, *Jacksonian Antislavery and the Politics of Free Soil, 1824–1854* (Chapel Hill, NC: University of North Carolina Press, 2004).

22. New England activities and E. Wright quoted, Zahler, *Eastern Workingmen*, pp. 88n., 98n.; "The Southport Convention," *American Freeman*, February 10, 1847, p. 1 on Clement; "Letter of I.P. Walker" [from *Waukesha Democrat*], *American Freeman*, January 31, March 14, 1849, which also includes a defense of Chase's resolutions in the legislature; Theodore Clarke Smith, *The Liberty and Free Soil Parties in the Northwest* (London: Longmans, Green & Co., 1897), pp. 210–13, 214–15, 215n.

23. Over twenty-five years later, shortly before his death, Smith wrote Ingalls "saying, he wanted to see Mr. Ingalls again, and hear him sing 'Acres and Hands'." Ingalls, *Reminiscences*, pp. 34, 43–4, also 29–30, 38, 39, 40, 167–8. On Jackson, see Commons et al., *Documentary History of American Industrial Society*, vol. 8, p. 26; Gerald Sorin, *The New York Abolitionists: A Case Study of Political Radicalism* (Westport, CT: Greenwood, 1971); Lewis Perry, *Radical Abolitionism: Anarchy and the Government of God in Antislavery Thought* (Ithaca, NY: Cornell University Press, 1973), p. 178n; Sewell, *A House Divided*, pp. 69, 76, 117.

24. L. A. Hine, *A Lecture on Garrisonian Politics, before the Western Philosophical Institute; Delivered in Cincinnati, Sunday, April 24th, 1853* (Cincinnati, OH: Longley, 1853), pp. 4, 14, 15, 16, 22–3, on Constitution and disunion, pp. 7–12, and electoral abstention, pp. 16–18. On Hine's later work, see "Xenia," *Emancipator*, June 30, 1877; "Workingmen's Party of the United States," *Emancipator*, August 18, 1877; "The Opening of the Ohio Campaign," *Emancipator*, September 1, 1877.

25. "Meeting in Philadelphia" and "Anti-Slavery Convention in the Assembly Buildings" [from the *Daily Republic*], *National Anti-Slavery Standard*, December 28, 1848, p. 123; excerpts from the *National Anti-Slavery Standard* of June 7, 1849 and the *Liberator* of June 8, 1849 in *The Frederick Douglass Papers: Series One. Speeches, Debates and Interviews, Vol. II: 1847–1854*, ed. John W. Blassingame et al. (New Haven, CT: Yale University Press, 1982), p. 202 and n. Philip Foner, *American Socialism and Black Americans From the Age of Jackson to World War II* (Westport, CT: Greenwood, 1977), p. 13 misquoted Charles Lenox Redmond as being "out of patience" with the National Reformers, but the original account clearly shows that Redmond was talking not about the NRA but abolitionists unwilling to accept the Free Soil party.

26. "Fourteenth Annual Meeting of the American Antislavery Society," *National Antislavery Standard*, May 18, 1848, p. 203, and Letter to *National Antislavery Standard*, May 25, 1848, p. 207.

NOTES

27. In addition to the resolutions passed at the 1848 National Industrial Congress, see West's letters in *National Antislavery Standard*, June 22, 1848, p. 12; and on "Self-Government," see *National Antislavery Standard*, March 22, 1849, p. 171.

28. John Lithgow, *Equality: or, A history of Lithconia* (Philadelphia, PA: the Liberal Union, 1837), pp. 26–7, 53 (the work originally serialized as "Equality—A Political Romance," *The Temple of Reason*, May 22–July 3, 1802, pp. 132–3, 141–2, 149–51, 157–9, 165–7, 172–4, 177–9). On Etzler, see Howard P. Segal, *Technological Utopianism in American Culture* (Syracuse, NY: Syracuse University Press, 2005), pp. 89–91. Etzler's publisher, Peter Eckler, later sold his operation to the *Truth Seeker*, the post-Civil War national weekly of the freethinkers. See George E. MacDonald, *Fifty Years of Freethought* (New York: Truthseeker Press, 1929), vol. 1, pp. 262 and n., 263f, vol. 2, p. 285. For the village as the result of collaboration between Evans and Masquerier, see "National Reform Settlement, No. II," *Young America*, January 17, 1846, p. 2; "Industrial Congress," *Voice of Industry*, June 18, 1847, pp. 1–2; Masquerier's "Diagram of the Proposed Village," *Young America! Principles and Objects of the National Reform Association, or Agrarian League; by a Member* (New York: [NRA], [1846?]), pp. 5–6; "Our Principles," *Working Man's Advocate*, April 6, 1844, p. 2, reprinted in Reeve Huston, *Land and Freedom: Rural Society, Popular Protest, and Party Politics in Antebellum New York* (Oxford: Oxford University Press, 2000), p. 140.

29. Norris, "The Land Reform Movement," pp. 73–82. See Don E. Fehrenbacher's *Chicago Giant, Biography of "Long John" Wentworth* (Madison, WI: American History Research Center, 1957), pp. 73, 74, 148, 197.

30. Seth Paine to *Albany Patriot*, July 7, 1847, which followed an earlier letter with similar complaints in the issue of June 2, 1847; Lovejoy quoted Edward Magdol, *Owen Lovejoy, Abolitionist in Congress* (New Brunswick, NJ: Rutgers University, 1967), pp. 81, also 41–5, 60–62, 78–9, 81, 88, 95. See also Owen Lovejoy, William F. Moore and Jane Ann Moore, *His Brother's Blood: Speeches and Writings, 1838–64* (Urbana, IL: University of Illinois Press, 2004). On Collins and Dyer, see Van Amringe's letter on Dyer, *Young America*, April 29, 1848, p. 4; Norris, "The Land Reform Movement," pp. 78–9n.; and James H. Collins, "Arrest of Fugitives in Chicago," *Wisconsin Freeman*, November 10, 1846, p. 2. Possibly the "Charles B. Dyer" associated with the Fourierists at Cincinnati. Commons et al., *Documentary History of American Industrial Society*, vol. 7, pp. 242, 248.

31. On Dyer's gubernatorial race, Paul Simon, *Lincoln's Preparation for Greatness: The Illinois Legislative Years* (Norman, OK: University of Oklahoma Press, 1965), p. 307. For Collins's insistence that their candidate in the Senate race "be a radical," see Magdol, *Owen Lovejoy*, pp. 118–19. Roy P. Basler, "Introduction" to John Lock Scripps, *Life of Abraham Lincoln*, ed. Roy P. Basler, notes by Lloyd A Dunlap (Bloomington, IN: Indiana University Press, 1961), pp. 17–18.

32. Frances M. Morehouse, *The Life of Jesse W. Fell* (Urbana, IL: University of Illinois Press, 1916), published as *University of Illinois Studies in the Social Sciences*, 6 (June 1916), pp. 265–393.

33. Smith, *The Liberty and Free Soil Parties in the Northwest*, pp. 98, 102, 132, 136, 146, 154–55. "Liberty State Convention," April 12, 1848, p. 2. A Janesville observer described it as "about three parts Democracy, one part Abolition, one or two *scruples* of Whiggery and a grain of National Reform," quoted in Richard N. Current, *The Civil War Era, 1848–1873: History of Wisconsin* (Madison, WI: Wisconsin Historical Society Press, 1976), pp. 202–3; Ms Rolls in Brotherhood of America Papers.

34. "Constitutional Convention" [from *Madison Expositor*], *Wisconsin Freeman*, November 10, 1846, p. 2; Warren Chase, "Association With Combination" [from *Boston Investigator*] *Young America*, July 11, 1846, p. 4; along with "Mr. Van Amringe's Mission," December 8, 1847, p. 2, "Land Reform" [from *Southport Telegraph*], *American Freeman*, April 12, 1848, p. 4.

35. "Reminiscences of the late Andrew E. Elmore of Green Bay, in an interview with Deborah Beaumont Martin," *Proceedings of the State Historical Society of Wisconsin at its Fifty-Eighth Annual Meeting, Held Oct. 20, 1910* (Madison, WI: State Historical Society of Wisconsin, 1911), pp. 190–92, 195–6; and Elmore's 1880 reminiscences in *The History of Waukesha County, Wisconsin* (Chicago, IL: Western Historical Company, 1880), pp. 358, 369, 371, 420, 491–2, 760, 763, with further references on pp. 420, 756, 760.

36. See *American Freeman* on "Mr. Van Amringe's Mission" [from *Young America*], December 8, 1847, p. 2, with subsequent reporting on his tour into April 1848, as well as his previously cited correspondence in *Young America*. "Land Reform in Wisconsin," *New York Daily Tribune*, April 3, 1850, p. 1.

37. "The Results" with "Election Returns," "Waukesha County Official Canvas," "Waukesha County Official Canvas," *Waukesha Democrat*, November 13, 20, 1849, all p. 2; Smith, *The Liberty and Free Soil Parties in the Northwest*, pp. 210–13, 214–15, 215n.

38. Parsons, "Wisconsin Phalanx," *Wisconsin Freeman*, June 12, 1845, p. 1, and Rounds in June 11, August 25, 1846. Originally from Southport, the Fourierists apparently kept close ties to the community. On C. J. Allen, see "Annual Meeting of the Wisconsin Anti-Slavery Society," *Wisconsin Freeman*, February 12, 1845, and his letters and reports in the *Wisconsin Freeman* issues of April 21, May 26, August 11, 1847.

39. "Mr. Van Amringe," *American Freeman*, January 12, 1848, p. 2; "The Chicago Industrial Congress," "National Labor Reform Congress," "Labor Movements— National Industrial Congress," "Labor Movements" with "Adjournment of the Fifth National Industrial Congress," *New York Daily Tribune*, June 12 (p. 3), 13 (p. 3), 15 (p. 2), 17 (p. 3), 1850. The *Freeman* serialized Van Amringe's eight lectures on "National Reform" through the first weeks of 1848, and later republished a series on "Homestead Exemption" and "Land Limitation" that ran into early 1849.

40. Ingalls, *Reminiscences*, pp. 26, 37, 47; Devyr, *Odd Book*, pp. 113, 115; Evans's sale of land August 7, 1849 to William Mason, mentioning Laura Evans and witnessed by Cecelia Evans in Book K5, pp. 404–6; Seaver in *Investigator*, October 17, 1849, quoted in Zahler, *Eastern Workingmen*, 39n.

41. Ingalls, *Reminiscences*, pp. 35, 37–38, 47; Devyr, *Odd Book*, pp. 50–51, 56–9, 60, 66; Devyr and Keyser, *Spirit of the Age*, December 29, 1849, p. 410, cited in James J. Martin, *Men Against the State: The Expositors of Individualist Anarchism in America, 1827–1908* (DeKalb, IL: Adrian Allen Associates, 1953), p. 117f.

42. Zahler, *Eastern Workingmen*, p. 88n. "Mr. Van Schaick on Land Reform," *New York Daily Tribune*, April 16, 1849, p. 2. In 1849, the state elections reported the Libertymen with only 1311, significantly less than the over 8500 polled two years before, and the "Workingmen's" party only 650, as opposed to over 1700. *Whig Almanac for 1850*, 44.

43. "The Independent Order of Liberals," and "Suggestions for the Independent Order of Liberals," *Independent Beacon*, vol. 1 (August 1849), pp. 8–10, and (October 1849), pp. 135, 136–8; Albert Post, *Popular Freethought in America, 1825–1850* (New York: Columbia University Press, 1943), pp. 108–9. See also "Peoples' Sunday Meetings" under its auspices. *Investigator*, February 14, 1849.

44. Zahler, *Eastern Workingmen*, pp. 45 and n., 53n; John H. Klippart, *Brotherhood of the Union: Address Delivered at Freedom, Portage County, Ohio; At a Festival of the B.U. (H.F.) C.A. of Circle No. 10.–98*. (Cleveland, OH: Sanford & Hayward, 1852), pp. 3, 6, 16; "Dr. Jaques on Land Monopoly in 1835," *Working Man's Advocate*, July 20, 1844, p. 1; "Man's Inalienable Right to Land," *The Radical*, I (April 1841), pp. 50–52; *Constitution ... of Nimisilla Circle of the BUCA, No. 9 of the State of Ohio, and 97 of the CA* (Canton, OH: A. McGregor, Printer, 1851), pp. 3–4; "The White Banner" [from New York *America's Own* of August 3], *New York Daily Tribune*, August 6, 1850, p. 6. See, in general, Roger Butterfield's "George Lippard and his Secret Brotherhood," *Pennsylvania Magazine of History and Biography*, 79 (July 1955), pp. 285–309.

45. From the *New York Daily Tribune*, see "The New-York City Industrial Congress," June 7, 1850, p. 4; "Brotherhood of the Union—Its Objects," July 3, 1850, pp. 2, 8; "Labor Movements," July 13, 1850, p. 3; "The White Banner" [from New York *America's Own* of August 3], August 6, 1850, p. 6; "Labor Movements," August 17, 1850, p. 4; "City Industrial Congress—Second Year" and "Brotherhood of the Union," October 23, 1851, pp. 5, 7; and, "Kossuth in New-York," *New York Daily Tribune*, December 8, 1851, p. 4; Also Nazarene Circle, "The Congress of Trades," *New York Herald*, August 15, 1850, p. 2, and Zahler, *Eastern Workingmen*, pp. 45, 53n.

46. William J. Simmons, *Men of Mark: Eminent, Progressive and Rising* (Cleveland, OH: G. M. Rewell, 1887), pp. 374–83, especially 374–5. On the Varneys, note that the correspondence of Warren and the Varneys from early 1847 is printed in Warren's *Practical Details in Equitable Commerce* (New York: Fowler & Wells, 1852); Masquerier wrote them [undated, ca. 1846], Lant Papers, and they published John Pickering's *The Working Man's Political Economy: Founded Upon the Principle of Immutable Justice, and the Inalienable Rights of*

Man (Cincinnati, OH: Thomas Varney, 1847). William V. Barr later shared a position later with black candidates on the United Labor ticket. Chicago *Daily Tribune*, February 27, 1887, p. 1, and *Labor Enquirer*, March 9, 1887, p. 4.

47. "The Land Question," and "Review of the Free Soil Movement," *Western Quarterly Review*, 1 (January 1849), pp. 28–44, 108–11; "H. H. Van Amringe, Esq.," and "Public Lands" [from *Ohio Organ and Sons of Temperance Record*], *Voice of Industry*, August 6, 1847, pp. 2, 4; *Wisconsin Freeman*, January 12, 1848. See "The Industrial Congress," *Cincinnati Gazette*, and the *Cincinnati Daily Commercial* for June 9, 1849. See also "Homes for All" [from Philadelphia *Dollar Democrat*], *Cist's Weekly Advertiser*, June 13, 1849.

48. Ingalls, *Reminiscences*, p. 56; Also mentioned is the participation of a Mr. Plotts and a Mr. Daniels, probably Naomit Plotts and Edward Daniels. For "Colonel" Daniel S. Curtiss of Mechanics State Council, San Francisco at the Cincinnati Congress of the National Labor Union, August 15–22, 1870, see Commons et al., *Documentary History of American Industrial Society*, vol. 9, p. 259. On Ceresco, see Joseph Schafer's "The Wisconsin Phalanx," *Wisconsin Magazine of History*, 19 (June 1935), pp. 454–74.

49. "The Secondary, Subsidiary or auxiliary principles" in "Fundamental Principles" published in "Adjournment of the Fifth National Industrial Congress," *New York Daily Tribune*, June 15, 1850, p. 3; "Letter of Alvan E. Bovay," *Albany Patriot*, January 26, 1848, p. 41.

50. Smith, *The Liberty and Free Soil Parties in the Northwest*, pp. 215, 234–5; and on Paine, *American Freeman*, December 6, 1848 and advertisements for his legal practice.

51. See John G. Gregory, "The Land Limitation Movement: A Wisconsin Episode of 1848–1851," *Parkman Club Publications*, No. 14 (Milwaukee, WI: Parkman Club, 1897).

52. "The North Star," *Voice of Industry*, December 31, 1847, p. 3; Ingalls, *Reminiscences*, p. 35; "Anti-Slavery Convention in the Assembly Buildings," *National Anti-Slavery Standard*, December 28, 1848, p. 123; "National Reform," in *The Life and Writings of Frederick Douglass*, ed. Philip S. Foner (5 vols.; New York: International Publishers, 1950–75), vol. 5, p. 111; and, *The Frederick Douglass Papers: Series One*, ed. John W. Blassingame et al. (5 vols.; New Haven, CT: Yale University Press, 1979), vol. 2, p. 307.

Chapter 7   Free Soil Radicalized: The Rise and Course of the Free Democrats, 1849–53

1. "The Hale Dinner," *Boston Herald*, May 6, 1853, p. 2; "The Ingraham Committee," "Society of Universal Democratic Republicans," presided over by John P. Hale, McMullen in Chair, "The Ingraham Committee and the Universal Democratic Republicanism," "The Neutrality Laws," *New York Times*, October 28, 1853, pp. 1, 5, November 11, 1853, p. 1, January 11, 1854, p. 5.

2. *History of Labour in the United States*, ed. John R. Commons, David J. Saposs, Helen L. Sumner, E. B. Mittelman, Henry Elmer Hoagland, John B. Andrews, Selig Perlman, Don D. Lescohier, Elizabeth Brandeis, and Philip Taft (2nd edition; 4 vols.; New York: Macmillan, 1947), vol. 1, p. 552 and n. For Philadelphia, see "A Review of the Industrial Union Movement" in *A General Report of the Industrial Union No. 1* (Philadelphia, PA: the Industrial Union, 1853), pp. 5–21; *Quaker City Weekly*, February 9(?), 1850. On Mills: John Bell Bouton, *Life and Choice Writings of George Lippard* (New York: H. H. Randall, 1855), pp. 91, 92; Roll of Members, Circle No. 92. The movement is also credited with fostering a succession of cooperative papers, including: Cincinnati *Nonpareil*; St. Louis *Signal*; Columbus *Fact*; Steubenville *Messenger*; Allegheny City *Enterprise*; Pittsburgh *Union*; Auburn *Herald*.

3. The standard sources from the Commons history through Sean Wilentz cover the NYCIC, though my *Young America* takes a somewhat different approach (see pp. 105, 106).

4. John H. Klippart, *Brotherhood of the Union: Address Delivered at Freedom, Portage County, Ohio; At a Festival of the B.U. (H.F.) C.A. of Circle No. 10.–98.* (Cleveland, OH: Sanford & Hayward, 1852), pp. 10–11; The Mr. Daniels referred to here is probably Edward Daniels, an abolitionist who later rode with John Brown in Kansas and turned up in land reform circles for many years after the war.

5. The *New York Daily Tribune* covered the "Walker boom" in the NYCIC through its regular columns on "Labor Movements."

6. "Labor Movements," *New York Daily Tribune*, May 30, 1851, p. 6. See also Merle Curti, "Isaac P. Walker: Reformer in Mid-Century Politics," *Wisconsin Magazine of History*, 34 (Autumn 1950), pp. 3–6, 58–62; and Amy Bridges, *A City in the Republic, Antebellum New York and the Origins of Machine Politics* (Cambridge: Cambridge University Press, 1984).

7. See piece from *Young America* reprinted in the *Independent Beacon*, vol. 1, pp. 509–12; *New York Daily Tribune*, April 9, 1851, p. 7.

8. *The Black Worker to 1869*, ed. Philip S. Foner and Ronald L. Lewis (Philadelphia, PA: Temple University Press, 1978), pp. 245–66.

9. Invitation from "Industrial Congress," *Voice of Industry*, June 11, 1847.

10. On Bowers, see Benjamin Quarles, *Black Abolitionists* (New York: Oxford University Press, 1969), pp. 7, 25, 26; William J. Simmons, *Men of Mark: Eminent, Progressive and Rising* (Cleveland, OH: G. M. Rewell, 1887), p. 202; and *A Documentary History of the Negro People*, ed. Herbert Aptheker (2 vols.; New York: International Publishers, 1971), vol. 1, pp. 105, 114, 176, 214.

11. Simmons, *Men of Mark*, pp. 374–83, especially 374–5. James M. Morris discusses the relationship of Clark and "William Haller: 'The Disturbing Element'," *Cincinnati Historical Society Bulletin*, 28 (Winter 1970), pp. 260, 265, 282–3, though he erroneously dates the inception of Haller's involvement as 1861 rather than ten or eleven years earlier. On the Varneys, see the letters in Warren's *Practical Details in Equitable Commerce* (New York: Fowler & Wells,

1852); Masquerier to the Varneys [undated, ca. 1846], in the Lant Papers, Missouri History Museum, St. Louis.

12. Hine noted with disgust that "one delegate declared that he would not sit with a colored man, and left the congress." *Cincinnati Daily Nonpareil*, June 11 (p. 2), 1851.

13. Van Amringe, *Wisconsin Freeman*, March 22, 1848; other expectations quoted in *Voice of Industry*, October 16, 1846.

14. "Call for a National Convention of the Liberty Party," *Frederick Douglass Paper*, June 26, 1851, repeated July 24, 1851, signed by, among others, Samuel R. Ward of Massachusetts, and James H. Collins of Illinois.

15. Jonathan Katz, *Resistance at Christiana: The Fugitive Slave Rebellion, Christiana, Pennsylvania, September 11, 1851: A Documentary Account* (New York: Crowell, 1974).

16. Published in our offices Fr. Schmidt, Washington DC. "Der National Demokrat," *National Era*, November 3, 1853, p. 175, c6–8. "Extracts from Our Correspondence," *Daily National Era*, February 8, 1854, p.2, c2.

17. *Proceedings of the Seventh Industrial Congress* ... (Washington, DC: n.p., 1852), p. 1; and, for Philadelphia's preparations, "The Great Mass Meeting at the Chinese Museum," in *The Jubilee Harbinger for 1854*, pp. 309–14.

18. *Proceedings of the Seventh Industrial Congress*, p. 2; letters to Pierce from Price, June 7; Gordon, June 14; Devyr, June 18, 23, 1852; A. G. H. Duganne, July 2; Price (with Croly, A. G. Levy, Commerford, and David Marsh), July 5; E. W. Capron, July 27, 1852. The last of Devyr's letters had several enclosures: a leaflet *To the Land Reform Forces of New York State* dated June 11; Cochrane's letter to Pierce of June 18, 1852 had several enclosures. Pierce got other letters from August G. H. Duganne and E. W. Capron.

19. See account of the "Meeting of Land Reformers in New York—Important Action" [from *New York Tribune*] in *Dollar Weekly Nonpareil*, August 12, 1852, p. 2, c5–6; "Meeting of the Independent Democrats at the Chinese Building," *New York Daily Tribune*, August 7, 1852, p. 5. William G. West is the delegate to Pittsburg. Other delegates included Leavitt and Russel T. Trall.

20. "Land Reform Meeting at Military Hall, Bowery," *New York Daily Tribune*, August 18, 1852, p. 7; Either that of August 12 or of August 16, 1852, both in SEN32A-J2, Box 150, f 8/9/52–2/22/53.

21. See "Land Reform," *New York Daily Tribune*, August 11, 1852, p. 5. In addition to those mentioned, Johnson, Wittenberg, and Bailey spoke.

22. Schuyler Marshall, "The Free Democracy Convention of 1852," *Pennsylvania History*, 22 (1955), pp. 146–67; "Free Democratic National Convention," *The National Era*, August 19, 1852, 2; Thomas H. McKee, *National Conventions and Platforms of All Political Parties, 1789–1900* (Baltimore, MD: Friedenwald Co., 1900), p. 77; Helene Zahler, *Eastern Workingmen and National Land Policy* (New York: Columbia University Press, 1941), p. 100 and n. The Free Democrats with land reform connections at the state convention included John Sheddon, William B. Thomas, and William J. Mullen. "Free Soil State Convention at Pittsburgh" and "The National Free Soil Convention," *New*

York Daily Tribune, August 11, 1852, p. 5. The overlap of program, leadership and participants indicate that M. Leon Perkal is mistaken in asserting that this current did not convince the Liberty Party. "American Abolition Society: A Viable Alternative to the Republican Party?" *The Journal of Negro History*, 65 (Winter 1980), pp. 57, 65.

23. In general, see Marshall, "The Free Democracy Convention of 1852"; Charles B. Going, *David Wilmot, Free Soiler* (New York: D. Appleton & Company, 1924; reprinted Gloucester, MA: P. Smith, 1966); Eric Foner, "The Workingmen Party Revisited," *Journal American History*, 56 (1969), pp. 262–79; Joseph G. Rayback, *Free Soil, the Election of 1848* (Lexington, KY: University Press of Kentucky, 1970).

24. "Land Reform Meeting at Military Hall, Bowery," *New York Daily Tribune*, August 18, 1852, p. 7; "CITY NEWS," *New York Herald*, August 19, 1852, p. 2.

25. *Young America! Principles and Objects of the National Reform Association, or Agrarian League. By a Member* (New York: [NRA], [1845]), p. 1; and Commerford, from regular NRA meeting, in *Working Man's Advocate*, January 18, 1845, and from "Land Reform," *New York Daily Tribune*, August 11, 1852, p. 5; "Address" in *Proceedings of the Seventh Industrial Congress*, pp. 12–13.

26. "Another Ticket and Platform," *New York Daily Tribune*, August 4, 1852, p. 4. This could be the Eliphalet Kimball, active in reform circles, who later wrote from New Hampshire to the Third Annual convention of the American Labor Reform League, though another man with the same name had been active in reform circles prior to his death in 1863. *The Word*, 2 (June 1873), p. 1.

27. Theodore Dwight, *The Roman Republic of 1849* (New York: R. Van Dien, 1851), pp. 198–208; Christopher Hippert, *Garibaldi and His Enemies: The Clash of Arms and Personalities in the Making of Italy* (Harmondsworth: Penguin Books, 1987), p. 104, 106, 108, 110; H. Forbes, "Italian Affairs in the Roman Republic and Its Calumniators," *National Era*, 4 (July 4, 1850), p. 105; George M. Trevelyan, *Garibaldi's Defence of the Roman Republic: 1848–9* (London: Longmans, Green, 1949), pp. 270, 350; André Viotti, *Garibaldi; the Revolutionary and His Men* (Dorset: Blandford Press, 1979), p. 89; "Italian Affairs in the Roman Republic and Its Calumniators," *National Era*, July 4, 1850, p. 105; "A Roman" letter to editor, June 25, "Garibaldi and Colonel Forbes," *New York Times*, June 28, 1859, p.1; H. Forbes, "Catechism of the Patriotic Volunteer," from his *Manual for the Patriotic Volunteer on Active Service in Regular and Irregular War* (2nd edition; 2 vols.; New York: W. H. Tinson, Printer, 1855), vol. 1, pp. viii, 9, 10. Emiliana P. Noether, "Roman Republic 1849"; "The State of Europe," London *The Times*, July 24, 1849; p. 6.

28. "Tuscany" under "Austria and Hungary," London *The Times*, October 20, 1849; p. 6; Dwight, *The Roman Republic of 1849*, pp. 208–9; "Garibaldi," London *The Red Republican*, July 6, 1850, p. 24; "Italian Affairs in the Roman Republic and Its Calumniators," National Era, July 4, 1850, p. 105; and, Forbes to F. B. Sanborn, January 9, 1858 in "Most Important Disclosures," *New York Herald*, October 27, 1859, p. 3; William J. Linton, *Threescore and Ten Years, 1820 to 1890* (New York: Charles Scribner's Sons, 1894), pp. 121–2, and his

European Republicans: Reflection of Mazzini and His Friends (London: Lawrence & Bullen, 1892), p. 124. See Trevelyan's description of Forbes in *Garibaldi's Defence of the Roman Republic*, p. 351.

29. Item from the *Tribune* under "Notice to Correspondents," London *The Red Republican*, October 26, 1850, p. 148; "The United States," *The Morning Chronicle*, September 24, 1850; Howard R. Marraro, *American Opinion on the Unification of Italy 1846–1861* (New York: Columbia University Press, 1932), pp. 62–3; Forbes to F. B. Sanborn, January 9, 1858 in "Most Important Disclosures," *New York Herald*, October 27, 1859, p. 3; "A Roman" letter to editor, June 25, "Garibaldi and Colonel Forbes," *New York Times*, June 28, 1859, p. 1.

30. Notices in *Red Republican*, 1 (November 16, 23, 1850, January 18, 1851), pp. 173, 180–81, 481. On the British associations, see Jamie L. Bronstein, *Land Reform and Working-Class Experience in Britain and the United States, 1800–1862* (Stanford, CA: Stanford University Press, 1999). See also Van Amringe, "National Reform—No. 1," *American Freeman*, January 19, 1848.

31. Two pieces entitled "The Ingraham Testimonial," *New York Herald*, September 9, October 28, 1853, both p. 4; "New York City," "The Koszta Affair," "New-York City. Republican Festival. Grand Celebration of the Universal Democratic Republicans. Processions, Banquets at the Shakespeare Hotel, Speeches, &c., &c.," and "Anniversary of the French Republic," *New York Times*, December 1, 1852 (p. 6), September 23 (p. 1), 1853, February 25 (p. 8), 1854, and February 26 (p. 2), 1855.

32. Jon Alexander and David Williams, "Andreas Bernardus Smolnikar: American Catholic Apostate and Millennial Prophet," *American Benedictine Review*, 35 (March 1985), pp. 50–63. See also Andrew B. Smolnikar, *Secret Enemies of True Republicanism* (Springhill, PA: R. D. Eldridge, 1859). For John H. W. Toohey's reply to Mr. Matthias, arguing for the compatibility of spiritualism with Christianity, see "New York Conference," *Spiritual Telegraph Papers*, 8, p. 160.

33. Arthur Lehning, "The International Association, 1855–1859," in his *From Buonarroti to Bakunin: Studies in International Socialism* (Leiden: E. J. Brill, 1970), p. 173; Marraro, *American Opinion on the Unification of Italy*, pp. 33–67, and his "Garibaldi in New York," *New York History*, 27 (April 1947), pp. 179–203, also in *Pages from the Garibaldian Epic*, ed. Anthony P. Campanella (Sarasota, FL: International Institute for Garibaldian Studies, 1984); Dwight, *The Roman Republic of 1849*, p. 208; H. Nelson Gay, "Garibaldi's American Contacts and His Claims to American Citizenship," *American Historical Review*, 38 (October 1932), pp. 5–6, 7.

34. Carl Wittke, *The Utopian Communist: A Biography of William Weitling, Nineteenth-Century Reformer* (Baton Rouge, FL: Louisiana State University Press, 1950). See also Boris Nicolaevsky, "Towards a History of 'the Communist League' 1847–1852," *International Review of Social History*, 1 (August 1956), pp. 234–52, and the latest contribution to the literature on his career in general, see Patrick Eiden-Offe, *Die Poesie der Klasse: romantischer Antikapitalismus und die Erfindung des Proletariats* (Berlin: Matthes & Seitz Berlin, 2017). On the Germans generally, see Carl Wittke, *Refugees of Revolution: The German Forty-*

Eighters in America (Philadelphia, PA: University of Pennsylvania Press, 1952); Bruce Levine, *The Spirit of 1848: German Immigrants, Labor Conflicts, and the Coming of the Civil War* (Urbana, IL: University of Illinois Press, 1992); Mischa Honeck, *We Are the Revolutionists: German-Speaking Immigrants and American Abolitionists after 1848* (Athens, GA: University of Georgia Press, 2011); and Alison Clark Efford, *German Immigrants, Race, and Citizenship in the Civil War Era* (Washington, DC: German Historical Institute; Cambridge: Cambridge University Press, 2013).

35. Hermann Kriege, *Dokumentation einer Wandlung vom Burschenschafter und Revolutionär zum Demokraten (1840–1850)*, ed. Heinrich Schlüter und Alfred Wesselmann (Osnabrück: Der Andere Verlag, 2002).

36. In addition to Levine's *Spirit of 1848*, see Honeck, *We are the Revolutionists*, and Efford, *German Immigrants, Race, and Citizenship in the Civil War Era*.

37. Karl Obermann, *Joseph Weydemeyer: Ein Lebensbild, 1818–1866* (Berlin: Dietz, 1968).

38. "The Convention of Infidels," "The Society of Universal Democratic Republicanism," "Universal Democratic Republican Societies of United States of North America," "Meeting of Liberal Societies," "Union of the Liberal Societies," *New York Times*, January 7 (p. 4), 1853, April 12 (p. 8), 27 (p. 3), May 25 (p. 4), July 6 (p. 4), 1854.

39. On the composition, see "Circular of the Convention of Liberals in America," October 9, 1854, in *The Liberator*, October 27, 1854. See also "Liberal Societies Represented in this Convention" in "Convention of Liberal Societies," *New York Tribune*, October 13, 1854, p. 3; "The Society of Universal Democratic Republicans," "Society of Universal Republicanism," "The Universal Republican Democratic Society," *New York Herald*, December 21 (p. 4), 1853, January 25 (p. 8), April 12 (p. 8), 1854. See too Mark Lause, *A Secret Society History of the Civil War* (Urbana, IL: University of Illinois Press, 2011).

40. Two articles under the heading "Free Democratic State Convention," and, "The Free Soil State Convention—Their State Ticket," *New York Herald*, February 23 (p. 1), 24 (p. 1), September 2, 1853 (p. 4). For William West running as an independent councilman Untitled classified ad, *New York Herald* (morning edition) October 31, 1853, p. 3, c5.

41. "The Organization," "Constitution of the Free Democratic League of the City and County of New York," *National Era*, December 16, 1852, p. 202, October 27, 1853, p. 171; "The Free Democratic League," "Meeting of the Free Democratic League," *New York Times*, October 26 (p. 5), October 29, 1853 (p. 4); "Review," and "The Origins of the Republican Party," *The Historical Magazine*, Second series, 1 (May 1867), pp. 307–8, 330, 331, 333, and Third series, 2 (December 1873), p. 329.

42. James Oliver Horton and Lois E. Horton, *In Hope of Liberty: Culture, Community, and Protest Among Northern Free Blacks, 1700–1860* (New York: Oxford University Press, 1997); John Stauffer, *The Black Hearts of Men: Radical Abolitionists and the Transformation of Race* (Cambridge, MA: Harvard University Press, 2001); James McCune Smith, *The Works of James McCune*

Smith: Black Intellectual and Abolitionist, ed. John Stauffer, foreword by Henry Louise Gates Jr. (Oxford: Oxford University Press, 2006), particularly "The German Invasion," *The Anglo-African Magazine,* 1 (February 1859), pp. 44–52, (March 1859), pp. 83–6; Richard J. Hinton, "John Brown and his Men," *Frank Leslie's Popular Monthly* (June 1889), p. 695, and, for the later New York City connection, Richard J. Hinton, *John Brown and His Men* (New York: Funk & Wagnalls Company, 1894]), pp. 162–3; James McCune Smith, "Human Brotherhood and the Meaning of Communipaw," *The Works of James McCune Smith,* p. 92.

43. See Lause, *A Secret Society History of the Civil War,* pp. 45–6, 57–9, 61–5. On Sickles shooting of his wife's lover, see "Les souteneurs de la Famille aux États-Unis," *Le Libertaire,* March 12, 1859, pp. 1–2. On Cuba: Tom Chaffin, *Fatal Glory: Narciso Lopez and the First Clandestine U.S. War against Cuba* (Charlottesville, VA: University Press of Virginia, 1996), pp. 121–2. Richardson Hardy, *The History and Adventures of the Cuban Expedition* (Cincinnati, OH: L. Stratton, 1850).

44. "The Anniversary Meeting of the American Abolition Society," *Radical Abolitionist,* 2 (June 1857), p. 94; M. Leon Perkal, "American Abolition Society: A Viable Alternative to the Republican Party?" *The Journal of Negro History,* pp. 59–60, 65–7, (Winter 1980), pp. 57–8; *Proceedings of the Convention of Radical Political Abolitionists, held at Syracuse, N.Y. June 26th, 27th, and 28th, 1855* (New York: Central Abolition Board, 1855), p. 4; Lysander Spooner in *The Unconstitutionality of Slavery* (Boston, MA: Bela Marsh, 1860), originally 1845.

Chapter 8   The Pre-Revolutionary Tinderbox: Universal Democratic Republicans, Free Democrats and Radical Abolitionists, 1853–6

1. "Circular of the Convention of Liberals in America," *The Liberator,* October 27, 1854, p. 172; Richard J. Hinton, "John Brown and his Men," *Frank Leslie's Popular Monthly* (June 1889), p. 695, and, for the later New York City connection, Richard J. Hinton, *John Brown and His Men* (New York: Funk & Wagnalls Company, 1894]), pp. 162–3; Benjamin Quarles, *Allies for Freedom: Blacks and John Brown* (Oxford: Oxford University Press, 1974), pp. 52–3.

2. Eugene W. Leach, *Racine County Militant: An Illustrated Narrative of War Times, and a Soldiers' Roster* (Racine, WI: E. W. Leach, 1914), pp. 25, 27, 52, 381; *Daily Free Democrat,* October 17, 1850, March 16, 1854, quoted in Larry Gara, *The Liberty Line: the Legend of the Underground Railroad* (2nd edition; Lexington, KY: University Press of Kentucky, 1996), pp. 103, 113, 135–6. On Booth, see Richard N. Current, *The History of Wisconsin: Vol. II. The Civil War Era, 1848–1873* (Madison, WI: State Historical Society of Wisconsin, 1976), pp. 219–22, 261, 277, and, for Booth's defense, 235, 260, 276.

3. Brotherhood of the Union in Brotherhood of America Papers, Pennsylvania Historical Society, Philadelphia; John G. Gregory, "The Land Limitation

Movement: A Wisconsin Episode of 1848–1851," *Parkman Club Publications*, No. 14 (Milwaukee, WI: Parkman Club, 1897), pp. 89n., 92, 102–4; *Dictionary of Wisconsin Biography* (Madison, WI: WHS,1960), pp. 42–3; Larry Gara, *The Liberty Line: the Legend of the Underground Railroad* (2nd edition; Lexington, KY: University Press of Kentucky, 1996), pp. 103, 113, 135–6; *History of Milwaukee, from its First Settlement to the Year 1895* (2 vols.; Chicago, 1895), vol. 1, pp. 89–90, 216–17, 231; and Vroman Mason, "The Fugitive Slave Law in Wisconsin," *Proceedings of the State Historical Society of Wisconsin at Its Forty-Third Annual Meeting* (Madison, WI: State Historical Society of Wisconsin, 1895), pp. 117–44.

4. Ethan J. Kytle, "'A Transcendentalist Above All': Thomas Wentworth Higginson, John Brown, and the Raid at Harpers Ferry," *The Journal of the Historical Society*, 12 (September 2012), pp. 283–308; Richard J. Hinton, "Wendell Phillips: a Reminiscent Study," *The Arena*, 13 (July 1895), pp. 226–9, 234; C. Carroll Hollis, "R. J. Hinton; Lincoln's Reluctant Biographer," *The Centennial Review*, 5 (Winter 1961), pp. 66–7. See also Ray Boston, *British Chartists in America, 1834–1900* (Manchester: Manchester University Press, 1971), p. 92; Hinton, *John Brown and His Men*, pp. 199–201, 203n.–4n.; William A. Phillips, *The Conquest of Kansas, by Missouri and Her Allies* (Boston, MA: Phillips, Sampson and Co., 1856), p. 43.

5. *Monthly Jubilee*, 4 (March 1854), p. 87; Jeriel Root, *Analysis of Theology, Law, Religion and the Rights of Man* (Peoria, IL: Benjamin Foster, 1855), pp. 33–4, 40; John H. Klippart, *Brotherhood of the Union: Address Delivered at Freedom, Portage County, Ohio; At a Festival of the B.U. (H.F.) C.A. of Circle No. 10.–98.* (Cleveland, OH: Sanford & Hayward, 1852), p. 14.

6. From *New York Herald* (morning edition); "The United Liberal Society of the United States," "The Meeting at Pythagoras Hall," "The News," and item under "The News," and "The United Liberal Societies," April 28 (p. 4, c5–6), 29 (p. 2, c3), May 12 (p. 4, c4, 1–3), 25 (p. 4, c2), 27 (p. 2, c4), 1854.

7. "Meeting of the United Liberal Societies," *New York Herald* (morning edition), June 22, 1854, p. 8, c4.

8. "Convention of Liberal Societies,' *New-York Daily Tribune*, September 28, 1854, p. 6, c4; "Convention of Liberal Societies," *New York Herald* (morning edition), December 14, 1854, p. 5, c6.

9. Douglas claimed to be "anxious that those lands should be sold, peopled and taxed" while he was "wedded to no particular plan." *The Letters of Stephen A. Douglas*, ed. Robert W. Johannsen (Urbana, IL: University of Illinois Press, 1961), pp. 132, 188. For the Whigs: Thomas A. Devyr, *The Odd Book of the Nineteenth Century, Or, "Chivalry" in Modern Days* [American section] (New York: the Author, 1882), p. 41; "An Act," *National Reform Almanac for 1849*, pp. 33–4. For the July 4, 1851 inquiry from Dr. William J. Young on behalf of the land reformers, see *The Papers of Daniel Webster*, ed. Charles M. Wiltse and Harold D. Moser (14 vols.; Hanover, NH: Dartmouth College by the University Press of New England, 1974–80), ser. 1: *Correspondence*, vol. 7, p. 491.

10. From *The Vanguard*, vol. 1: see "Letter from W. Denton," (August 22, 1857), p. 196. Francis E. Hyer, "Missouri, Texas and Yucatan, Considered in Reference to Associative Movements," (August 29, 1857), p. 106 [*sic* 205]; Denton, "Kansas the Place for Reformers," (October 31, 1857), p. 260; William McDiarmid, "Extracts from Correspondence," (February 13, 1858), p. 374.

11. Warren's ideas appeared in various forms over the years before its final version as *Equitable Commerce: a New Development of Principles as Substituting for Laws and Governments* (New Harmony, IN: for the Author, 1846.). On Warren's Time Stores and push-back, A. Miltenberger, "'Cost the Limit of Price,'" and Alfred Cridge, "Remarks," *The Vanguard*, 1 (February 27, 1858), p. 386.

12. Stephen Pearl Andrews built them into *The Science of Society* nos. 1 and 2 (New York: Fowlers and Wells, 1852); Edward N. Kellogg, Labor and Other Capital (New York: for the Author, 1849). Edward F. Underhill took up the ideas of Kellogg, Warren and Andrews of Modern Times to the abolitionists in his "Cost the Limit of Price," *The Liberator*, October 14, 1853, p. 164; Cridge, "Remarks' in response to A. Miltenberger, "'Cost the Limit of Price,'" *The Vanguard*, 1 (February 27, 1858), p. 386.

13. On Newberry, see George E. McNeil, *The Labor Movement: The Problem of To-Day* (New York: The M. W. Hazen Co., 1887), p. 102; and his obituary, "Dr. Edward Newberry," *New York Times*, November 8, 1897, p. 8. Newberry embraced land reform along with spiritualism and phrenology, eventually moving to the Modern Times community where he carried his dental equipment in a hollow walking stick.

14. Albert Parry, *Garrets and Pretenders: A History of Bohemianism in America* (New York: Covici, Friede, 1933). On Clapp's earlier arrest in Lynn, see "Land of the Free and Home of the Brave," *Voice of Industry*, April 10, 1846, p. 2, but see generally Mark Lause, *The Antebellum Crisis and America's First Bohemians* (Kent, OH: Kent State University Press, 2009).

15. Theodore Clarke Smith, *The Liberty and Free Soil Parties in the Northwest* (London: Longmans, Green & Co., 1897), pp. 274, 280, 281, and quote from 282; Bovay quoted Frank A. Flower, *History of the Republican Party* (Springfield, IL: Union Publishing Company, 1884), pp. 147–8, 149–53; Eric Foner, *Free Soil, Free Labor, Free Men: the Ideology of the Republican Party before the Civil War* (New York: Oxford University Press, 1970); Hendrik Booraem V, *The Formation of the Republican Party in New York: Politics and Conscience in the Antebellum North* (New York: New York University Press, 1983); William E. Gienapp, *The Origins of the Republican Party, 1852–1856* (New York: Oxford University Press, 1987); Allan Nevins, *Ordeal of the Union* (2 vols.; New York: Scribner's Sons, 1947), vol. 2, pp. 322–3; *New York Daily Tribune*, June 17, 1856, p. 4.

16. Letter to the ULS. "The Polish Exiles," and "Free Democratic League," *New York Herald* (morning edition), June 30 (p. 2), and November 3 (pp. 5–6), 1854; "New-York City" "Union of the Liberal Societies," *New York Times*, July 6, 1854, p. 4.

17. "Catechism of the Patriotic Volunteer," from Forbes, *Manual for the Patriotic Volunteer on Active Service in Regular and Irregular War* (2nd edition; 2 vols.; New York: W. H. Tinson, Printer, 1855), vol. 2, pp. 59–95, with the party descriptions on pp. 84–5; "The Society of Universal Democratic Republicanism," "Meeting of Liberal Societies," "Convention of Liberal Societies," "Red Republican Demonstration. Celebration of the 22d September," "Liberal Societies," "Convention of Liberal Societies," *New York Times*, April 12 (p. 8), August 31 (p. 8), September 21 (p. 1), 23 (p. 1), 28 (p. 4), October 13 (p. 8), 1854; and Forbes, *Manual for the Patriotic Volunteer*, vol. 2, pp. 66–7.

18. "The Saratoga Convention," *New York Daily Tribune*, August 17, 1854, p. 4; "Anti-Nebraska Meeting at Saratoga," and "Temperance Meeting in Saratoga," both in the August 18 issue; "Anti-Nebraska Convention at Auburn," September 27, 1854, pp. 4–5, and, on the seceding group, September 27, 28, 1854.

19. "New-York City" "Convention of Liberal Societies," *New York Times*, October 13, 1854, p. 8.

20. From the *New York Times*, see "Political Intelligence" on "The 'Practical Democrats'," October 18, 1854, p. 8; and, "The Liberal Societies on Politics," October 20, 1854, p. 3. The well-indexed contemporary press extensively covered Practical Democrats and the American Democrats, and they are covered extensively in Mark Lause, *A Secret Society History of the Civil War* (Urbana, IL: University of Illinois Press, 2011). Participants mentioned included all the prominent land reformers still in the city. See also "A Letter to the American Slaves from those who have fled from American Slavery," *Proceedings of the Black State Conventions, 1840–1865*, ed. Philip S. Foner and George E. Walker (2 vols.; Philadelphia, PA: Temple University Press, 1979–80), vol. 1, p. 50.

21. "New-York City. Meeting of the Liberal Societies.—The Soule Affair.—Maine Law," *New York Times*, November 16, 1854, p. 8, from which the Poles were absent owing to preparations for their anniversary.

22. "Democratic Glorification," *New York Daily Tribune*, November 11, 1854. Also "Tammany Union and Harmony Demonstration," March 8, 1855; Amy Bridges, *A City in the Republic, Antebellum New York and the Origins of Machine Politics* (Cambridge: Cambridge University Press, 1984), pp. 116n.61, 116, 117nn.63–4; and *A Documentary History of American Industrial Society*, ed. John R. Commons et al. (10 vols., reprinted; New York: Russell & Russell, 1958), vol. 8, pp. 27, 287, 288, 301.

23. "New-York City" for "The City Poor. Meeting of the Unemployed," *New York Times*, December 22, 1854, p. 2; "Meeting of the Unemployed Workingmen in the Park," *New York Tribune*, December 23, 1854, p. 5.

24. Untitled items, "Interview of the Committee of Unemployed Laboring Men with Mayor Wood," *New York Tribune*, January 5, 1855, p. 7. "The Unemployed: Large Meeting in Hope Chapel," *New York Times*, January 9, 1855, p. 4.

25. "The City Poor. Meeting of the Unemployed," The Labor Movement. Second Meeting of the Unemployed," "Meeting of the Unemployed Workingmen in the Park," "The Labor Movement" on the "Workingmen's Conference," "Workingmen's Mass Meeting. Gathering at the Broadway Tabernacle," Letter

from Ben Price on "The Tabernacle Meeting," *New York Times*, December 22 (p. 2), 23 (pp. 3, 5), 1854, January 19 (p. 4), 30 (p. 4), and 31 (p. 3), 1855.

26. "Circular of the Convention of Liberals in America," *The Liberator*, October 27, 1854, p. 172; "Meeting of the Liberal Societies," *New York Times*, January 17, 1855, p. 4. On Davis's role, see "Labor. Condition of the Unemployed Poor," *New York Times*, March 1, 1855, p. 2.

27. "Labor. Condition of the Unemployed Poor," *New York Times*, March 1, 1855, p. 2.

28. Arthur Lehning, "The International Association, 1855–1859," in his *From Buonarroti to Bakunin: Studies in International Socialism* (Leiden: E. J. Brill, 1970), their American branches, 198–201; "Universal Democratic Republicans," *New York Daily Tribune*, March 7, 1855, p. 7. See also James H. Billington, *Fire in the Minds of Men: Origins of the Revolutionary Faith* (New York: Basic Books, 1980), pp. 326, 328; and, for G. Bonnin, Forbes, and others on, "Les Collectivistes Français (Les précurseurs théoriques)," *La Revue Socialiste*, 5 (March 1887), p. 221n.

29. Ruth Miller Elson, *Guardian of Tradition: American Schoolbooks of the Nineteenth Century* (Lincoln, NE: University of Nebraska Press, 1964), p. 38; *American Authors, 1600–1900*, eds. Stanley J. Kunitz and Howard Haycraft (New York: H. W. Wilson Company, 1938), p. 98; *National Reform Almanac for 1849* (New York: Young America, 1848), p. 20.

30. Bruce Levine, *The Spirit of 1848: German Immigrants, Labor Conflict, and the Coming of the Civil War* (Urbana, IL: University of Illinois Press, 1992); and Mischa Honeck, "We Are the Revolutionists: Forty-Eighters, Abolitionists, and the Struggle to Overthrow Slavery" (Ph.D. diss., University of Heidelberg, 2008).

31. "Minutes of the Convention," *Proceedings of the Convention of Radical Political Abolitionists, held at Syracuse, N.Y. June 26th, 27th, and 28th, 1855* (New York: Central Abolition Board, 1855), p. 10–51, 63. See also M. Leon Perkal, "American Abolition Society: A Viable Alternative to the Republican Party?" *The Journal of Negro History*, Winter 1980, pp. 58–60, 65–7.

32. "Minutes of the Convention," *Proceedings of the Convention of Radical Political Abolitionists*, pp. 52, 64–5; "Anti-Slavery Convention," *New York Daily Times*, June 28, 1855, p. 4, also "Radical Anti-Slavery Convention," *Liberator*, 25 (July 6, 1855), p. 107. On McIntosh. "The Labor Question," and "Things in General," *Boston Investigator*, January 13, 1864, p. 286; and, "The Cincinnati Movement," *Socialist*, September 21, 1878, p. 5.

33. "Minutes of the Convention," pp. 62–3; "The Abolition Convention," *New York Daily Times*, June 29, 1855, p. 1; and Perkal, "American Abolition Society," p. 58. Bonnie Laughlin-Schultz, *The Tie That Bound Us: The Women of John Brown's Family and the Legacy of Radical Abolitionism* (Ithaca, NY: Cornell University Press, 2018).

34. "General Convention of Radical Political Abolitionists, at Boston," *Liberator*, 25 (October 5, 1855), p. 179.

35. "Free Democratic Convention," *Ohio State Journal*, January 18, 1853, p. 3, "Free Democratic Convention in Pennsylvania," *New York Herald*, May 25, 1854, p. 8; Untitled on Pennsylvania," two entitled "Free Democratic Convention" on Massachusetts and Vermont, *Boston Herald*, June 4 (p. 4), September 15 (p. 4), 1853, July 14 (p. 2), 1854. "Extract from Our Correspondence," "To the Free Democracy of the State of New York," *National Era*, February 16 (p. 27), 1854, August 16 (p. 13), 1855. See also Robert S. Dabney's *A Defence of Virginia*. "Review," *The Historical Magazine*, second series, 3 (January 1868), p. 61; "More Fusion," *New York Times*, August 7, 1855, p. 4; *Brooklyn Daily Eagle*, August 8, 1855, p. 2, and those scattered sources on the party across the country.

36. Joshua King Ingalls, *Reminiscences of an Octogenarian* (New York: M. L. Holbrook & Company; London: L. N. Fowler, 1897), pp. 153, 156, 157–8, 159; *Free Love in America: A Documentary History*, ed. Taylor Stoehr (New York: AMS Press, 1979), pp. 6, 23, 319–21; and see also Lause, *The Antebellum Crisis and America's First Bohemians*, pp. 35–41.

37. The *New York Daily Tribune* closely followed the development of the Republican organization in the city and state from September through October; On Williamsburg, Devyr, *Odd Book*, pp. 66–9, 101–2. "A Circular" of the Democratic order, in *New York Daily Tribune*, March 4, 1856; "Voice of the Radical Democracy of New York," May 19, 1856; A. S. Diven and Benjamin Welch, Jr. at Democratic-Republican convention, July 19, 1856. See also Charles E. Heller, *In Advance of Fate: a Biography of George Luther Stearns, 1809–1867* (Amherst, MA: University of Massachusetts, 1985).

38. "Convention of Radical Abolitionists," *New York Daily Times*, February 17, 1857, p. 1.

39. *The Correspondent*, 2 (January 19, 1828), pp. 401–2. See also 2 (February 9, 16, 23, 1828), pp. 35–7, 46, 51–2, 65–6; Devyr, *Odd Book*, p. 115; "The Complimentary Ball" [from *Young America*], *Voice of Industry*, March 12, 19, 1847; Lewis Masquerier, *Sociology* (New York: the Author, 1877), p. 99; Fitzwilliam Byrdsall, *The History of the Loco-Foco or Equal Rights Party* (New York: Clement & Packard, 1842), pp. 14–15; *Investigator*, October 17, 1849, quoted in Helene Zahler, *Eastern Workingmen and National Land Policy* (New York: Columbia University Press, 1941), p. 39n.

40. On Evans's death, see the untitled notice, *New York Daily Tribune*, February 7, 1856, 7; see also Masquerier, *Sociology*, p. 99, which mistakenly dates the death on March 25, though correctly giving it as February 2 on p. 102. "Land Reform Meeting," and "The Land Reformers" with "The Land Reform Testimonial to the Memory of the late George H. Evans," *New York Herald*, February 17 (p. 5), April 13 (pp. 1, 5), 1856.

41. "The New Land-Grab," *New York Daily Tribune*, March 5, 1855, and "Kansas" by "B." of Iowa Point (the small community where Barr had settled), *New York Daily Tribune*, February 23, 1858. For the presence of social radicals in the settlement of Kansas and the struggle over its future, see Mark A. Lause, *Race*

and Radicalism in the Union Army (Urbana, IL: University of Illinois Press, 2009), pp. 9–24.

42. For this sketch of John Brown's activities in Kansas, see the biographical sources, particularly David S. Reynolds, *John Brown, Abolitionist: The Man Who Killed Slavery, Sparked the Civil War, and Seeded Civil Rights* (New York: Alfred A. Knopf, 2005).

43. Russell K. Hickman, "The Vegetarian and Octagon Settlement Companies," *Kansas Historical Quarterly*, 2 (November 1933), pp. 377–85; Daniel C. Fitzgerald, *Ghost Towns of Kansas: a Traveler's Guide* (Lawrence, KS: University Press of Kansas, 1988), pp. 130–33.

44. From *The Vanguard*, 1: see Denton, "Letter from William Denton," (October 10, 1857), p. 254; Denton, "Kansas the Place for Reformers," (October 31, 1857), p. 260; Denton, "Notes from the Lecturing Field," (November 7, 1857), p. 268; and, Henry Hiatt, "Letter from Kanzas," (March 6, 1858), p. 395. See also F. G. Hunt, "Letter from Kansas," (January 16, 1858), p. 339.

45. Leon Hühner, "Some Jewish Associations of John Brown," *Publications of the American Jewish Historical Society*, No. 23 (1915), pp. 55–78. John Mead, "Declarations of Liberty Representations of Black/White Alliances Against Slavery by John Brown, James Redpath, and Thomas Wentworth Higginson," *Journal for the Study of Radicalism*, 3 (Spring 2008), pp. 111–43.

46. Ingalls, *Reminiscences*, p. 35, 49; Hinton, *John Brown and His Men*, pp. 16, 35, 679; Phillips, *The Conquest of Kansas*, p. 332.

47. Nicole Etcheson "'Our Lives, Our Fortunes, and Our Sacred Honors': The Kansas Civil War and the Revolutionary Tradition," *American Nineteenth Century History*, 1 (2000), pp. 62–81.

48. The Kansas Indian named Tooley is quoted by John Speer in *Transactions of the Kansas State Historical Society*, 5 (1896), p. 111. On the Ottawas, Wilbur H. Siebert, *The Underground Railroad from Slavery to Freedom*; introduction by Albert B. Hart (New York: Macmillan Co., 1898), pp. 37, 38, 91–2. See also, on Jones, the explanation of John Brown Relics and Manuscripts, John T. Jones to John Brown, October 13, 1857, John Brown Papers, Kansas Historical Society; Hinton, *John Brown and His Men*, pp. 81–2, and, for the attack on Jones, Thomas Goodrich, *War to the Knife: Bleeding Kansas, 1854–1861* (Mechanicsburg, PA: Stackpole Books, 1998), pp. 158–9; and Reynolds, *John Brown*, pp. 157–8, 170, 173–4, 203; as well as Lause, *Race and Radicalism in the Union Army*.

49. Larry J. Schmits, "Quindaro: Kansas Territorial Free-State Port on the Missouri River," *The Missouri Archaeologist*, 49 (December 1988), pp. 89–145; Steve Collins, "In the Eye of the Border Storm: The Quindaro Regional Underground Railroad Stations," unpublished manuscript, Kansas Community College, Kansas City, Kansas, 1999; and Diane Eickhoff, *Revolutionary Heart: The Life of Clarina Nichols and the Pioneering Crusade for Women's Rights* (Kansas City, KS: Quindaro Press, [2006]).

50. Hinton, "Wendell Phillips: a Reminiscent Study," pp. 235–6. See also William E. Connelly, "Col. Richard J. Hinton," *Transactions of the Kansas State Historical Society, 1901–1902*, ed. George W. Martin, VII (Topeka, 1902), pp. 490, 493.

On Kansas: Richard J. Hinton, "Making Kansas a Free State," *The Chautauquan: a Weekly Newsmagazine* (1880–1914), 31 (July 1900), pp. 345–51; Hinton, "Wendell Phillips: a Reminiscent Study," pp. 226–41.

51. On Sumner: "Indignation Meeting in New York," May 31, 1856; and S. E. Church at the "Free Speech in Brooklyn," June 2, 1856; Ingalls, *Reminiscences*, p. 34. See also "National Radical Abolition Convention" preceded that of the Republicans by a day, *New York Daily Tribune*, May 29, 1856; and see also "Radical Abolition State Convention," September 19, 1856. "Republican State Convention," *New York Daily Tribune*, May 29, 1856; "Gerrit Smith, Again" and "A Second Letter from Mr. Geritt Smith," in *New York Daily Tribune*, August 17, 1855.

52. "Discussion in the National Abolition Convention," *Radical Abolitionist*, 1 (July 1856), p. 104.

53. Oswald Garrison Villard, *John Brown: 1800–1859: A Biography after Fifty Years* (Boston, MA: Houghton Mifflin Company, 1910), p. 248.

Chapter 9   The Spark: Small Initiatives and Mass Upheavals, 1856–60

1. "Radical Abolition Convention," *The National Era*, 1 (May 1, 1856), p. 70. The calls are at "The Liberty Party" and "The Radical Abolitionists," *New York Times*, April 12 (p. 4), May 29 (p. 1), 1856. See also "Call for a National Convention" two issues, "The National Nominating Convention" with "Minutes of the National Abolition Convention," and "Discussion in the National Abolition Convention," *Radical Abolitionist*, 1 (April, May, June, July 1856), pp. 68–9, 79–80, 94–5, 97–104.

2. "Minutes of the National Abolition Convention," and "Discussion in the National Abolition Convention," and The National Nominating Convention," *Radical Abolitionist*, 1 (June 1856), pp. 94, 96.

3. "National Land Industrial Congress," *New York Daily Times*, June 7, 1856, p. 8, col. 1.

4. "Republican Convention at Philadelphia," *Radical Abolitionist*, 1 (July 1856), pp. 105–6. On Vermont, Massachusetts and Pennsylvania, see Helene Zahler, *Eastern Workingmen and National Land Policy* (New York: Columbia University Press, 1941), p. 101. Only a short while earlier, the Philadelphia *Public Ledger* which had supported National Reform measures objected in 1854 to the further questioning of candidates for local offices about slavery and land reform. *Public Ledger*, May 25, 1854, quoted Zahler, *Eastern Workingmen*, p. 83n.

5. "Great German Fremont Meeting," *New York Times*, August 22, 1856, p. 1. See also Justine Davis Randers-Pehrson, *The Turbulent Life of a German Forty-Eighter in the Homeland and in the United States* (New York: Peter Lang, 2000).

6. "Great Convention at Pittsburgh," *New York Daily Tribune*, September 18, 1856, p. 4; "Special Notices," "Mechanics to the Rescue," *New York Times*, September 2, 1856, p. 3; "Political Notices," "Free Territory for Free Labor," *New York Times*, September 11, 1856, p. 6; "Political Notices," "Free Territory

for Free Labor," *New York Times*, September 22, 1856, p. 3; "Political Notices," "Free Territory for Free Labor," *New York Times*, September 30, 1856, p. 3; "Political Notices," "Huzza for the Natick Cobbler," *New York Times*, October 4, 1856, p. 6; "Free Labor. Senator Wilson before the Mechanics and Working-Men of New-York," *New York Times*, October 6, 1856, p. 1; "Free Labor. Senator Wilson before the Mechanics and Working-men of New-York," *New York Times*, October 11, 1856, p. 4; "Political Miscellany," *New York Times*, October 11, 1856, p. 4; "Political Notices," "Mechanics and Workingmen, to the Rescue!" *New York Times*, October 21, 1856, p. 3.

7. "The Mechanics' and Workingmen's Meeting in the Park," *New York Times*, October 29, 1856, p. 1.

8. "Radical Abolition Convention," *The National Era*, 1 (May 1, 1856), p. 70; "The Radical Abolitionist State Convention," *New York Times*, September 19, 1856, p. 4; "The Platform Examined," "New York State Convention of Radical Abolitionists" with "Items," and "Annual Meeting of the American Abolition Society," *Radical Abolitionist*, 1 (July 1856), p. 107, and 2 (October, December 1856), pp. 31, 41–5; "Kansas. Convention of Kansas Aid Committees at Buffalo," *New York Times*, July 11, 1856, p. 8; M. Leon Perkal, "American Abolition Society: A Viable Alternative to the Republican Party?" *The Journal of Negro History*, Winter 1980, pp. 61–3.

9. "The Anniversary Meeting of the American Abolition Society," *Radical Abolitionist*, 2 (June 1857), p. 93, and for issues from vol. 3: "The Prospect of Kansas," and "Notice of the Annual Meeting of the American Abolition Society," (September 1857), p. 12 with "Annual Meeting of the American Abolition Society at Syracuse, N.Y.," (October 1857), pp. 18–22. "The Annual Meeting," "Abolition in Vermont," and "May Anniversary of the American Abolition Society," *Radical Abolitionist*, 3 (October 1857), p. 22 (February 1858), pp. 54–6 (May 1858), pp. 73–6; and; "State Anti-Slavery Convention," and "Anti-Slavery Convention in Vermont: Wednesday—Morning Session," *Liberator*, August 26, 1859, and September 3, 1858, pp. 135, 142, 148.

10. "Free-Soil Meeting," "Meeting of the Workingmen's State Central Committee," "The Mechanics' and Workingmen's State Central Committee," and two articles entitled "The Land Reformers," *New York Times*, January 28 (p. 1), July 1 (p. 1), 2 (p. 4), 1857, January 29 (p. 1), March 11 (p. 4), 1858.

11. "New-York City," "The European Revolutionists—Celebration of the 24th of February 1848," *New York Times*, February 25, 1857, p. 8.

12. Lehning, "International Association," pp. 179–81, 187–8, 198–9, note 1, citing the first number of the *Bulletin International*, as quoted in *Le Prolétaire*, June 17, 1857. See also Billington, *Fire in the Minds of Men*, pp. 326–9; "Address to Bedini," "Universal Democratic Republicans," and "Italian National Society," *New York Daily Tribune*, February 1 (p. 3), 1854, March 7 (p. 7), 1855, November 23 (p. 7), 1859.

13. "The Orsini and Pierri Sympathizers," and "Practical Socialism in New York," *New York Times*, April 14 (p. 4), June 22 (p. 5), 1858. See also Mischa Honeck, "'Freemen of All Nations, Bestir Yourselves': Felice Orsini's Transnational

Afterlife and the Radicalization of America," *Journal of the Early Republic*, 30 (Winter 2010), pp. 587–615.

14. For his earlier presence, see John Allen, "Introductory," and "Loaves! Loaves!," *Voice of Industry*, June 19, 1846, July 3, 1847, both p. 2.

15. Valentin Pelosse in both "Mais qui est Déjacque?" pp. 9–14 and "Essai de Biographie de Joseph Déjacque," pp. 15–28 in *Joseph Déjacque: La Question Révolutionnaire, l'Hujmanisphere, A Bas les chefs!, La Liberation des noirs Americains*, ed. Valentin Pelosse (Paris: Editions Champ Libre, 1971). His exchanges included, from Brussels, two socialist and refugee French journals, *Le Bien-Etre Sociale* and *Le Proletaire*, to London *L'Association Internationale*, and from private addresses, to Geneva the Swiss political and humoristic journal, *Le Carillon St-Gervais*.

16. "News of the Day," *New York Times*, June 24, 1858, p. 4; "The Republican Celebration by the International Society," *New York Times*, June 24, 1858, p. 4.

17. "Orsini and Pierri Meeting in Boston," and "Personal," *New York Times*, May 1, 3, 1858, both on p. 1; "From Boston," *Cincinnati Enquirer*, May 1, 1858, p. 2.

18. "The Orsini Conspiracy in England," and Untitled items "Orsini Demonstration in Chicago," *New York Times*, May 3 (p. 4), 21 (p. 2), 1858; "Appendix VIII. A Manifesto by the Central International Committee Sitting in London, June 24, 1858," in Lehning, "International Association," pp. 241–6; "The Orsini Demonstration," "'Romantic' Career of Captain de Ruido, Once Sentenced to Death on the Guillotine," *Cincinnati Enquirer*, May 18, 1858, p. 3, April 18, 1896, p. 14, and "The Orsini Demonstration in Cincinnati" [from *Cincinnati Gazette*], *New York Herald*, May 21, 1858, p. 2.

19. "The Prospect of Kansas," *Radical Abolitionist*, 3 (September 1857), p. 12.

20. Richard J. Hinton, "Making Kansas a Free State," *The Chautauquan: a Weekly Newsmagazine* (1880–1914), 31 (July 1900), pp. 349–50; Edward J. Renehan described them as "well organized, meticulous, and circumspect" in *The Secret Six: The True Tale of the Men who Conspired with John Brown* (New York: Crown Publishers, 1996), pp. 146, 147.

21. "Freedom by Means," *New York Independent*, November 15, 1855, p. 363. See also Thomas R. Marshall, "When Kansas Bled," *New York Times*, September 16, 1925, p. 27.

22. Forbes to Dr. S. G. Howe, May 14, 1858 and Forbes to F. B. Sanborn, April 24, 1858, in "Most Important Disclosures," *New York Herald*, October 27, 1859, p. 4; and Jeffery S. Rossbach, *Ambivalent Conspirators: John Brown, the Secret Six, and a Theory of Slave Violence* (Philadelphia, PA: University of Pennsylvania Press, 1982), p. 133. One suspects that this is the reason Adam Zamoyski described Forbes as "a detestable character" in *Holy Madness: Romantics, Patriots, and Revolutionaries, 1776–1871* (London: Weidenfeld & Nicolson, 1999), p. 366.

23. Renehan, *The Secret Six*, pp. 152, 160, 161, 153, 163–4, 167, 168; Richard J. Hinton, "John Brown and his Men," *Frank Leslie's Popular Monthly* (June 1889), p. 695. A "Letter from Paris" exaggerated his prison time and described him as having been long active in the Kansas struggle appeared in the *New York*

Herald, which allowed a letter to the *New York Times* to appear, correcting and disparaging Forbes's career. Untitled items "Garibaldi and his Former English Lieutenant" and "A Roman," letter to editor, June 25, "Garibaldi and Colonel Forbes," *New York Times*, June 24 (p. 2), 28 (p. 1), 1859.

24. Franklin Benjamin Sanborn, *Recollections of Seventy Years* (2 vols.; Boston, MA: Richard G. Badger, the Gorham Press, 1909), vol. 1, p. 135; and Nat Brandt, *The Town That Started the Civil War* (Syracuse, NY: Syracuse University Press, 1990), pp. 154–5, 173–6, 200; David S. Reynolds, *John Brown, Abolitionist: The Man Who Killed Slavery, Sparked the Civil War, and Seeded Civil Rights* (New York: Alfred A. Knopf, 2005), p. 240, but see also pp. 113–14, 191, 234, 240–44, 258; Daniel C. Littlefield, "Blacks, John Brown, and a Theory of Manhood," *His Soul Goes Marching On: Responses to John Brown and the Harpers Ferry Raid*, ed. Paul Finkelman (Charlottesville, VA: University Press of Virginia, 1995), p. 79; Albert J. von Frank, "John Brown, James Redpath, and the Idea of Revolution," *Civil War History* 52 (June 2006), pp. 42–160.

25. "George DeBaptiste," *Detroit Advertiser and Tribune*, February 23, 1875. Lambert's statement that John Brown drew upon "this body" before the Harpers Ferry raid, easily misunderstood as a claim about the influence of the specific secret society, actually seems to refer to the fugitives in Canada, as his next remarks are on the Chatham convention. "Freedom's Railway," *Detroit Tribune*, January 17, 1887, p. 2.

26. "The Anniversary Meeting of the American Abolition Society," *Radical Abolitionist*, 2 (June 1856), p. 94; "The Anniversary Meeting of the American Abolition Society," *Radical Abolitionist*, 2 (June 1857), p. 96.

27. The proceedings are in Osborne P. Anderson, *A Voice from Harper's Ferry: the Unfinished Revolution* (New York: World View Publishers, 1974; original 1861), pp. 39–43; Reynolds, *John Brown*, pp. 261–4, but see also pp. 113–14, 191, 234, 240–44, 258.

28. From the *New York Times* for 1858: "The Land Reformers," October 5, p. 1; "The Rev. John Pierpont's Address to the New-York Spiritual Association," October 11, p. 5; "City Politics" October 14, p. 5; "The Political Campaign. Celebration of the Opposition Triumphs. Meeting of Americans and Republicans in the City Hall Park," *New York Times*, October 22, p. 1.

29. "Mass Meeting of Germans to Organize an Independent Political Party," *New York Times*, October 14, 1858, p. 5.

30. From the *New York Times* for 1859: "Manifestation of the Solidarity of the Nations," two pieces under "City Intelligence," January 15, 18, 19, all p. 5.

31. "Land for the Landless," *National Era*, July 14, 1859, p. 112, and, "Distribution of the Public Lands," and "The Freedom of the Public Lands—Timothy Davis, M.C., of Iowa, and the Land Reformers," *New York Times*, July 21 (p. 4), August 9 (p. 3), 1859; Perkal, "American Abolition Society," pp. 63–5; and campaign coverage in both the *Gerrit Smith Banner* in New York City, and Goodell's *Radical Abolitionist*.

32. "The Liberty Party," *New York Daily Times*, April 12, 1856, p. 4; and, from *Radical Abolitionist*, 4: "Voting for Morgan to Keep Out Parker" with

"'Don't Throw Away Your Votes!'" and "'We Must defeat the Pro-Slavery Democracy'," with "'The Republican Party Must be Preserved,'" (October 1858), pp. 20, 22–3; and "N.Y. Tribune vs. Gerrit Smith," (November 1858), pp. 26–7.

33. *Proceedings of the National Emigration Convention of Colored People; Held at Cleveland, Ohio* (Pittsburgh, PA: n.p., 1854). See also Christopher Dixon, "Nineteenth Century African American Emigrationism: the Failure of the Haitian Alternative," *The Western Journal of Black Studies*, 18 (Summer 1994), pp. 77–88; and Matthew Clavin, "A Second Haitian Revolution: John Brown, Toussaint Louverture, and the Making of the American Civil War," *Civil War History*; 54 (June 2008), pp. 117–45.

34. James McCune Smith, "For the Radical Abolitionist!," *Radical Abolitionist*, 4 (September 1858), p. 32.

35. R. J. M. Blackett, "John Sella Martin: The Lion From The West," in *Beating Against the Barriers: Biographical Essays in Nineteenth-century Afro-American History* (Baton Rouge, LA: Louisiana State University Press, 1986); Philip S. Foner and Robert J. Branham, "An Appeal for Aid to the Freedman," *Lift Every Voice: African American Oratory, 1787–1900* (Tuscaloosa, AL: University of Alabama Press, 1998).

36. *"No Struggle, No Progress": Frederick Douglass and His Proverbial Rhetoric for Civil Rights*, ed. Wolfgang Mieder (New York: P. Lang, 2001), p. 154; *The Radical Abolitionist* includes material from the District of Columbia, Virginia, Kentucky, Missouri, Arkansas, and North Carolina.

37. From the *Radical Abolitionist*, 4: "'The New Republican Platform,'" (October 1858), p. 24; "'Era of Good Feeling,'" and "The Pennsylvania Election," (November 1858), pp. 27, 29; and, James Redpath, "Who Were the True Friends of Kansas?," (September 1858), p. 12; "The Parties" [from *North-West Excelsior*], *The Vanguard*, 1 (February 27, 1858), p. 395. See also *The Past and Present of Lake County, Illinois* (Chicago, IL: William E Baron & Co., 1877), p. 240. See also *Slavery Limitation Abandoned in theory and practice by the defenders of the Crittenden-Lecompton Compromise*, Annual Report of the American Abolition Society (New York: American Abolition Society, September 1858); and Perkal, "American Abolition Society," pp. 64–5.

38. The press generally covered the February debates in Congress, particularly the *New York Daily Tribune*, and Wade quoted in William K. Wyant, *Westward in Eden: the Public Lands and the Conservation Movement* (Berkeley, CA: University of California Press, 1982), p. 60; "Cassius M. Clay on Free Labor, Slavery, Poverty and Things in General," *New York Times*, December 27, 1858, p. 2.

39. Joshua King Ingalls, *Reminiscences of an Octogenarian* (New York: M. L. Holbrook & Company; London: L. N. Fowler, 1897), p. 35; meetings, including those held in German were announced in the *Gerrit Smith Banner*, October 18, 1858. The *New York Daily Tribune* covered the campaign through October to the general election; Commerford to Johnson, December 17, 1859 in *The Papers of Andrew Johnson*, ed. LeRoy P. Graf and Ralph W. Haskins. Editorial associates: Harry T. Burn, Jr. and Patricia P. Clark (20 vols.; Knoxville, TN:

University of Tennessee Press, 1967–), vol. 3, pp. 356–8; L. A. Hine, *A Lecture on Garrisonian Politics, before the Western Philosophical Institute; Delivered in Cincinnati, Sunday, April 24th, 1853* (Cincinnati, OH: Longley, 1853), pp. 12, 20.

40. Beriah Green, "A Faithful Testimony," *Liberator*, 28 (February 5, 1858), p. 24.
41. "New York Correspondence," *National Era*, November 10, 1853, p. 179.
42. Untitled item, "A Case for the Underground Railroad.—Slavery of Women.— Mrs. Julia Branch," *New York Times*, June 28, 1858, p. 4; "'The Cause and Cure of Evil,'" *New York Times*, September 2, 1858, p. 4. William Goodell letter to *New York Tribune*, reprinted under "The Rutland Convention," *Radical Abolitionist*, 4 (July 1858), [first page of the issue]; Untitled item "The Free-Lovers at Utica," *New York Times*, September 15, 1858, p. 4.
43. April John Cook has to marry Mary Kennedy, who is pregnant. A few months after the wedding, she gives birth to a son. Steven Lubet, *John Brown's Spy: the Adventurous Life and Tragic Confession of John E. Cook* (New Haven, CT: Yale University Press, 2014).
44. Renehan, *The Secret Six*, pp. 179–80.
45. Hinton, "John Brown and his Men," *Frank Leslie's Popular Monthly* (June 1889), p. 695, and Hinton, *John Brown and His Men*, pp. 513n, 514n, 520, 672–5, 673; Statement of Richard J. Hinton, John Brown Papers, Kansas Historical Society. Probably Hinton, whose letter to the *Chicago Tribune* was misinterpreted as an argument that the Indian nations were "deeply interested in slaves." "The Two Systems—the Future, " *National Era*, June 17, 1858, p. 94. Richard Realf to John Brown, February 10, 1858, John Brown Papers, Kansas Historical Society. See also Ludwell H. Johnson, *Red River Campaign: Politics and Cotton in the Civil War* (Kent, OH: Kent State University Press, 1993), pp. 6–7, which further discusses on pp. 7–8 the influence of Edward Atkinson's 1861 tract *Cheap Cotton by Free Labor* (Boston, MA: A. Williams, 1861). Phillips also cited later works by Atkinson.
46. "Kansas. The Insurrectionary Movement in Southern Kansas—General News," *New York Times*, January 18, 1859, p. 8; Renehan, *The Secret Six*, pp. 172, 176–7.
47. Franklin B. Sanborn, "John Brown and His Friends," *The Atlantic Monthly*, 30 (July 1872), p. 55.
48. Jerry Thompson retrieved from www.tsha.utexas.edu/handbook/online/ articles/view/CC/fco73.html; Rodolfo Acuña, *Occupied America: A History of Chicanos* (2nd edition; New York: Harper & Row, 1981); Arnoldo De León, *They Called Them Greasers: Anglo Attitudes Toward Mexicans in Texas, 1821–1900* (Austin, TX: University of Texas Press, 1983); Charles W. Goldfinch and José T. Canales, *Juan N. Cortina: Two Interpretations* (New York: Arno Press, 1974); J. Fred Rippy, "Border Troubles along the Rio Grande, 1848–1860," *Southwestern Historical Quarterly*, 23 (October 1919); Paul Schuster Taylor, *An American-Mexican Frontier, Nueces County, Texas* (Chapel Hill, NC: University of North Carolina Press, 1934); Jerry Don Thompson, *Sabers on the Rio Grande* (Austin, TX: Presidial, 1974).

49. "Witnesses and Testimony at the Trial of John Brown," retrieved from www. civilwar.org/learn/primary-sources/witnesses-and-testimony-trial-john-brown.

50. On the treatment of Copeland and Green, the two African American raiders brought to trial, see Steven Lubet, "Execution in Virginia, 1859: The Trials of Green and Copeland," *North Carolina Law Review*, 91 (2013) pp. 1785–1816.

51. "The Republican Celebration by the International Society," *New York Times*, June 24, 1858, p. 4.

52. Benjamin N. Kinyon, "The Foundation of Governments, and Ownership of Property," *Banner of Light*, May 6, 1865, p. 2; Cora L. V. Tappan, quoted in Kerber, "Abolitionist Perception of the Indian," p. 295, cited by Elliot West, "Reconstructing Race," *Western Historical Quarterly*, 34(1) (2003): p. 47.

Epilogue   Survival and Persistence:
The Lineages and Legacies of the Early American Movement

1. Thomas Featherstonhaugh, "The Final Burial of the Followers of John Brown," *The New England Magazine*, new series, 24 (April 1901), pp. 128–34; Gordon Iseminger, "The Second Raid On Harpers Ferry, July 29, 1899: the Other Bodies That Lay a-Mouldering in Their Graves," *Pennsylvania History*, 71 (Spring 2004), pp. 129–64.

2. "Telegraph to the Herald," with "The John Brown Revolution" and "A New John Brown Party in Massachusetts" [from *Boston Traveler*], February 22, 1860, p. 4, and April 20, 1860, p. 2; "The Kansas War," *Boston Herald*, April 11, 1860, p. 4; untitled, *Louisville Daily Journal*, February 17, 1860, p. 3; "Another Insult to Virginia" [from the *Petersburg Express*], *Memphis Daily Appeal*, April 13, 1861, p. 2. See also Mark A. Lause, *Race and Radicalism in the Union Army* (Urbana, IL: University of Illinois Press, 2009) on the John Brown connections.

3. "Red Republicanism in the United States," *New York Times*, December 31, 1856, p. 4; and, J. R. Y. "The Private Soldier," *Philadelphia Press*, May 18, 1863; Seaver, *Occasional Thoughts* (Boston, MA: J. P. Mendum, 1888), pp. 16, 37, 49–50, 154.

4. Richard J. Hinton, "Wendell Phillips: a Reminiscent Study," *The Arena*, 13 (July 1895), pp. 237, 238; T. W. Higginson, March 24, 1860, Richard J. Hinton Papers, Box 1, f1, A, 12 (March 1860).

5. J. K. Hudson, "The John Brown League," and O. E. Morse, "An Attempted Rescue of John Brown from Charleston, Va. Jail," John Brown Papers, Kansas Historical Society. See also *The Narrative of John Doy, of Lawrence, Kansas* (New York: T. Holman, for the Author, 1860); Richard J. Hinton, *John Brown and His Men* (New York: Funk & Wagnalls Company, 1894]), pp. 512, 520–25. Also involved were Joseph Gardner, Silas S. Soule, J. A. Pike.

6. Hinton, "Wendell Phillips: a Reminiscent Study," pp. 236–7; "Twenty-Ninth Anniversary of the Polish Revolution," *New York Herald*, November 30, 1859, p. 5; "Spiritual Lyceum and Conference [One hundred and Fourth Session],"

Herald of Progress, July 7, 1860, pp. 3–4; and "La Guerre Servile," *Le Libertaire*, October 26, 1859, pp. 1–2. Forbes, as part of his immersion into American radicalism also attended spiritualist activities. See Harrison D. Barrett, *Life Work of Mrs. Cora L. V. Richmond* (Chicago, IL: Hack & Anderson, printers, for the National Spiritualists Association, 1895), p. 131.

7. Jackson in "Discussion in the National Abolition Convention," *Radical Abolitionist*, 1 (July 1856), p. 97.

8. "Political Anti-Slavery Convention," *Liberator*, May 10, 1860, p. 3.

9. "Radical Abolition National Convention," *The Principia*, 1 (September 15, 1860), p. 345, and "Letter of Gerrit Smith," pp. 345–46.

10. L. A. Hine, *A Lecture on Garrisonian Politics, before the Western Philosophical Institute; Delivered in Cincinnati, Sunday, April 24th, 1853* (Cincinnati, OH: Longley, 1853), pp. 12, 20; Richard J. Hinton, "Making Kansas a Free State," *The Chautauquan: a Weekly Newsmagazine* (1880–1914), 31 (July 1900), p. 347.

11. Bovay in "Emigration to Oregon" in *Working Man's Advocate*, December 28, 1844; "Discussion in the National Abolition Convention," *Radical Abolitionist*, 1: (July 1856), p. 98, speech continuing briefly on p. 99. See also David Roediger, *Seizing Freedom: Slave Emancipation and Liberty for All* (New York: Verso. 2014).

12. Henry George, *Progress and Poverty* (New York, n.d.), pp. 530, 534; Jamie L. Bronstein, *Land Reform and Working-Class Experience in Britain and the United States, 1800–1862* (Stanford, CA: Stanford University Press, 1999), pp. 69–70.

13. Philip J. Schwarz, *Migrants Against Slavery: Virginians and the Nation* (Charlottesville: University Press of Virginia, 2001), pp. 150–68, 234n33; Benjamin Quarles, *Allies for Freedom and Blacks on John Brown* (Oxford: Oxford University Press, 1974), pp. 173–4; Orin G. Libby, "The Geographic Distribution of the Vote of the Thirteen States on the Federal Constitution, 1787–8," *Bulletin of the University of Wisconsin. Economics, Political Science, and History Series*, 1 (1894–96), pp. 1–116; and Orin G. Libby, "A Study of the Greenback Movement, 1876–1884," *Transactions of the Wisconsin Academy of Sciences, Arts, and Letters*, 12 (Part 2: 1900); and Orin G. Libby, *The Arikara Narrative of Custer's Campaign and the Battle of the Little Bighorn* (Norman, OK: University of Oklahoma Press, 1920).

Index

CPSIA information can be obtained
at www.ICGtesting.com
Printed in the USA
LVHW111716110919
630726LV00006B/121/P